MegaMyths

of

Politics, Economics, and Religion

Also by
Eugene Schwarz

His Word, Our Guide;
Biblical Origins of the Christian Church

MegaMyths

of

Politics, Economics, and Religion

By

Eugene Schwarz

MegaMyths

of

Politics, Economics, and Religion

ISBN: 978-1-46792-806-9

eBook ISBN: 978-1-61914-682-2

Printed in the United States of America

Most of the data used in this book is based on U.S. government sources. It is in the public domain, and is freely available on the Internet and in print. Where brief references are made to material from specific non-governmental sources, the organizations and authors are identified in the body text.

Material from the following organizations and individuals is used with their permission:

Organization and topic   Page

Dr. Joseph Hanlon, Jubilee Research,
    Debt of U.S. Supported Dictatorships   15

Center on Budget and Policy Priorities,
    Income Share of Top One Percent of Households   24
    Uneven Distribution of Income Gains   25

Center for Responsible Politics
    Active Lobbyists and Total Spending   108

Families USA
    Prescription Drug Cost VA vs. Medicare Part D   137

Health Care for America Now
    Insurance Company Profits and CEO Compensation   149
    Insurance Company Repurchases of Their Own Stock   150

Kaiser Family Foundation
    U.S. Regional Incarceration Rates   213

Dennis Chaltry (personal friend)   Cover Photo

Contents

Independent Thinking 1

We Cannot Afford It. 6

Small Government..28

Fair Tax...38

Immigration Reform...54

Public welfare...66

Free Market Economics..85

Government of the People, by the People, and for the People 108

Retirement Security... 117

Quality Health Care 126

No Child Left Behind... 168

Winning the War on Drugs.. 191

Gun Control 199

Correctional Institutions... 210

Just War. 222

Separation of Church and State... 237

Race for Space 263

Freedom of Speech.. 271

Conclusion 275

Tables and Charts

Chapter Title and Topic   Page

We cannot afford it.
Great Depression Statistics, 1929-1934 8
Deficit Spending and Unemployment, 1933-1939 9
Debt of U.S. Supported Dictatorships, 1965-1996 15
Oil Prices, Effect on Economy, 1972-1976 22
Income Share of Top One Percent of Households, 1913-2007 24
Uneven Distribution of Income Gains, 1946-1976 and 1976-2007 25

Fair Tax
Median Household Income vs. Tax Expenditures, 2007 39
Income and Taxes by Income Rank, 2007 40
Individual vs. Corporate Revenues and Taxes, 2007 42
Effect of 1986 Tax Reform by Income Group 45
Effect of 2001-2003 Tax Cuts by Income Group 46
Tax Cuts, Deficits, and National Debt, 1980-1983 and 2000-2003 46
Proposed Gross Revenues Tax System 2007 Data 47

Immigration Reform
Balance of Trade with Mexico, 1992-2006 55

Public welfare
Welfare Cost for Families and Children, 2000-2008 67
Minimum Wage Increase and Effect on Unemployment 68
Psychological Distress by Poverty Level, 2008-2009 79
Psychological Distress of Those Below Poverty Level, 1997-2009 79
Aid to Needy Families with Children 83

Free Market Economics
Bank Failures, 1929-1938 89
Bank Failures, 1980-1989 89
Bank TARP Funds and CEO Pay, 2007 102

Government of the People, by the People, and for the People
Active Lobbyists and Total Spending, 1998-2010 108

Retirement security

U.S. Households and Income by Age, 2009 118

Hypothetical Retirement Savings Plan 120

Quality health care

Health Care Expenditures, 2006 Country Comparison 126

Infant Mortality, 2010 Country Comparison 127

Life Expectancy at Birth, 2010 Country Comparison 128

Insured and Uninsured Population, 2009 129

Uninsured Persons Percent by Family Income, 2009 129

Unemployment and Underemployment by Household Income, 2009 130

Health Care Expenditures by Payer, 2008 131

Health Care Spending per Beneficiary by Demographic, 2008 132

Health Care Usage by Age 2007-2008 134

Administrative Efficiency Medicare vs. Private Insurers, 2005 135

Medicare Expenditures by Type, 2008 135

Prescription Drug Cost VA vs. Top Medicare Part D Insurers 137

Medicaid Spending by Type of Service, 2008 140

Medicaid Spending per Beneficiary by Basis of Eligibility, 2008 141

Health Status in Relation to Poverty Level 141

Timeline for Tricare (Military Insurance) Cost Expansion 142

Military Health Care Increases by Type, 2000-2005 143

Tricare Beneficiaries by Eligibility, 2005 144

Tricare vs. Civilian Insurance Cost Comparison, 2002 144

Tricare vs. Federal Employees Health Plan Out-of-Pocket, 2005 145

Estimated Effect of Tort Reform 147

Insurance Company Profits and CEO Compensation, 2000 and 2007 149

Insurance Company Repurchases of Their Own Stock, 2003-2008 150

Medicare vs. VA Health Care Costs, 2008 157

Winning the war on drugs

Teenage Substance Abuse, 2009 192

Incarcerations by Type of Crime, 1980-2008 198

Gun Control

Causes of Death by Mechanism and Intent, 2007 203

Correctional institutions

Recidivism Rate of Released Offenders, 1994-1997 209

World Incarceration Rates, 2006-2008 210

U.S. Regional Incarceration Rates, 2009 211

Death Row Inmates Exonerated Since 1973 by State 213

Racial Characteristics of Incarcerated Populations, 2008 219

Separation of Church and State

Teenage Substance Abuse by Grade and Type, 2009 239

Sexual Activity of Teenagers 2009 239

Teenage Violence by Grade and Type, 2009 240

Men and Women in the Labor Force, 1950 and 2000 240

Teenage Childbearing, 1970-2007 242

Women Using Contraception by Type, 2008 242

Abortions by Age Group, 2006 250

Abortions to Unmarried Women by Race, 2006 250

Women Having Abortions by Race, 1997-2006 251

Number of Abortions Reported, 1973- 2007 252

Median Household Income by Race, 2008 253

Unemployment Rate by Education Level and Race, 2009 253

Persons Below Poverty Level by Race, 2008 254

Persons with Fair or Poor Health by Race, 2009 254

Race for space

World Population, 1950-2050 262

Preface

Much of what we accept as fact regarding some of the most important issues of life, even if it made sense at some point in time, was never true or is now untrue. Whether the topic is politics, economics, education, business, the environment, crime, health, or almost any other domain, we either cling to outdated notions or accept as gospel what is neatly packaged for us. We let politicians, religious leaders, educators, judges, business leaders, economists, and experts of all sorts, often with a vested interest in promoting a particular point of view, do our thinking for us. It is easier than examining the facts for ourselves, even when it is possible to ascertain what they really are.

Ideas are being packaged and sold to us just as soaps and detergents were a few decades ago. As in the case of products, behind each package of ideas, there are those who have something to gain, and it is usually at our expense. What makes one pair of denim jeans worth $80 when a nearly identical pair at Wal-Mart or K-Mart sells for $20? Someone must have persuaded you that a fancy stitch on the pocket or a 10-cent label is worth $60. We similarly overpay for our ideological labels.

Most of us get our information from one or two sources, typically TV cable news channels. On every issue, two positions are presented, each a package of ideas that we must accept in total in order to retain our right to their label. When each side presents "experts" with diametrically opposing views, they cannot both be right, but they can both be wrong, and often are. It is difficult to discern whether they are representing our own ideas or shaping them. We should always ask why there are only two potential solutions to every problem, who gains from each solution, and who pays for it.

Someone must be benefiting from the polarization and acrimonious division caused by the politicization of social issues. How else can we explain the repeated straight party line votes in Congress, other than invisible hands are pulling the strings on both sides of the aisle? It is inconceivable that no one has independent views. Viewed through the lens of politics, everything seems crystal clear. One must be either liberal or conservative, Republican or Democrat, pro life or pro abortion, etc. Can these simplistic labels really define who we are? This book is not about politics. It is about thinking for ourselves, recognizing the difference between ideals and ideology, and examining the individual ideas in a package rather than the label on it.

My training as an industrial engineer and experience as a management consultant and senior executive in international business taught me that evaluating all available current and historical data is essential for understanding problems and formulating solutions. When you examine the available data, you will see that much of what we have been led to believe on major social issues is based on misconceptions, myths, or anachronisms. I call them MegaMyths. Both the data and common sense suggest rethinking is necessary if we are to resolve them. We will examine a number of proposed solutions. I believe you will find them logical, effective, and fair. At the very least, I hope you find them interesting and even stimulating.

Acknowledgements

My deepest gratitude to my loving wife, Rosemarie, whose unflagging support, proof reading, editing, and endless patience made it possible to devote countless hours to the task.

I am indebted to the many experts whose work is reflected in these pages. Many of them work in government agencies responsible for the issues examined here; consequently, their names do not appear in their product. Their work is in the public domain, and I have made extensive use of it. To them, I say "Thank you!"

Those whose identities and product titles are known to me are included in the text, tables, and charts, whenever possible. My expertise is not in any of their fields. I am merely a trained observer and analyst. Their research has made this work possible, and I am profoundly grateful.

Independent Thinking

People are generally most comfortable in large like-minded groups, somewhat like herd animals. Perhaps it is a defensive mechanism. Separating oneself from a herd might expose one to predators. We fear isolation and rejection, so we rarely challenge the dominant bull. Consider the following examples.

Aristarchus of Samos (310 – c. 230 BC), an ancient Greek astronomer and mathematician, proved that the sun, not the earth, was the center of the solar system. In about 250 BC, his contemporary, the Greek philosopher Eratosthenes proved mathematically that the earth is round, and calculated its circumference with astonishing accuracy. A few educated people may have believed the truth over the next seventeen centuries, but they chose not to challenge the powers who, based on an incorrect literal interpretation of the Bible, insisted that the sun circled a flat earth. It wasn't worth getting burned at the stake. Copernicus and Galileo had proofs for their hypotheses, but those in power were not interested in examining the evidence.

For much of human history the king decided the religion of his people. Egyptian Pharaoh Amunhotep IV, dictated monotheism in the form of sun worship. The sons of Constantine declared Christianity the religion of the Roman state, and applied the death penalty to those caught practicing pagan rituals. Invariably, when a ruler accepted Christianity, his or her subjects were also Christianized. Henry VIII made himself head of the Anglican Church, and his subjects were obligated to join it. Stalin changed Russia into an atheist society. More recently, the Taliban in Afghanistan and fundamentalist Muslims in other countries dictated the religious beliefs and practices of their subjects.

The most egregious example of mind control is the way Hitler took control of Germany. Good people stood by silently as he broke treaty agreements, made racism a national policy, and started wars of conquest to steal the land and wealth of other nations. He packaged his plan as patriotism. Of course everyone wanted to be patriotic. As long as he was winning, he had overwhelming support. Businessmen, farmers, and other professionals all had something to gain. Morality was whatever the Fuehrer said it was. Never mind that more than fourteen million people, mostly Russians, Poles, and Jews, were put to death, in addition to the many battle casualties. Fortunately for the world, Hitler, convinced of his own genius, could not accept advice from anyone, not even his most competent military advisors. Hitler's all-consuming ambition led him to make the military decisions that led to his ultimate failure.

It is no different in the corporate world. Disagreeing with the boss can be dangerous to one's future. Why else would executives of cigarette companies have sat silently while decisions were made to increase the nicotine content of cigarettes, and therefore their addictive properties? Did anyone not know that cigarettes cause cancer, heart disease, and lung disease? It would be hard to find an industry where the old adage of 'might makes right' does not apply.

In every domain there are people who have a vested interest in preserving the status quo. They have the resources to manage the complexity for their own benefit. They labor under the assumption that their individual good is synonymous with the common good. It often is not. There are many domains within which the experts are wrong, whether through faulty logic, vested interest, inadequate information, fear of change, or social conditioning. It takes courage to break free from the comfort of the herd.

Changing one's mind is many times more difficult than making it up correctly in the first place. This was clearly demonstrated by an experiment performed by Dr. Marvin E. Mundel, professor of Industrial Engineering at Purdue University in 1940s. The classroom was set up with a slide projector. As students entered, they were handed two slips of folded paper containing an identification number. Only the students knew their own numbers. Before the projector was turned on, the students were instructed to observe the blurred image on the screen, write down what they thought the object was and the time of observation, as soon as they were able to, and drop it into a box. Every minute the focus on the projector was adjusted slightly to make the image clearer. A student could change his or her mind about the identity of the object by repeating the process. On the blackboard were rows representing increments of time and columns corresponding with the numbers on the slips of paper. The results were entered on the blackboard. Invariably, the early entries were wrong. Furthermore, those who were the earliest to guess the object's identity incorrectly the first time were usually last to change their minds, long after the rest of the class had identified the object correctly as a fire hydrant. The early group was more concerned with being first in what they perceived to be a competition. The last group was more concerned with getting it right.

Social pressure (the herd instinct) often causes us to make decisions we would not make if we were acting independently. This was proven in experiments conducted by social psychologist Solomon Asch in the early 1950s and later corroborated by several researchers. In one set of experiments, two cards were prepared, one had a single line, and the other had three lines of varying lengths. The lines were marked a, b, and c. Only one line matched the length of the line on the first card. In trials where the subject did not know how others in a group had answered, the subject almost always gave the correct answer. When the subject was last in a group of participants, and the other participants were secretly told to select the wrong answer, the subject often chose the same incorrect answer as his peer group. After many trials, 37% of subjects gave the same incorrect answer as their peer groups. Only about 25% were able to resist their influence. The subjects who gave the incorrect answers had difficulty changing their minds when confronted with the correct answer. This may explain how spin-doctors get us to polarize around obviously incorrect ideas.

David Eagleman, a neuroscientist at Baylor College of Medicine, in his book *Incognito: The Secret Lives of the Brain,* addresses many ways by which our perceptions of truth can be altered. In the *illusion-of-truth effect* experiments (page 65), subjects were made to believe that something is true even after they were later told it is false. The subconscious mind accepts it as true merely based on repetition or exposure. Marketing and public relations firms, political advisers, and news media are well aware of these and similar effects. Therein lies the danger of allowing overconcentration of news and other media outlets in too few hands.

In the realm of politics, party allegiances seem to dictate one's position on war, abortion, national health care, environmental protection, taxation, gun control, and myriad other issues. It is distressing to see the strength of opinions people express without a clear grasp of their validity. When asked for facts to support their opinions, they conveniently repeat sound bites of pundits on their favorite TV news channel without any credible supporting evidence. Most people consider the issues too complex for the common person, so they must simply accept one party line or the other. The party line is often drafted by some of the thirty-five thousand registered lobbyists in Washington, D.C., representing powerful corporations and special interest groups. The spin-doctors perpetually bombard us with the vision their patrons wish us to have, often at the expense of the truth. How can we make correct decisions when so much spin is put on every issue? One need only look at the prescription drug plan, energy bill, proposed immigration reform bill, and health care reform bill to realize that they were not working on our behalf.

There were times when investigative reporters ferreted out the facts behind many issues and events of the day, not just here but around the globe. News budgets have been slashed. Now, we get an hour of non-stop coverage of the latest hurricane, tornado, flood, house or forest fire, or gaffs by political candidates or their acquaintances on every television news channel. During the last presidential campaign, several cable news channels devoted nearly half an hour each to a fist bump by Barack and Michelle Obama and her style of dress. It is not news, but it is cheap. The Internet and cell phones have made us all reporters of sorts. To be sure, we can access a lot of information online, but one has to be relatively knowledgeable about the issues to weed out the trivialities, misinformation, and disinformation.

Much of the dumbing-down of America can be traced back to the consolidation of media ownership in the hands of an ever-smaller number of similarly minded ideologues. That guarantees our continuing ignorance of the facts. Distortion of facts and statistics has left people confused and distrustful. The only solution seems to be to find someone we can trust to interpret for us. But, who can that be?

How do we know that we are not being manipulated by special interests with the resources to do so?

There is an old adage: "Those who do not learn from history are destined to repeat it." When circumstances demand change, we tend to negotiate the least possible change. Patch upon seemingly innocuous patch is applied until the level of complexity exceeds most people's capacity to understand. The result is grossly inefficient systems that force us to seek the assistance of experts. A perfect example of this is our system of taxation. The patches rarely cure the problem, but, because they are incremental changes to familiar structures, they give us the illusion of control. The devil we know is always less frightening than the devil we don't know.

Educating oneself on important issue takes a lot of work. Some of the data is spread over many university and government databases. Some is only available by paid subscription. Some statistics are gathered in a way that makes them virtually meaningless, unemployment being a prime example. Others are structured in a way that makes meaningful analysis extremely difficult. Books on an issue can be very one-sided. Getting the information is only the first hurdle. Criticism of the status quo can get one labeled as unpatriotic. There is nothing unpatriotic about wanting to understand and improve our systems and processes. It may in fact be unpatriotic not to want to do so.

My family and I experienced Soviet communism and Nazi fascism in Eastern Europe. We came here as refugees after World War II. The U.S. gave us the blessings of liberty and opportunity. I love this country, and am profoundly grateful to be living in a democratic society. That does not mean it is without flaws. If democracy and capitalism are to survive, we must strive to correct them. Let's begin by understanding them.

Progress is impossible without change, and those who cannot change their minds cannot change anything.

George Bernard Shaw (1856-1950), Irish writer.

We Cannot Afford It.

In my travels, I noticed that people in economically depressed societies suffer from many maladies including missing or rotten teeth. They simply have no money for dental care, or anything else for that matter. Their governments cannot afford to provide dental care. Dentists from other countries won't go there because there is no money to be made. So people continue to live with pain and discomfort while their government officials typically enjoy lives of luxury. I picked this example to make a bigger point - what the role of government should be. If the government had hired some dentists, those dentists' income would flow to home builders, grocers, clothiers, farmers, auto makers, bankers, mechanics, and many other businessmen and workers, all of whom would pay a portion back to the government in taxes, and ultimately repay the government investment. If the government fails to provide the needed stimulus, most people will continue to live in misery.

The difference between what the government spends on dentists and what ultimately comes back as taxes is a form of inflation. The government typically does not have the money to hire the dentist, but it does control the money supply. It could issue (print) just enough money to hire the dentists. The dentists' earnings would then flow down to other members of the economy, all of whom would pay taxes. As long as everyone in the chain pays a fair and relatively equal share in taxes, inflation can be controlled. As each of the businesses in the chain get more business, their efficiency increases, and they can produce more products and services for less money. That productivity gain offsets inflation. The system is in balance. If one link in that chain does not pay its fair share of taxes in relation to its income, or if government spends on non-productive ventures that do not bring back money in taxes, inflation increases and the government must borrow money to cover the deficit or print more money.

Of course, the government could borrow enough money to hire the dentists. The loan would have to be repaid with interest. That would require higher tax rates to cover the additional burden of interest. Since the loan repayment would go to a foreign entity, the government could never recoup its investment, consequently it would be trapped in a vicious cycle of either printing money or borrowing more money and raising tax rates so high that they deprive most of its population of disposable income, thereby depressing the economy further. That is why third world countries that borrow money to stimulate their economies cannot generally control inflation or achieve prosperity. Printing money causes immediate inflation while borrowing merely spreads it out over time and makes it more difficult to measure. Before we explore alternative courses of action, let's give our hypothetical country a name just so we don't confuse it with ours. How about RISC—Republic Investigating Sources of Capital?

Even if the government of RISC did hire the dentists, it could never recoup its investment because most of its citizens have no disposable income. That would leave the government with two choices: either (1) get money directly into people's hands, or (2) go the socialist route of paying the dentists itself, and providing free dental care.

The socialist choice (2) cannot work because the cost is far greater than it can ever recover from its tax revenues. It improves dental health, but does nothing to otherwise raise the earnings of its citizens or, consequently, increase tax revenues. The socialist government has no choice but to pay dentists much less and to ration the amount of dental care a citizen can receive. Inevitably, quality declines and the government must print more money to hide its continuing budget deficits.

A government handout (1) can have some stimulative effect, but the effect is slow acting and often temporary. If the handout is only large enough to cover the cost of the dentists, it affects only a small segment of the economy and does not increase the citizens' disposable income. It cannot generate sufficient tax revenues to repay the government. The resulting budget deficits can only be reduced by raising taxes or printing money. We have already shown that borrowing money to cover budget deficits guarantees failure. What other alternatives can there possibly be?

Isn't a free market economy supposed to restore equilibrium? If that is true, their government could just do nothing. We tried that once.

After the stock market crash of 1929, we actually ran a budget surplus. President Hoover promised to stimulate the economy by building infrastructure, but only within the bounds of fiscal discipline. The stimulus was too little and too late. By 1931, government revenues plummeted causing a sizeable deficit, and unemployment hit 15.9%. This was at a time when most households had a single earner. By 1933, unemployment hit 24.9%, tax revenues dropped to half their 1929 level, approximately 9800 banks had failed, and crime increased dramatically. It took eight more years of huge tax increases and enormous deficit spending to stabilize the economy and stimulate growth. The free market would eventually have restored equilibrium without government intervention; it just might not have happened in one lifetime.

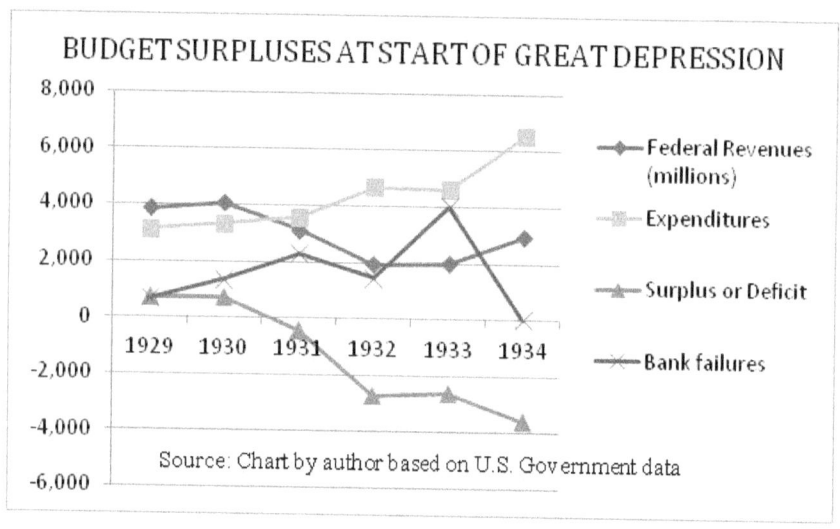

Some argue that the massive government spending during the Great Depression did nothing to rebuild the economy – that it was World War II. It is a specious argument. Prior to the war, lack of consumer demand due to severe poverty prevented the rebuilding of the private sector economy. It was massive deficit spending by the government to rebuild our military that gainfully employed everyone that could work. By 1944, unemployment averaged only 1.2%. Greater disposable income increased demand for goods and services and restored the economy. It could do so now if we had not exported most of our industrial jobs to other countries, or if we had the political will to commit to several years of all-out rebuilding of our infrastructure. The Vietnam War and the race for dominance in space had a similar effect in the 1960s. The wars in Iraq and Afghanistan do not have the same potential because they are less destructive of military hardware so less needs to be replaced. Unlike the space race, they are not spawning much new civilian technology.

Please note that extremely high tax rates on the wealthy during the Great Depression only applied to a handful of people – those earning the equivalent of tens of millions of dollars today – an inadequate tax base to refuel the economy. High taxes may have prevented a total collapse of the economy, but they did little to reignite consumer spending. Those who were working were only working thirty hours per week – also not enough to reignite the consumer economy. In the following table, you can plainly see that huge deficit spending was responsible for reducing unemployment. Political pressure to reduce spending in 1937 and 1938 in an attempt to cut the deficit only served to deepen the recession. Cutting government spending increased unemployment from 14.3% in 1937 to 19.0% in 1938. It was only when everyone was put to work in World War II that enabled consumers to refuel the economy. These lessons should not be lost on us.

EFFECT OF DEFICIT SPENDING ON UNEMPLOYMENT 1933-1939							
(Millions of Dollars)	1933	1934	1935	1936	1937	1938	1939
Federal Revenues	1,997	2,955	3,609	3,923	5,387	6,751	6,295
Federal Expenditures	4,598	6,541	6,412	8,228	7,580	6,840	9,141
Unemployment Rate %	24.9	21.7	20.0	16.9	14.3	19.0	17.2
Top Income Tax Rate %	63	63	63	79	79	79	79
For Income Over $MM	1.0	1.0	1.0	5.0	5.0	5.0	5.0
Source: Table by author based on U.S. Government data.							

Getting back to RISC, couldn't the government reduce taxes to stimulate the economy? If their tax codes are progressive like ours, with the rate of taxation increasing with one's income, any across-the-board tax cut would benefit most the small number of people at the top of the economy. The vast majority would receive little benefit. The tax cuts would merely reduce government revenues and increase the deficits. The Great Depression happened while the top income tax rate was only 25%, the lowest in the past century, following two dramatic tax cut from 67% to 43% in 1924, and to 25% in 1926 . It is interesting to note that the severe recession in the early 1980s followed huge tax cuts from 70% to 50%. The 1990-1991 recession followed further tax cuts to 31%. The 2001-2003 recession also followed large tax cuts. I am not implying that the tax cuts directly caused the recessions, but they were a contributing factor. Dollars must flow through the economy to stimulate consumer demand. Each of the tax cuts gave a windfall to the already wealthy who had no need to spend more of it on goods and services. Their money became what I call "lazy money". It was parked in passive long term investments. As a consequence, money tightened for the majority of people, spending declined, and the economy collapsed. The problem has been exacerbated in the last three decades by the decline in real wages and the growth of derivatives as investment vehicles, which are actually a form of gambling – bets on what the working economy will do – dollars that do not actually produce useful products or services. If the tax cuts had been gradual and done only while the economy was experiencing surpluses, they might not have been so damaging.

President John F. Kennedy was credited with stimulating economic growth by cutting taxes. We must remember that the top personal tax rate at that time was an outrageous 91% on incomes over $400,000. He proposed cutting them to 70% in 1962, but the tax cuts were not enacted until February of 1964, three months after his assassination. Before the tax cuts could have any measurable effect, the productive capacity of the U.S. was fully engaged in supporting the Vietnam War. There is no way to determine which the actual cause of that recovery was. However, there was a tax increase that led to a balanced budget under the Clinton administration. In 1993, the top tax rate was increased from 31% to 39.6%. By the end of that administration and the first year of the next, we had four years of budget surpluses totaling $559 billion, and unemployment hit a 31 year low of 4.0%.

Up to the last thirty years, the wealthiest U.S. individuals and corporations made their fortunes during and after the Great Depression in spite of atrociously high income tax rates. Those with deep pockets bought up failing companies for a fraction of their worth. They kept their personal income low, but invested heavily in research and development and expanding the asset base of their businesses. Who can forget the dramatic growth of companies like General Electric, Boeing, Coca Cola, Procter and Gamble, the auto makers, appliance manufacturers, electronics firms, oil companies, and those involved in the space race, nuclear power, construction, engineering, and consumer goods? They understood that wealth formation is as much a product of the growth of the value of their stock as of personal income. Their pricing strategy minimized their taxes and helped to increase consumer demand. They were willing to pay their workers more in preference to paying more in income taxes. This is not a suggestion that high taxes are a good thing, but merely that low taxes don't guarantee a healthy economy.

Doesn't putting more money into the hands of businessmen motivate them to invest in new business ventures that would stimulate the economy and create jobs? For example, RISC could set up dental clinics. After all, RISC has a desperate need for them. But, the unemployment rate is high and people's income is at the subsistence level. They cannot afford dental care. It would be a foolish businessman indeed who would set up clinics under those circumstances. Smart businessmen do not expand operations in the absence of current or projected demand. It is people with sufficient disposable income who create the demand. What does that say about the wisdom of those who militate for lower wages and oppose increases in the minimum wage? In 1982, the average pay of U.S. corporate CEOs was 42 times that of their average workers. By 2002, it was 419 times. Now it is even higher. Yet, between 1981 and 1990 and then between 1996 and 2007, there were no minimum wage increases. This reduced the real incomes of the poorest among us. We rank 93rd in the Central Intelligence Agency wage equality index out of 135 countries listed. Obviously, putting money in the hands of the already wealthy has done nothing to improve the economy. Unemployment is more than 9%, more than one million homeowners have lost their homes, 50 million people have no health insurance, 15% of our population is living in poverty, and bankruptcies have reached an alarming rate.

The above statement might tempt one to hang a 'liberal' or 'left wing' label on me, but that would be incorrect. I am a firm believer in democracy, capitalism, the right to life, the right to keep and bear arms, just and efficient government, low but fair taxes, one man=one vote, moral and fiscal conservatism, and personal responsibility. That does not obviate my right to question the degree to which we adhere to those ideals.

Whether we examine the situation in our imaginary country, RISC, or the U.S., it should be apparent by now that the situation requires government intervention, but that there are no quick fixes. Any action taken must be gradual, but on a large enough scale and over a long enough period of time to permit balance to be restored. Many would fear that level of government involvement in the economy might lead to socialism and oppressively large government. What possible other solutions can there be?

RISC could approach the IMF (International Monetary Fund) or World Bank for assistance. We have already shown that it is extremely difficult to refuel a depressed economy on credit. Nonetheless, RISC felt it had no choice. The banks agreed to the loans, but the loan agreements had more than 100 requirements RISC would have to meet. The requirements included spending cuts, lowering taxes, raising interest rates to control inflation, deregulation, privatization of its infrastructure, and favorable treatment of foreign corporations. If you were paying attention, then you realize that this is not a prescription for economic recovery.

Several corporations were anxious to acquire RISC's hydroelectric power plants, its water and waste treatment plants, and its transportation system. Petroleum, gas, and mining interests were also vying to further develop its natural resources. RISC consulted other countries that had taken advantage of such loans. They found that the proposed economic policies increased unemployment, reduced tax revenues, and greatly increased the cost of living for its citizens. Instead of controlling inflation, they increased it. The companies took possession of the participating countries' natural resources and exported them, but returned very little to the countries' citizens. Why would any country agree to such terms? The answer is not a mystery—bribes.

Take Nigeria as an example. With most of its Gross Domestic Product coming from its vast oil and gas reserves, why is Nigeria forced to borrow money from the IMF? Nigerians have long complained that they are not benefiting from the wealth under their communities. Seventy percent of Nigeria's citizens live on less than $2 a day. Deregulation has resulted in exorbitant fuel price increases further aggravating their plight. Nigerian rebels have been sabotaging oil company installations and pipelines in protest. Halliburton and its former subsidiary KBR have agreed to pay $579 million in fines for bribing Nigerian officials in excess of $180 million, some of which occurred while former Vice President Cheney was Chief Executive Officer of the company. He has recently been indicted by the Nigerian government on corruption charges. Halliburton was part of a consortium including Italian and Japanese companies.

Two decades ago, Brazil was one of the world's biggest debtor nations. Inflation was rampant. The American Chamber of Commerce in Brazil listed nearly all of our Fortune 500 companies as members. U.S., Japanese, German, Belgian, and other foreign corporations controlled most major industries there, and were exporting its vast natural resources. While I was there, unemployment was 26%, and people were living under bridges and sleeping in cardboard boxes on the grassy boulevards in the centers of streets. The crime rate was so high that most streets were empty after 7:00 PM. Today, Brazil is becoming an economic powerhouse. It has since repaid all of its debt to the IMF, and has been lending money to it. President Lula convinced other South American countries to jointly renegotiate their deals with the IMF. Its state-controlled oil company, PetroBras, is likely the engine behind Brazil's recovery. Brazil learned from other South American countries.

In 1997, Bolivia secured a loan from the World Bank. The agreement required Bolivia to agree to deregulation, privatization, and pegging its exchange rates to the dollar.. Prices for gasoline increased 10% and diesel 23%, which caused prices for other goods to increase also. Many Bolivians were living on $2.50 per day. Some of its water and sewer systems were turned over to a French-led group. Water prices increased 35%, and the cost of hooking a home up to the water system increased by hundreds of dollars. A popular uprising forced a change in the government. Under the new president, Evo Morales, Bolivia took control of its oil and gas reserves. Foreign oil companies will continue to make a profit as contractors performing drilling, refining, and distribution operations, but will not actually own the oil and gas.

In 1999, Venezuelans elected Hugo Chavez to be their President. He nationalized the oil industry and initiated social programs to lift the people out of poverty. Venezuela repaid all of its debt to the IMF five years ahead of schedule and broke off its relationship with it. Now, Chavez is attempting to displace the IMF by lending directly to other South American countries. We do not agree with Chavez's communist leanings, but cannot deny that some of his actions have improved the circumstances for Venezuela's poor. It is uncertain as to what degree the oil companies have been compensated for their assets.

RISC learned that, in addition to the economic damage, some suffered life-threatening environmental damage. Ecuador is reportedly suing Chevron for environmental damage done by Texaco before its acquisition by Chevron. Nearly a thousand crude oil waste pits and billions of gallons of toxic wastewater were dumped into the environment, apparently prior to Texaco turning control of operations to PetroEcuador in the 1990s. They may be responsible for the 1401 cancer deaths in the Lago Agrio region.

The International Monetary Fund was founded at the end of World War II for a noble purpose. It aided the reconstruction of war ravaged countries by stabilizing the world financial system and lending to members in financial difficulty. The IMF website describes it this way: *The International Monetary Fund (IMF) is an organization of 186 countries, working to foster global monetary cooperation, **secure financial stability**, facilitate international trade, **promote high employment** and **sustainable economic growth**, and **reduce poverty around the world**.* Until the early 1980s, it may have indeed achieved some of those purposes. Since then, it seems to increasingly serve corporate interests. It is chaired by our Treasury Secretary, Timothy Geithner, with Federal Reserve Chairman, Ben Bernanke, as an alternate. The United States has 17% of the total votes, almost three times the number of votes as Japan and Germany, and nearly four times as many as France and England. Major decisions require a supermajority of 85% of the votes. The US is the only nation that can individually block any proposal. Over the years, the IMF has supported a considerable number of dictatorships around the world that were friendly to US and European corporate interests. With rare exception, those countries owed more to the IMF at the end of each dictatorship than at the beginning. See the chart below. It is painfully clear that the IMF is not serving the interests of democracy, US strategic interests, or the people of its client countries. It may indeed be sowing the seeds of anti-Americanism.

DICTATORS' DEBTS BY COUNTRY							
Based on a 1998 Jubilee Research report by Joseph Hanlon							
		In Power		Debt $ billion		Increase	
Country	Dictator	from	to	start	end	$ bn	* %
Algeria	military	1991	**1996	28.2	33.3	5.1	15%
Argentina	military	1976	1984	9.3	48.9	39.6	81%
Bolivia	military	1962	1980	0.0	2.7	2.7	100%
Brazil	military	1964	1984	5.1	105.1	100.0	95%
Chile	Pinochet	1974	1989	5.2	18.0	12.8	71%
El Salvador	military	1979	1994	0.9	2.2	1.3	59%
Ethiopia	Mariam	1977	1991	0.5	4.2	3.7	88%
Haiti	Duvalier	1971	1986	0.0	0.7	0.7	100%
Indonesia	Suharto	1967	1998	3.0	129.0	126.0	98%
Iran	Shah	1953	1979	0.0	4.5	4.5	100%
Kenya	Moi	1979	**1996	2.7	6.9	4.2	61%
Liberia	Doe	1979	1990	0.6	1.9	1.3	68%
Malawi	Banda	1964	1994	0.1	2.0	1.9	95%
Nigeria	Buhari/Abacha	1984	1998	17.8	31.4	13.6	43%
Pakistan	Zia-ul Haq	1977	1988	7.6	17.0	9.4	55%
Pakistan	military	1990	**1996	20.6	29.9	18.7	63%
Paraguay	Stroessner	1954	1989	0.1	2.4	2.3	96%
Philippines	Marcos	1965	1986	1.5	28.3	26.8	95%
Somalia	Siad Barre	1969	1991	0.0	2.4	2.4	100%
South Africa	apartheid		1992		18.7	18.7	100%
Sudan	Nimeiry/al-Mahdi	1969	**1996	0.3	17.0	16.7	98%
Syria	Assad	1970	**1996	0.2	21.4	21.2	99%
Thailand	military	1950	1983	0.0	13.9	13.9	100%
Zaire/Congo	Mobutu	1965	1997	0.3	12.8	12.5	98%
* Increase as % of end debt ** Still in power in 1996.		TOTAL		104.0	554.6	460.0	83%

One must ask why so many countries in the world are running perpetual budget deficits and borrowing money from international bankers. Is it not because government debt is one of the most secure investments? Neither the debtor countries nor the world community are willing to let them default. The countries are kept in a depressed state. Only the bankers benefit.

Confronted with these disturbing facts, RISC could not accept the IMF loan agreement, and it had insufficient clout to get it modified. The only immediately available natural resource RISC had was cheap labor. In order to attract foreign manufacturers, RISC created a free trade zone where they could build plants to produce goods for export. In return, they would receive free land for their facilities, be able to import materials duty free, and not be required to pay RISC income taxes. The employment related taxes and workers' income taxes were a help, but it would take many years to effect a recovery.

That was the situation in the Dominican Republic (DR) about twenty years ago. Its economy was largely based on sugar exports until world sugar prices plummeted in the early 1980s. More than a third of its workforce was unemployed. The Reagan administration established the Caribbean Basin Initiative (CBI) to aid struggling countries in the region. The DR set up free trade zones (FTZ) to attract foreign manufacturers. The tax benefits under CBI, low labor cost, and proximity to the US made setting up operations there appealing. I was there investigating just such a venture. My guide was an official of their economic development commission (He considered himself quite the philanthropist for employing three maids in his home at 50 cents per day each). He explained the workings and benefits of the FTZ. When a container of goods was ready for shipment, we could call for a customs inspector to check the shipment. Slipping him a few dollars would assure prompt release. I protested having to bribe a government official. He explained that we would be doing the country and the inspector a favor because the bus fare to get to the factory was more than his pay. The deal breaker was the unreliability of DR's electrical distribution system. Power could be interrupted several times a day, sometimes for several hours. The country's three power distribution systems were all operating at a loss. The reasons were clear. Few could afford to pay for electricity, much of the power being generated was stolen by illegal hookups, and DR had no domestic source of fuel. Oil prices had increased many fold from 1973 to 1980, and continued high through 1985. The collapse of sugar prices and increase of oil prices forced the DR to turn to the IMF. The IMF imposed austerity programs that resulted in massive price increases for basic goods, which provoked widespread strikes and protests. During the early 1990s, oil prices were about half of what they were a decade earlier. The economy took off and hundreds of companies set up operations in the FTZs. The boom did not significantly reduce poverty. In 1996, the power distribution systems were privatized, but were unable to make a profit, so they were bought back by the government. Hurricanes, the global recession, and a fivefold increase in oil prices over a recent six year period is reversing much of the gain.

In 1971, the United States established the Overseas Private Investment Corporation (OPIC) to help US corporations set up operations in developing countries ostensibly to aid their economic development. OPIC provides financing for such projects and political risk insurance for US corporations setting up operations in foreign countries, including the DR. Much of its support has gone to corporations like oil companies, Coca Cola, Union Carbide, and Motorola, corporations that very probably did not need assistance. OPIC's operations blur the distinction between government and business. They involve insurance brokers, money fund managers, and other business interests. If it has not had a significant impact on poverty either here or in other countries, whose economy is it developing? How does moving our industries overseas help our economy? Here is a clue: it does not!

This appears to be a recurring theme around the world. Governments of the developed countries (the G8), their banks, and the energy industry's giants, which are in the best position to lead the world out of poverty into prosperity, are responsible for the policies that are doing the exact opposite. They have convinced most of us that economics is too complicated for us to understand. It is only complicated because many economists, playing with complex mathematical models based on often faulty assumptions, either don't look at real world results or look at them through the lens of political ideology. It would be very helpful if laymen could understand what money is and how it works.

Before currency was invented, people did business by barter – two chickens for ten pounds of potatoes, etc. Both commodities had to be available and needed at the same time. Hauling all those chickens and potatoes around was quite a pain, so currency was invented to represent the value of the chickens and potatoes. That allowed people to market their produce and spend their earnings whenever they chose. The most common medium of exchange was precious metals, usually gold or silver. There was a limited supply of these, so economies could only expand as quickly as additional quantities could be obtained. Weighing the gold at every transaction slowed down the pace of business, and there was always the opportunity for cheating. To make business more convenient, governments began to issue coins of known weight and purity. The total amount of coins had to equal the value of all the chickens and potatoes.

Consider this example. If the total economy consists of ten chickens and ten coins we'll call dollars, then each chicken is worth one dollar. If the chicken farmer decides to grow ten more chickens, but the government does not increase the money supply, you now have twenty chickens represented by ten dollars. The chickens are devalued to a half dollar each. Constricting the money supply this way is called deflation. That is what happens in a tight money situation. Since the chickens were raised at a cost based on a one dollar price, the farmer cannot recover the cost of raising his chickens. Banks will not lend money to a business that cannot generate a profit, especially when money is tight. If he has limited resources, his business must fail.

There are several possible reasons for tight money, including the government failing to increase the supply when needed, high interest rates that make it difficult to borrow, and some segments of the economy getting a disproportionate share of the money, and leaving less for the remainder of the economy to share—which is currently the case with health care, energy, finance, and defense sectors.

Of course, even if the government did increase the money supply, if the farmer doubled the number of chickens when there was no demand for that many, the farmer would be forced to lower the price to stimulate demand. At some point, he could no longer make a profit, and the business would fail. That is currently the situation with our auto industry. Cars are lasting longer and there are far too many auto manufacturers serving a smaller domestic market.

What if the farmer has ten chickens and the government increases the money supply to twenty dollars? His ten chickens are now represented by twenty dollars. The chickens are each worth two dollars. That is called inflation. If a person had saved two dollars before the onset of inflation, those two dollars would each only buy half a chicken. The savings are devalued. If the inflation continues unabated, the previous day's earnings cannot buy the current day's needs, and people are thrown into poverty. Saving money becomes extremely difficult and pointless.

In the late 1970s and early 1980s, oil-fueled hyperinflation caused prices for domestic materials and goods to skyrocket. Domestic manufacturers found it more profitable to either purchase or manufacture their products in Japan, Mexico, Taiwan, China, Korea, and other countries. The Federal Reserve jacked up interest rates to unprecedented levels to stop the runaway inflation, throwing the country into deep recession. At the same time, the administration slashed the top tax rate from 70% on incomes over $215,400 to 50% on incomes over $85,600, and mounted an enormous expansion of defense spending on the Strategic Defense Initiative, or Star Wars. Budget deficits climbed from $41 billion in 1979 to $298 billion in 1983, with no way to pay for them. High interest rates increased the demand for dollars, and foreign money came flooding in. By February of 1982, the prime rate was 21.2% and, by October, unemployment was 10.8%. Unemployment did not fall below 5% again until 1997. The flight of manufacturing was irreversible. One can readily see that OPIC exacerbated the problem.

Not everyone loses in a period of high inflation. For example, if a person bought a house, a car, or a business on credit at a reasonable fixed rate of interest, and that person's income kept pace with inflation, those loans would be repaid with less valuable dollars.

As you can see, too many dollars can have the same result as too few dollars. Too few dollars causes the price of chickens to fall. Too many chickens also causes the price to fall. Conversely, too many dollars causes the price of chickens to rise, and too few chickens causes the price to rise. This is called the law of supply and demand. As long as there is healthy competition among chicken farmers, an adequate supply of chickens, and enough dollars to purchase them, the system will be in balance. What is true of chickens is true for all assets, but it is not easy to maintain that balance over thousands of commodities and asset classes.

Someone has to control the amount of money in the system so that it represents the value of all assets plus enough to provide for creation of additional assets to meet future needs. Those assets are created by businesses that cannot issue money, so they borrow money from the currency the government issued. That money must be repaid with interest low enough to make creation of new assets affordable, yet high enough to cover the rate of inflation. Someone has to control the interest rates as well. If too many assets are being created, interest rates must rise to slow down the inflation. If too few assets are being created, interest rates must be lowered to stimulate growth. That's the job of our Federal Reserve System (FED). It was created in 1913 to control the money supply and interest rates, primarily to protect against bank failures, but also to achieve maximum employment. Since its creation, more than 11,000 banks have failed and unemployment has been as high as 25% and is currently around 10%. The Federal Reserve is run by bankers. Why can they not get it right?

The problem is competition, but not the competition between chicken farmers for market share, nor even competition between chicken farmers and beef and pork raisers. That is fair competition and good capitalism. The problem is competition for favored treatment from the government. Chicken farmers could form an association to promote the interests of chicken farmers. They could hire lobbyists to funnel money to those politicians likely to support special tax breaks for chicken farmers, restrictions on beef and pork imports, and relaxation of environmental regulations requiring them to clean up chicken droppings. Once their profitability is enhanced, they could agree to restrict the supply of chickens. In the presence of strong demand and restrained competition, the price of chickens must inevitably rise. Their tax savings become an increased burden on the individual taxpayer, and their higher prices on every consumer. The higher prices also increase inflation. Because they do not operate in a vacuum, the prices of other meats can rise as well to maintain relative price parity. If all this is too hypothetical, let me cite a real world example.

In 1979, oil prices increased 68% from the previous year due to a perceived shortage of oil. My company was using several million pounds annually of styrene plastic, and had a supply agreement with Amoco that dictated quantities and prices. Amoco violated the agreement on both counts, severely restricting the quantity and increasing the price by about 50%. When I threatened to sue, their representative told me that it was my prerogative to do so, but it would not change their position. A business associate, whose brother was an attorney representing a group of investors, offered to contact his brother on our behalf. A few days later, he returned with an inventory of many available petrochemical products including six million metric tons of the type of styrene we were using. The materials were sitting on barges in Shreveport, Louisiana. We could buy any quantity we could use, under three conditions: the price was several cents higher than the then current market price, we would have to buy several months of supply, and the shipment would be placed on a ship of foreign registry and brought in through another port. I did not take advantage of the offer because another source offered to supply us on somewhat better terms.

The energy sector has by far the greatest impact on our economy. Oil and gas power our transportation systems, heat our homes, and cook our food. Most plastics used in the products we buy come from oil, as do many chemical compounds. Natural gas is the source of most of our nitrate based agricultural fertilizer. Participants in this sector, perhaps more than any other, should compete for our business, but they do not. In 1928, the major oil producers met in Achnacarry Castle in Scotland to forge an agreement that would bring order to the petroleum market. Since then, oil producers have acted in concert to control supplies and prices with impunity. For several decades, they were granted an exemption from taxes on 27.5% of their sales. It was called the oil depletion allowance. By 1975, it had been lowered to 15% and restricted to independent oil producers only. In 1973, in retribution for our support of Israel in the Arab Israeli War, Saudi Arabia took control of 25 % of Aramco, the Arab-American Oil Company. In 1980, Saudi Arabia assumed 100% control. Subsequently, US oil producers were granted a first year tax deduction of 70% of the cost of drilling wells, with the remaining 30% to be deducted over the next five years. With Saudi Arabia, Venezuela, and other countries nationalizing their oil and mineral resources, it has become more profitable for oil companies to drill in the US where, in addition to having us pay for the drilling, they can control prices and increase their profits. That is what was behind the push for more domestic drilling. Whether it is smart to further deplete our limited reserves is yet another question.

The energy sector is our greatest source of inflation. I estimate their impact to be about 40%, meaning that a 10% increase in oil prices raises our cost of living 4%. While not the only cause of recessions, this chart shows that the mid-1970s recession began with a tripling of oil prices. Oil price increases fueled inflation, the FED responded by raising interest rates, and the country was thrown into recession. The chart is annual, but on a month by month scale the sequence of events is unmistakable.

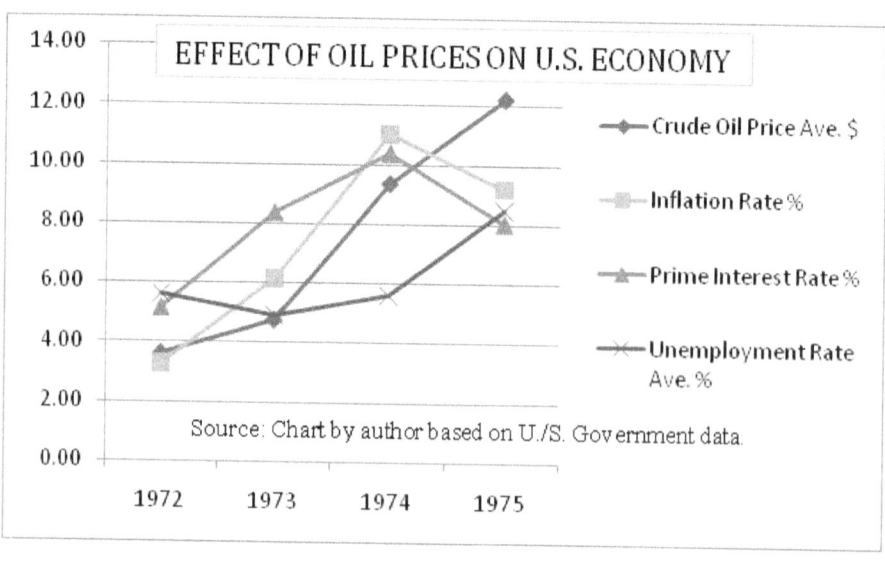

The 2001 recession followed a 45% increase in oil prices between 1999 and 2000. The 2008 recession followed a 97% increase in oil prices from 2007. The only winners in this game are the oil companies and speculators. The current recession is a prime example of the convergence of multiple causes. Oil prices went from an annual average of $22.81 per barrel in 2002 to $64.20 in 2007 to $126.33 in 2008, causing prices of nearly everything to rise. This was during the eleven years without an increase in the minimum wage. Deregulation allowed banks to charge any rate of interest they wanted. Home mortgage and credit card interest rates climbed. Dramatic increases in health care costs, energy, and education also added fuel to the fire. The average consumer's disposable income plummeted. By 2009, unemployment was 10.2%. The recession was blamed entirely on the so-called housing bubble (covered in a later chapter), but, as you can see, that is only part of the story. Every time there is a huge disproportion of income, the excess goes into passive long-term investments that do not trickle through to the general economy. The oil companies, insurance companies, universities, and banks all acted in unison. Capitalism only works when there is competition. Where are the competitors? Obviously, deregulation in this case did not promote competition. Two-thirds of our economy is based on consumer spending. The policy failures that have allowed real incomes for the vast majority to decline are directly responsible for the current financial crisis.

The following charts by the Center for Budget and Policy Priorities (*http://www.cbpp.org/cms/index.cfm?fa=view&id=2908*) demonstrate that both crises occurred coincident with the dramatic increase in income of the top one percent of earners and consequent erosion of income for the majority of consumers. The first chart shows the huge increases in the income of the top 1% of households leading up to the Great Depression and the current financial crisis. The increase appears to coincide with the tax cuts in the 1980s and 2000s.

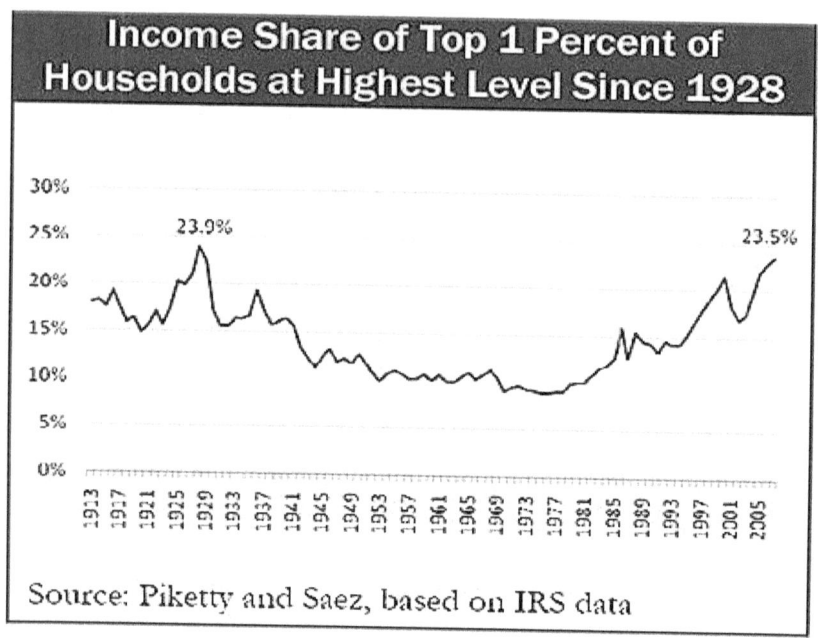

On examining why the income growth of the top one percent was so low during the period when top income tax rates ranged from 70-92%, the only logical conclusion is that it was kept low voluntarily to avoid paying too much to the IRS. Corporations also kept their profits moderate for the same reason. They poured their money into expansion of product lines, research and development, and capital investments, all of which increased the value of their companies and the wealth of their stockholders. They could afford to pay higher wages and provide better benefits for their workers. Businesses benefitted from enabled consumers, and workers from low unemployment. The subsequent erosion of wages and benefits is an unintended consequence of the tax cuts. Money that was once used to expand industrial activity and national infrastructure has been corralled by the financial sector, which now is the largest sector of our economy, but produces nothing. It is **lazy money**!

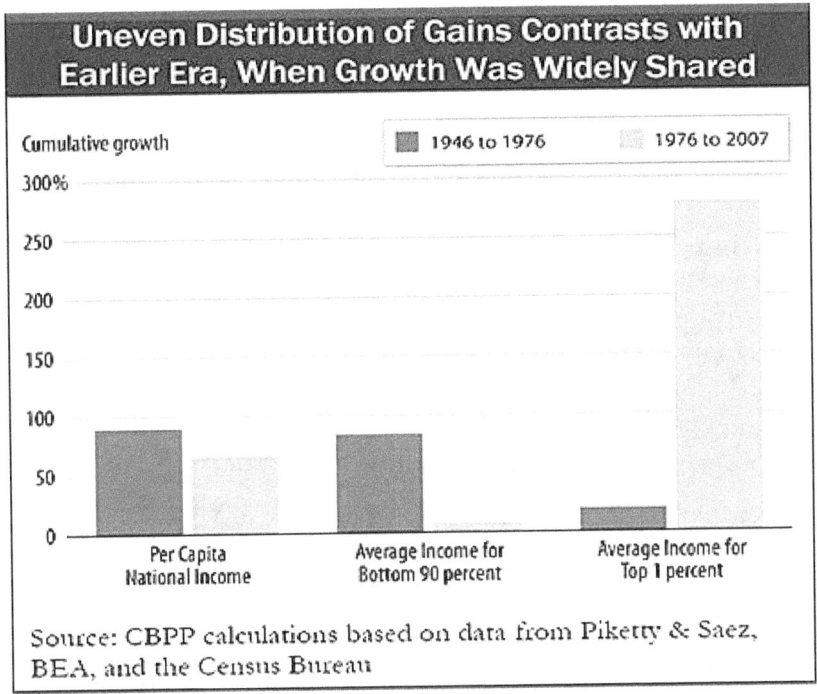

Uneven Distribution of Gains Contrasts with Earlier Era, When Growth Was Widely Shared

Cumulative growth   ■ 1946 to 1976   ▨ 1976 to 2007

Per Capita National Income	Average Income for Bottom 90 percent
Average Income for Top 1 percent	

Source: CBPP calculations based on data from Piketty & Saez, BEA, and the Census Bureau

Where did we get the idea that all deregulation is good? Don't our politicians know the difference? You may have heard the old adage "You gotta dance with the one who brung you." It takes a lot of money to get elected to Congress. If you want to keep your job, you have to keep the money coming. Who will you listen to, the $10 individual donor, whose opinion hardly matters, or the big-bucks donor who can just as easily finance your opponents campaign? If that donor is a major advertiser in, or perhaps owns, numerous media outlets, you will be disinclined to oppose his interests even when you know they are not in the interest of your constituents. It then becomes necessary to sell the donor's ideology to the public. Those media outlets really come in handy. When that donor corporation is part of an industry association, its power is greatly magnified.

We are caught in a paradoxical situation. If we don't spend enough over a long enough period of time, the economy may not recover fully for decades. If we do spend enough, the deficits will increase our national debt to a point where interest payments will absorb more of our revenues than any other expense. During the 1980s, interest payments were as high as 21% of our revenues. They will be even higher now. Our revenues are completely inadequate to meet our needs, so the spending can only be financed by huge tax increases, which is politically unacceptable, or borrowing, which requires more revenues to offset interest costs. Our trading partners are already balking at buying more treasury notes, so we may not be able to borrow the amounts needed, even if we want to. In order to attract investors to our government debt, we will be forced to raise interest rates, which will slow down the economy and lead to deeper recession. We could drastically reduce spending, but that will only increase unemployment and reduce revenues. A radical overhaul is needed to avoid the recurring boom and bust cycles that have plagued our personal and national economies. That is the only way we will be able to restore fiscal responsibility and avoid becoming RISC. The question we must ask ourselves is not "Can we afford to do it?", but "Can we afford not to do it?"

In addition to overhauling our system of taxation, financing of political campaigns, and regulating what financial institutions can do with our money, we must deal with several other issues that affect our economic future: immigration, welfare, health care, and education. We will address each in subsequent chapters. For now, let's recap what we should have deduced from this chapter.

1. Spending cuts and other austerity measures cannot refuel depressed economies.
2. Tax cuts do not refuel depressed economies, but tax increases may.
3. Borrowed money cannot refuel deeply depressed economies.
4. Economies are refueled by consumers with disposable income.
5. Full recovery from deep recessions usually takes many years.
6. Government subsidies to any business or person are a tax on all others.
7. Banks, insurance companies, and investment firms gamble with our money.

8. The current system of taxation and deregulation of the financial sector, or failure to enforce existing regulations, are directly responsible for the present financial crisis.
9. Some forms of deregulation stifle competition.

"Gold will be slave or master."

Horace (65 BC-8 BC), ancient Roman poet

Small Government

President Ronald Reagan, speaking at a Texas fundraising dinner in 1982, quoted Oliver Wendell Holmes, Justice of the Supreme Court, as saying, *"Keep government poor and remain free."* There is no record of Holmes having ever said that, but it did not matter. Along with another of his quotes, *"Government is not a solution to our problem, government is the problem,"* it set the antigovernment tone for politicians for decades to come. Is it not ironic that the very politicians who are the government and who are vying for government positions want us to believe that government is a bad thing?

Ronald Reagan's career as a movie actor began during the Great Depression. The top income tax rate went from 25% on incomes over $100,000 to 63% on incomes over $1,000,000 just as he was getting started. He was right to be upset about the terrible waste in government and the outrageous tax structure, but these were issues related to lack of proper government oversight and a terrible system of taxation more than the size of Government. The Great Depression became a crisis due to government inaction, but it began with corporate failures. The cost of World War II and the arms race that followed, the creation of the Federal bureau of Investigation and the Central Intelligence Agency, and reconstruction after the war all had to be repaid somehow. If the notion that cutting taxes would reduce the size of government and force it to cut spending was correct, why did his administration nearly triple the national debt from $908 billion in 1980 to $2,602 billion in 1988? One can always blame Congress, but the President has the power to veto any bill. Many of Reagan's achievements deserve praise, but small government and fiscal responsibility are not among them.

As this is being written, Haiti is recovering from a devastating earthquake that has claimed more than 200,000 lives in Port Au Prince. Haiti is a small country adjoining the Dominican Republic on the island of Hispaniola. It has a small government—so small that it could not provide the most basic of needs to its people or its business community. Most of the deaths occurred because thousands of buildings collapsed. Hundreds of thousands of people were left homeless. Emergency services were nonexistent. Food, water, tents, and medical care had to be provided by other nations. Haiti does not have the resources to rebuild. That raises a question: Is it small government that is good, or is it efficient government that provides maximum freedom, opportunity, order, and protection for its citizens?

History is full of examples that might help to answer that question. Let's begin with the country of my birth, Poland. Few people realize that Poland was the largest country in central Europe and one of the leading powers in the thirteenth through seventeenth centuries. It had a long history of religious freedom, one of the oldest universities, and was a center of science, culture and art. In 1572, because there was no male successor to the throne, Poland's Royal Republic was established. Kings were thereafter elected by the estate-owning gentry, which was about 10% of the population, the largest voting class in Europe. The king had to agree to a contract that protected the privileges of the gentry and the rights of citizens. The political system featured a parliament and a senate, with a group of senators acting as the king's overseers. The parliament could overrule the king. Representatives had the right of 'free veto', which allowed any representative to veto any legislation passed in a session, effectively overruling the majority. This system was called the 'Golden Freedom'. It was carried to an extreme in the late seventeenth century when the free veto was extended to regional parliaments. In 1683AD, the Polish army, under King Jan Sobieski, with 10,000 German auxiliaries defeated the large Turkish Islamic force at Vienna, preventing the invasion of Europe. This was to be the last display of Poland's power. The nineteen or so families that controlled the economy would not agree to any spending bill. Their representatives simply vetoed anything that might increase their taxes. They achieved small government at the expense of its institutions, education, and infrastructure. Within 100 years, Poland became one of the weakest countries in Europe, and was partitioned between Russia, Prussia, and Austria. It would not regain its independence until after World War One, despite the best efforts of some heroic men, two of whom, Tadeusz Koszciuszko and Kazimierz Pulaski, helped us gain our independence by commanding forces in the American Revolutionary War.

History is full of examples worth considering. The Roman Empire had grown so large that, even with its advanced road system and Mediterranean fleet, it became ungovernable. They split the empire into eastern and western regions each with their own administrations. In the fourth century, the Emperor Constantine reconsolidated them and moved the headquarters of the Roman Empire from Rome to Constantinople. His successors completed the move by mid century. Much of the money and power went with them. The city of Rome was reduced from about 1,000,000 people to less than 100,000. With greatly reduced commerce and government institutions, wealthy landholders (lords) exchanged some of their lands for military service and oaths of loyalty from their supporters (barons or knights). They, in turn, rented out some of their lands to their supporters (villeins). The peasants (serfs) attached themselves to their lords in exchange for protection and work. Under the feudal system, whoever owned the land (fiefs) essentially owned the people who worked it. With no significant central government presence, the warlords were the only protection against the frequent incursions by marauding barbarian tribes. Each warlord taxed his subjects, charged tolls for the use of his roads, established duties on goods passing through his fiefdom, and provided services for travelers, often at exorbitant prices. Most commerce came to a halt because of the dangers and cost of travel. Literacy declined, and Europe sank into the Dark Ages. About ninety percent of the population were little more than slaves.   Europe began to recover only when strong central governments were reestablished by the most powerful nobles, giving rise to nations, particularly Germany and France. In contrast, the Eastern Roman Empire, which we now call the Byzantine Empire and which had a strong central government, survived for another thousand years despite continual battles with Arab then Turkish Islamic forces.

Rome gained its wealth through conquest. Its soldiers fought willingly because they got some share of the spoils. Once it had defeated wealthier nations, the cost of conquest exceeded the benefits. All that could be gained was cheap labor—slaves. The Roman historian Tacitus wrote that, early in the second century, a senator became angry when he was bumped by someone on the street . He asked the senate to pass a law requiring slaves to wear identifying clothing. The senate conducted a census to determine who the slaves were. When the senate learned that nearly eighty percent of the city's population were slaves, the senators wisely decided not to pursue the matter. When a majority of the population has no stake in the success of a nation, its loyalty cannot be assured, and it can only be controlled by force. In a society where the only medium of exchange is cheap labor, there is no opportunity for broad based commerce to flourish.

At first glance, it might appear that the problem of Poland and Western Rome was lack of military strength. Closer examination shows that they were oligarchies governed by elite moneyed minorities that sought to preserve their disproportionate advantage. Their senates were a sham, only representing special interests. Without a strong middle class, the tax base was eroded until it could no longer support a strong military or other necessary institutions.

Spain also gained its wealth through conquest. After discovering the Americas, it decimated and enslaved its native populations, and exported their precious metals, as well as new agricultural products like potatoes, tomatoes, corn, and tobacco to Spain. The great increase in the amount of gold, the primary medium of exchange, caused hyperinflation. High prices hammered the poor and hindered exports. The nobility made little attempt to develop Spain's internal economy, partly because of class consciousness, and partly out of desire to increase their profits. They opted to import much cheaper foreign goods. Its government remained highly concentrated. The disparity between rich and poor increased. When the inward flow of gold slowed, Spain's wealth continued to drain out. Spain never regained its economic or military strength.

Spain's situation in the 1500s closely resembles that of the United States in recent decades. Foreign products were much cheaper, so domestic manufacturers sourced their products from foreign suppliers. They made more profit and gave the consumer a better deal. In the process, unemployment increased and wages decreased. In the end, the consumer was worse off. Only those at the top of the economic pyramid were better off. It's the old ballpark analogy. If you stand up, you can see better; if everyone stands up, only the tallest will see well. If you save much of your income, you will be better off; if everyone does so, the economy will be depressed, and you will be forced to exhaust your savings, unless you have very deep pockets.

Long-term security and prosperity can only be achieved when economic, political, popular, and military power is kept in balance internally and internationally. If a country with a small government has a weak military, it is inevitably overrun by foreign powers or overthrown by popular revolution. If it has a strong military, it invariably becomes a military dictatorship. There are far too many military coups that can be used as examples, so we will examine a recent one.

In February of 2010, the government of Niger, an African country, was toppled in a military coup. It was one of about thirty countries in Africa that have experienced military coups in recent years. Its strongman president, Mamadou Tandja, whose term should have ended in December, pushed through a new constitution that removed term limits and granted him virtually totalitarian powers. Tandja was democratically elected in 1999 after a series of coups and rebellions. Niger exports cattle, agricultural products, and uranium. The uranium mines are foreign owned. The decline in worldwide uranium demand has had a negative impact on its economy. Foreign companies have taken out licenses to exploit Niger's gold and other mineral deposits. China's National Petroleum Corporation has been licensed to develop Niger's oil industry, including a refinery and pipeline. Niger is heavily dependent on IMF, World Bank, and various United Nations programs for support. Niger's population is about 15 million, of which 5 million are in the workforce, and fewer than 80,000 actually earn salaries and wages. Average wages are less than $2 per day. The logical conclusion is that people with no economic power have no political power. They cannot resist either their military or their politicians.

There are also numerous examples of foreign countries overrunning those with small governments. Nazi Germany's defeat of Poland in World War II is a prime example. People sometimes joked about Poland's elite cavalry, the Ulani, charging German tanks on horseback. These brave souls were charging past the tanks to attack the infantry behind the tanks. Poland had no equipment capable of stopping the tanks. The Polish army was actually not defeated in the field. It had limited radio equipment, so it had to rely on the nation's civilian telephone and radio networks, the first infrastructure the Germans knocked out. Hundreds of thousands of Polish troops were left directionless. Many of them made their way out of the country. Near the end of the war, many thousands of Polish troops were fighting alongside the allies on the western front. One need only look at the casualty lists at Monte Casino in Italy to see that the largest number were Polish. Twenty years after regaining its independence was simply not enough time to rebuild its economy and, consequently, its military.

Nazi Germany, on the other hand, poured its resources overwhelmingly into its military. Its industrial sector saw it as a tremendous opportunity. The alliance of politics, military, and business defines fascism. The combination sucked the lifeblood out of its economy and its people. The importance of maintaining that critical balance of powers cannot be overstated. We should all remember President Eisenhower's warning, as he was leaving office, concerning the danger in the ever-growing power of the military-industrial complex.

Even if a country with a small government and weak military is not overrun by a foreign power, the result can be equally grim— warlords fighting for control of the government, civil war along ethnic, religious, or political grounds; or lawless elements terrorizing their neighbors for personal gain. In the recent past Rwanda, Sudan, Somalia, and Kenya have had thousands of people killed when their governments were either unwilling or unable to maintain order. The Khmer Rouge in Cambodia killed nearly two million of their countrymen in an attempt to force communism upon them.

We all want to be secure in our persons, in our livelihood, in our possessions, in our intellectual pursuits, and in our liberties. That security comes at a price. It cannot be achieved by force of arms alone. We want to live in an orderly society where our neighbors' freedoms do not encroach upon ours. We want building codes to protect the value of our properties, police protection to protect us against criminal and reckless behavior, fire departments to provide emergency services, street and road maintenance to protect our vehicles, water systems that provide clean safe water, protection against unsafe products and services, and countless other regulations and items of infrastructure. It should be readily apparent that small and/or poor government is not capable of providing all the services needed to provide the order and security necessary for economies to flourish and people to prosper.

Much of the economic growth we have experienced has been based on basic research conducted and/or funded by the government. Here is just a brief sample. It includes nuclear power, radar, jet planes, integrated circuits that made modern computing possible, the Internet, satellite TV, GPS systems, airport scanners, and more than a third of medical research. The business community's research and development efforts are generally aimed at short term profit. It is quite good at commercializing the product of basic research, but rarely engages in it. Poor governments cannot afford to pursue the basic research that leads to innovative technologies that drive economic growth and ensure our long term security.

We want the benefits that government can provide, but without waste, inefficiency, and fraud. We want a government small enough to listen to us, not an arrogant bureaucracy that instills a sense of powerlessness in individuals. We want a fair system of taxation that does not punish success or impoverish the already poor. We want government operations to be transparent—free of obfuscation, misinformation, and disinformation— so we can make informed decisions. We want a method of financing political campaigns that does not unduly favor powerful special interests over individual citizens.

There is much that the private sector does better than government. For example, communist countries that dictated which products to produce, how to produce them, in what quantities, and what prices to charge, have invariably failed miserably at it while private sector corporations often get it right. On the other hand, the private sector is just as riddled with waste, inefficiency, and fraud as the public sector. Many companies I have invested in over the past decade have been involved in litigation with their stockholders, customers, and the Securities and Exchange Commission. Many have participated in accounting scandals, been fined, or had their executives prosecuted and imprisoned. Most of us have heard of Adelphia, AIG, AOL, Bristol-

Myers Squibb, Chiquita Brands International, Enron, Freddie Mac, Halliburton, Health South, Madoff, MCI World Com, Merck & Co., Qwest, Tyco, Union Carbide, Waste Management, and many others.

As of 2008, the federal government was spending about $400 billion per year on private contractors throughout the government. The cost for them is considerably higher than it would be if government employees were doing the work. It may look like smaller government, but it is an illusion. It is nothing more than patronage of the same sort as was practiced by powerful political machines in the past. You may recall that it was contractors in the State Department that accessed confidential records of presidential candidates in the 2008 election. There were more than 180,000 private contractors in Iraq—more than the 169,000 US military personnel. Blackwater alone held about $1billion in federal contracts. Halliburton received contracts worth up to $7 billion without competing bids. The Congressional Conference Report accompanying the Intelligence Authorization Act For Fiscal Year 2008 states the following: *The Intelligence Community employs a significant number of "core" contractors who provide direct support to Intelligence Community mission areas and are generally indistinguishable from the United States Government personnel whose mission they support.* **Because of the cost disparity between employing a United States civilian employee, estimated to cost an average of $126,500 annually, and a core contractor, estimated to cost an average of $250,000 annually, the conferees believe that the Intelligence Community should strive to reduce its dependence on contractors.** You may recall that Mussolini had his 'Blackshirts', and that Hitler consolidated his power by forming the SA 'brownshirts' that morphed into the SS. Does anyone think it is a good idea for a private army-for-hire to exist on our soil? Some things should never be privatized.

There are proponents of small government who would prefer states to provide all necessary regulation and services. While, superficially, it might appear to be smaller government, the staff required and the cost, in the aggregate, is far greater. Much of a state's infrastructure (interstate highways, airports, railroads, telecommunication systems, electrical power generating and distribution facilities, oil and gas pipelines, etc.) exists to support interstate commerce. Business activity is hampered and cost of doing business increases if every state regulates them individually. Furthermore enforcement becomes more difficult, often resulting in protracted litigation with mortgage lenders, tobacco and energy companies, and polluters. As employment becomes more transitory, people need to move from state to state in search of work. They can lose their unemployment insurance and other state-provided benefits at the time they can least afford to lose them, and could lose their health insurance as well. The amount of time state legislatures spend on conflicting laws increases cost and creates confusion. Firearm laws are a good example. Until recently, possession of a semiautomatic rifle in one county could get you a mandatory sentence of one year in jail in another. In one state, you may keep a loaded handgun in your vehicle for protection; in many others, even those with much higher crime rates, that protection is denied you. There is no easy way for travelers to know the rules current in each town.

Many issues are beyond the capability or means of state and local governments to resolve, among them are national defense, national security, disaster relief, consumer protection, disease control, medical research, basic scientific research, protection of natural resources, immigration, space exploration, interstate commerce, international commerce, international law, and international relations. The cost and complexity of such efforts and the need for continuity dictates a dedicated civil service at the national level which is independent of politics—people who have a stake in preserving their system of government.

The examples in this chapter are representative of what has happened and continues to happen in the real world. They do not require proof by complex mathematical formulas or philosophical arguments—just some common sense. We can summarize this chapter as follows:

1. Small and/or weak governments cannot provide long term security or prosperity.

2. Business and financial interests are generally concerned more with their own short term profits than long term general prosperity.
3. An inadequate tax base ultimately leads to national decline.
4. Cheap labor is not a solid foundation for a strong domestic economy.
5. Failure to reinvest in a domestic economy drains a nation's wealth.
6. Much, and possibly most, long term national economic growth stems from research conducted by or funded by government.
7. Elimination of waste, inefficiency, and fraud is a better objective than small government.
8. Privatization of essential government functions increases the cost and complexity of government.
9. Having individual states regulate interstate activity and issues increases the aggregate cost and complexity of government.
10. Long-term security and prosperity can only be achieved when economic, political, popular, and military power is kept in balance.

"If liberty and equality, as is thought by some, are chiefly to be found in democracy, they will be best attained when all persons alike share in government to the utmost."

Aristotle (384-322 BC), ancient Greek philosopher.

Fair Tax

Hardly anyone believes that our system of taxation is fair. Most people have no idea how much of their income goes to taxes, what taxes they are paying, and who is paying most of them. Federal progressive income tax rates appear to punish the successful, but the revenues derived from them are smaller than those from the myriad hidden taxes that masquerade as user fees and product cost borne by most of us. When we consider all forms of taxation, like state income taxes, property taxes, sales taxes, vehicle license fees, utility taxes, excise taxes, entertainment taxes, tolls, duties, etc., they exceed what we pay in federal income taxes. Politicians love user-based taxes because they are easier to pass. All taxes on products and services get passed through to the consumer. Because they are applied at the point of sale, they are perceived as product cost, so consumers rarely complain. Don't be misled; they are taxes, and they must be paid even when one has little or no income.

Before currency was invented and most societies were agrarian, most business was done by barter. People's livestock, produce, and labor were the only basis for collecting taxes. One could be wealthy without having money as such. Today, that is no longer the case, but property taxes continue to be levied. Because they are community based, the wealthiest communities have excellent schools and services, while the poorer, which are far greater in number, receive the bare minimum. The property tax is usually hidden in a mortgage or rent payment, so we sometimes forget that it is a tax. Worst of all, it doesn't care whether the taxpayer had any income at all. Some states have exorbitant vehicle license fees based on the value of the vehicle. This is just another property tax. The sixty year old person who cannot find a job, whose unemployment compensation has run out, and who is still too young to collect social security, must nevertheless pay his property tax or lose his home or his car. After a lifetime of good citizenship and taxpaying, that is hardly fair.

In the accompanying table, you can see that in 2007 the federal government spent $2.73 trillion compared to state and local governments, which spent $2.66 trillion, mostly from user based taxes. Data for 2007 was used because it preceded most of the financial meltdown. The numbers for 2008 and 2009 were much worse. If the expenses were equally divided across households, they would have amounted to $46, 168. Corporations paid $11,611 of that. The budget deficit added $1,378 to our national debt. The remaining $33,179 was paid by the median household in all forms of taxation. That is 66.1% of their income.

TAXES MEDIAN HOUSEHOLD PAID IN 2007		
Income and Tax/Expenditure	Amount	% of MHI
Median household income (MHI)	**$50,233**	**100%**
Federal spending per household (1)	$19,364	38.5%
State and local spending	$26,804	53.4%
Taxes paid by corporations (2)	$11,611	23.1%
Taxes to be paid by households (3)	**$34,557**	**68.8%**
Taxes deferred by budget deficit	$1,378	2.7%
Net taxes paid in current year	**$33,179**	**66.1%**
Source: Table by author based on Internal Revenue Service data.		
1. Excludes transfers to states and local governments.		
2. May include deductible taxes paid to foreign countries.		
3. Taxes required to avoid budget deficits.		

There should be no doubt that our system of taxation is broken. For any fix to be fair, it must follow this rule: one's obligation to society must be proportional to the benefit one receives from it. It is difficult to determine how unfair the federal system is because IRS statistics are often three or more years out of date, show taxable income rather than total revenues, and are not structured in a way that facilitates analysis. The following table should give some indication. When we factor in all Social Security and Medicare taxes, the rate of tax actually paid is little different between the highest and lowest earners. Those who argue that Social Security is an insurance program not a tax must explain why so much of the premiums are transferred to the general fund to reduce deficits. One might argue that it is unfair to include the employer's portion in the tax paid by the employee, but the fact that those amounts would otherwise be available for wages and employers claimed employment taxes as deductions suggests their inclusion is reasonable. If we factor in all the state and local user-based taxes, it should be obvious that the bottom half of taxpayers pay proportionally far more in taxes than any of the top tiers and cannot pay more. That is the justification for the progressive income tax, and that is why true tax reform must look beyond individual income taxes.

2007 IRS Income and Taxes by Income Rank								
Income Rank	* AGI Range $		Average AGI $	Income Tax Paid	** FICA Tax Est.	Medicare Tax Est.	Total Tax Est.	Tax %
	From	To						
Top 1%	410,096	>	1,423,580	319,645	6,045	41284	366,974	25.78%
2-5%	160,041	410,095	227,950	39,939	6,045	6611	52,594	23.07%
6-10%	113,018	160,040	132,316	16,749	6,045	3837	26,631	20.13%
11-25%	66,532	113,017	85,891	8,102	10,768	2491	21,361	24.87%
26-50%	32,879	66,531	47,490	3,328	7,266	1377	11,971	25.21%
Low 50%	<	32,879	15,287	457	2,339	443	3,240	21.19%
* Adjusted Gross Income			** FICA and Medicare includes employee and employer's share.					
Source: Table by author based on IRS data.								

When all forms of taxation are considered, you are paying far more in taxes than you ever imagined. We have been told that the reason is entitlements like Social Security and Medicare. That is partially true, but they are large enough issues to deserve separate chapters. For now, we will address the tax system itself and the various proposals that have been put forth to reform them.

One tax reform proposal is the Fair Tax. It is a National Sales Tax or consumption tax on individual income. Don't be fooled into thinking there is anything fair about it. It must be paid when one has little or no income. Consider this example. A household making $50,233 per year would probably spend about one-third ($16,744) on goods and services subject to the sales tax. If the tax was set at 20%, the tax would amount to $3349, or 6.7% of income. Another household making one hundred times that income ($5,023,300) might spend $251,000 on taxable products and services. Their tax would be $52,000, or 1.0% of income. It would allow the wealthy to escape taxation on most of their income. One estimate of the tax rate proposed was 23%. Keep in mind that they did not propose eliminating Social

Security, Medicare, state and local, and other taxes. No matter how it is structured, it would place an increased burden on the middle class. Most of us would be paying significantly more than we are now paying.

Some countries have introduced a Value Added Tax (VAT) to try to overcome some of the inequities of profit-based taxes. VAT has also been proposed here. It is essentially a sales tax paid on the purchase of goods and services at every stage of the supply chain. At each stage, one pays to the government the VAT it collects from its customers less the VAT it has paid to its suppliers. In practice, while it may overcome some problems in the current income tax system, it has the exact same effect as the National Sales Tax. It only taxes the income used for taxable product and services while leaving investment income untouched. Consequently, it shifts the burden onto the lower and middle class earners.

While progressive income tax rates are very high (35%) for the highest earners, and one is tempted to believe they are actually paying them, the chart above shows that not to be the case. It has not prevented the number of billionaires in the U.S. from swelling to nearly 400. Much of their income comes from capital gains, which get preferential tax treatment. Proposals continually reappear for the complete elimination of capital gains taxes as a means of encouraging capital investment. They don't make a lot of sense since capital gains are not realized until the assets are sold. When demand is strong, corporations tend to hold on to their assets in order to benefit from the increased profits. Businesses invest in plants and equipment in response to demand, not sell-off of assets.

Several proposals have been aimed at the complete elimination of corporate income taxes. As you can see from the above charts and tables, taxing individual income alone cannot come close to meeting our needs even if drastic spending cuts were made, unless of course we were willing to bear even higher tax rates. Corporations must pitch in. A July 2008 Government Accountability Office (GAO) report shows that in one eight year period, 1998-2005, in at least one year, 72% of Foreign Controlled Domestic Corporations (FCDCs) paid no U.S. income tax, while 55% of United States Controlled Corporations (USCCs) paid no U.S. income tax. One year might be considered a fluke, but 34% of FCDCs and 24% of USCCs paid no U.S. income tax in at least four of the eight years. With ever more domestic business being done by FCDCs, the tax loss is significant.

Many corporations do pay taxes, some at high rates, but taken in the aggregate, corporations are getting a free ride. The problem lies in the very concept of taxing profits, which are subject to manipulation, and the many complex, often irrational, exemptions, exclusions, and deductions that have been written into the tax codes to benefit special interests. A corporation can deduct all of its expenses, but individuals only a small portion.

2007 TAX DATA	Individual	Corporate
Number of Returns	142,978,806	5,868,849
Gross Receipts *	$10,797,957,158,000	$28,762,923,553,000
Deductions	$2,110,238,389,000	$27,514,638,096,000
Taxable Income/AGI	$8,687,718,769,000	$1,248,285,457,000
Taxes Paid	$1,955,642,048,000	$368,481,478,000
Taxes % of Taxable	22.51%	29.52%
Taxes % of Receipts	18.11%	1.28%
* Note that corporate receipts are nearly triple those of Individuals.		
Source: Table by author based on U.S. Internal Revenue Service data		

Much tax avoidance is based on country of incorporation. A company can incorporate in the Cayman Islands or other tax haven and pay no U.S. income tax. Multinational corporations can have subsidiaries in dozens of countries. It is virtually impossible to determine profitability under those circumstances. Transfers between subsidiaries can be priced in a way to generate losses (or at least reduced profits) where tax rates are highest. The effect can be seen in a Forbes report on 2009 taxes paid by the largest twenty-five U.S. corporations. Exxon Mobil had sales of $311 billion, on which it made a profit of $37.3 billion and paid taxes of $17.6 billion, but none of it was paid to the U.S. Chevron had sales of $172 billion, on which it made a profit of $18.5 billion and paid taxes of $8.0 billion, but only $200 million was paid to the U.S.

A May 5, 2009, article by David Evans in Bloomberg states that in 2004 there were 12,748 U.S. companies registered in the Cayman Islands. Their address is a five-story building in Grand Cayman. Among the companies listed are Intel, Coca Cola, Oracle, and Seagate. The often-stated reason for this is to simplify the determination of taxes due to various countries where multinational corporations operate. I have read estimates of tax revenue loss to the United States that exceed $200 billion a year. I attempted to find a list of these companies, and was shocked that there is none that is readily available to the public. How can it be that something as important as this can be kept from us? Obviously neither the companies nor the politicians want us to know. I did find fragmentary references that included several of the financial firms involved in our economic meltdown, including Citigroup, Morgan Stanley, Bank of America, Goldman Sachs, and J.P. Morgan; information technology firms, including Intel, Hewlett-Packard, Oracle, Apple, and Seagate; government contractors like Boeing, Halliburton, KBR, Martin Marietta, Altria, and Tyco; Pharmaceutical companies like Merck, Pfizer, and Schering Plough; Transocean of Deepwater Horizon oil spill fame; and many others including General Motors, Procter and Gamble, FedEx, Del Monte, Sprint, and Global Santa Fe, just to name a few.

You may not be aware of it, but if a corporation loses money, you will pay to make them whole. For example, one company that helped to precipitate the current financial crisis, Citigroup, had sales of $80 billion and losses of $7.8 billion, which gave it a tax loss carry-forward of $6.7 billion. One of my former clients had a loss of $768,000 after a small acquisition. Accelerated depreciation, write-down of assets, and other devices were used to generate that paper loss. The after-tax loss was $112,000. Who do you think made up the difference? You did.

Of course, a corporation does not have to actually lose money to have us give them our money. General Electric had 2009 sales of $157 billion, on which it made $10.3 billion, but it got $1.1 billion tax loss carry-forward. It won't be paying taxes here for quite a while. The same is true of Bank of America. It had sales of $120 billion, on which it made a profit of $4.4 billion, but got $1.9 billion back in tax loss carry-forward.

At the end of 2010, the Bush Administration's tax cuts were due to expire at the same time as unemployment insurance benefits for the long-term jobless. The Obama Administration pressed to have the tax cuts expire for the top two tax brackets, those earning more than $250,000 per year. The only way they could get the unemployment benefits extended was to push back the tax cut expiration for two years. That deferral will increase the deficit and the national debt by many billions of dollars per year. The argument for continuing the tax cuts was its effect on small business. It is an utterly disingenuous argument. Business income taxes are paid on profits, not revenues. A business with a profit of $250,000 might have sales in excess of $2.5 million. Most small businesses do not come close to that. However, many millionaire hedge fund managers, partners in law firms, and others who file their business income on personal returns but have minimal business expenses, are classified as small businesses and would be affected. S corporations are also classed as small businesses, although some have revenues of hundreds of millions of dollars. The profits or losses of S corporations are divided among those who own them. S corporations pay no income taxes. Their profits or losses are divided among the partners who pay the taxes individually. There are many ways that the corporations' financials and partners' earnings can be manipulated to reduce their tax liability. Most of them are too complex for anyone who is not a tax professional to understand.

Tax systems based on profits or income after deductions have a number of inherent flaws, not the least of which is that they are subject to manipulation. The number of companies whose executives have been indicted or sued for misrepresenting their companies' earnings for years clearly shows that profits are not easily verifiable, even by experts. That makes enforcement extremely difficult, and forces government to get involved in the minutiae of a business or household budget. The result is complex rules and regulations and, inevitably, loopholes. The very complexity of the income tax codes makes it virtually impossible to catch tax cheats. IRS enforcement budgets have been slashed over the last several years, so the IRS concentrates its efforts on the simpler tax returns where the amounts recovered are a pittance compared to what is lost due to under-reporting of income and the use of various tax shelters and sophisticated tax avoidance schemes. We know how ridiculous it is, but what can we do about it?

Attempts to reform the methods of taxation and the income tax codes to make them more equitable have failed miserably. In 1986, the Reagan administration proposed, and Congress enacted, the Tax Reform Act (TRA86). The following table clearly shows that only the top 10% of earners received a significant benefit, while most of the bottom 90% received a mere pittance. The employment taxes in this table are only those paid by the employee.

EFFECT OF 1986 TAX REFORM ACT BY INCOME RANK				
$ millions		**Top 1 %**	**Top 2-10 %**	**Bottom 90%**
1986	Income (AGI)	$ 285,197	$ 601,313	$ 1,637,614
	Income Tax	$ 94,491	$ 106,212	$ 166,276
	Employment Tax	$ 3,066	$ 27,591	$ 114,440
	Tax Percent	34.2%	22.3%	17.1%
1988	Income (AGI)	$ 473,527	$ 759,009	$ 1,891,620
	Income Tax	$ 113,841	$ 122,570	$ 176,350
	Employment Tax	$ 3,679	$ 33,114	$ 140,844
	Tax Percent	24.8%	20.5%	16.8%
Change in tax % paid		**-27.4%**	**-7.8%**	**-2.2%**
Source: By author based on U.S. Internal Revenue Service data				

Every tax cut in the last thirty years has had a disproportionate benefit to the highest earners. The cuts in the tax rates are offset by increases in employment taxes, changes in deductible limits, and changing the income threshold for each tax rate. In the above table, the highest tax rate in 1986 was 50% on incomes over $175,200. In 1988, it was 28%, but on incomes over $29,750. TRA86 was riddled with exemptions for wealthy contributors to political campaigns. Donald L. Barlett and James B. Steele of the *Philadelphia Inquirer* won a Pulitzer Prize in 1989 for their 15 month investigation into TRA86. It was reformulation and not reform.

Effect of 2001 Tax Cut by Income Group			
Dollars in millions Based on IRS data	Top 1 Percent	Top 2-10 Percent	Bottom 90 Percent
2000 Income (AGI)	$ 1,336,773	$ 1,618,613	$ 5,087,204
Income Tax	366,929	293,221	613,592
Employment Tax	44,304	94,385	341,368
Total Tax Percent	30.8%	23.9%	18.8%
2004 Income (AGI)	$ 1,306,417	$ 1,742,858	$ 5,568,706
Income Tax	306,902	260,371	530,988
Employment Tax	45,459	97,373	370,025
Total Tax Percent	27.0%	20.5%	16.2%
Change in tax % paid	-12.3%	-14.3%	-13.8%
Source: Table by author based on IRS data.			

The 1982 and the 2001 tax cuts greatly increased budget deficits and debt. The 2001 tax cuts reduced taxes for everyone, but they were not accompanied by controls on spending, so they turned four years of surpluses into huge budget deficits and increased debt.

Effect of Tax Cuts on Deficits and National Debt				
Year	1980	1981	1982	1983
Top Rate, All income	70	69.125	50	50
For Income Over	215,400	215,400	85,600	109,400
Federal Revenues (millions)	517,112	599,272	617,766	600,562
Expenditures	590,941	678,241	745,743	808,364
Surplus or (Deficit)	(73,830)	(78,968)	(127,977)	(207,802)
National Debt (millions)	907,701	997,855	1,142,034	1,377,210
Tax cuts ocurred in shaded years.				
Year	2000	2001	2002	2003
Top Rate, All income	39.6	39.1	38.6	35
For Income Over	288,350	297,350	307,050	311,950
Federal Revenues (millions)	2,025,457	1,991,426	1,853,395	1,782,532
Expenditures	1,789,216	1,863,190	2,011,153	2,160,117
Surplus or (Deficit)	236,241	128,236	(157,758)	(377,585)
National Debt (millions)	5,674,178	5,807,463	6,228,236	6,783,231
Source: Table by author based on U.S. Government data				

The time has come to face reality. Individual income is an inadequate tax base to meet our national needs. In an increasingly global economy, we must develop a system of taxation that is independent of the country or state of incorporation or location of facilities. It cannot be based on profits because they are not easily verifiable, encourage cheating, and invite government intrusion into business operations and personal lives. It must not discriminate on the basis of marital status or number of dependents. It must not give preferential treatment on the basis of type of corporation, organization, or association. Furthermore, it must be totally free of subsidies, exemptions, exclusions, and deductions. It must apply only one tax rate to all individuals and entities regardless of income level or profit. Finally, it must be simple, understandable, and enforceable.

My proposal requires the elimination of all forms of taxation except one — **a single flat rate income tax on gross receipts of all individuals, corporations, and organizations without exception, payable in the country and state from which money is received, with no exemptions, deductions, exclusions, or subsidies, and no place to hide.** Using the 2007 example in the table above, we can see what the tax rate would be.

PROPOPSED GROSS REVENUES TAX SYSTEM		
2007 Gross Receipts, Spending, & Tax Rates		
Individual ($10.8 trillion)	$10,797,957,158,000	
Corporate ($28.8 trillion)	$28,762,923,553,000	
Total Receipts	$39,560,880,711,000	**Tax (3)**
Federal Spending	$2,729,000,000,000	**6.90%**
State & Local Spending (1)	$2,195,000,000,000	**5.55%**
Total Spending & Tax Receipts (2)	$4,924,000,000,000	**12.45%**
1. Excludes intergovernmental transfers from federal.		
2. There are no budget deficits at the proposed tax rates.		
3. Tax rates apply equally to individuals and corporations.		

Keep in mind that in 2007 we were fighting two wars and running budget deficits. In this proposal, which bases taxes on actual expenditures, there are no budget deficits. Ending our wars and simplifying government operations under other proposals in later chapters would permit us to pay off the national debt in one generation. Forbidding deficit spending and requiring a supermajority popular vote to increase the tax rate would enforce fiscal discipline. Ultimately, it should easily be possible to reduce federal and state taxes combined below ten percent overall.

The beauty of this system is that taxes are directly proportional to prices. If prices for a commodity or service double, so do the taxes. Industries that have most egregiously raised prices, and the speculators dealing in their commodities, would all pay a fair share. In the end, the consumer always pays the accumulated taxes in the supply chain, but the burden would be least on those who consume the least in products and services. Likewise, those businesses that are most efficient in their use of materials, labor, and services would be rewarded for their efficiency instead of being penalized for their success.

Some might worry that businesses might not be able to make a profit. If all businesses, including foreign businesses, are taxed at the same rate and receive no subsidies of any kind, then all would be competing on a level playing field. Each would set prices at a level sufficient to make a profit and pay its taxes. We should not have to subsidize them. If we want less government interference in business, then we must recognize that businessmen are the ones responsible for setting prices and controlling costs to achieve profits. As long as all competitors are playing by the same rules and managing their affairs competently, they should be able to make money.

Our foreign trading partners would also pay tax on their sales into the U.S. That would enable more efficient domestic businesses to compete with those of foreign countries. It would reduce the relative cost of imports for countries with the lowest tax rates, which are typically the poorest. There is always a chance that some countries would resist adopting such a system, but they would be foolish not to since they would be denying themselves a revenue stream. Even without broad international agreement, if the United States adopted a gross revenues tax system, others would be forced to follow out of self-interest.

As with most changes, there can be unintended consequences. That is why the transition must be made slowly, allowing adequate time for adjustment. I believe a ten-year period would be appropriate. Each year, the current tax rates for every form of taxation, all user fees, and subsidies would be reduced by ten percent from the original, and the gross receipts tax would increase by ten percent. The process would essentially add two lines to a tax return. The impact would be apparent after the first year.

At the end of the ten year conversion period, tax returns could be as simple as two lines, identifying information, and any census or statistical data required by the government. Every month, your employer would remit to the federal, state and local governments your tax payment without any action on your part. The employer would pay his taxes on the same basis. Once per year, on a date appointed for you, you would file a supplemental return for any unreported income received, such as cash payments, tips, etc.

Two industries would require somewhat different treatment than most. The money deposited by clients in financial institutions is held for the clients' benefit, and should not be taxed. All other financial institution receipts that are not customer deposits should be taxed at the flat rate. Like financial institutions, insurance company premiums are held for the benefit of the insured. Any receipts in excess of claim payments should be taxed at the flat rate.

The proposed tax rates could be reduced significantly if additional sources of income are included in the gross revenues tax program. For example, the sale of property could be taxed at the flat rate on actual cash received at closing, after paying off the mortgage and realtors, less the initial payment or down payment. It eliminates the need for capital gains calculations and a host of complex regulations. Inheritance should be taxed similarly on actual cash value received, after paying off funeral and other estate expenses. It is, after all, just income, which, by the way, was not earned by the recipient. Any new trusts should all be created with after-tax income, with no tax due until funds pass to a beneficiary. Then, any amount received should be taxed at the flat rate.

Gifts are easily abused so all gifts should be made with after-tax money. There should be no tax to the recipient unless the gift is subsequently sold.

Since the proposed system of taxation is not based on profits, we should seriously consider how to redefine non-profit institutions. Only organizations that are supported by voluntary contributions and do not charge for their services should be exempt from taxes, providing they are not affiliated with for-profit businesses and do not engage in political activity. Many HMO's (Health Maintenance Organizations) started out as non-profits and were converted into for-profit businesses making their chief executives billionaires, and causing premiums to skyrocket. Such transfers or liquidation of assets should be taxed on the full value of the receipts to the seller/transferor or transferee.

I anticipated the cries of "Double Taxation!" Under the current system, consumers are always taxed twice—first by paying the taxes imbedded in the prices of goods and services, then by paying taxes on the money earned or otherwise received. It is only fair that businesses be taxed in the same way.

I also anticipated that some will argue in favor of gasoline taxes, cigarette taxes, alcohol taxes, and other forms of economic micromanagement in order to limit consumption. That is a form of price control that unduly punishes consumers. There is no place for price controls in a truly capitalist society.

Any tax reform scheme must be understandable and agreeable to the populace and the business community for it to succeed in the long term. I have tried to anticipate some of their questions that might arise, and to provide concise answers. It is my fervent hope you will see the merits. A constitutional amendment might be required to prevent Congress from imposing any other types of taxes or granting exemptions and subsidies. Much of the information the government currently collects by separate forms for numerous agencies can be inferred from a one-page tax return, then distributed to the appropriate agencies. The savings for businesses and government alike would be substantial. It might even be possible to replace the census taking process by incorporating it into a mandatory tax return.

Consider some of the benefits:

- Reduced cost of living for most people.
- A larger tax base makes it possible to eliminate deficits and reduce the national debt.
- The charade of raiding the Social Security and other funds to reduce deficits goes away when all government obligations are paid from the general fund.
- Less bureaucracy. The IRS would be free to concentrate on investigation and collection in an environment that makes cheating extremely difficult.
- Accountants would be free to concentrate on business profits, and helping people to manage their resources.
- Everyone would understand the tax codes, so the level of frustration would be dramatically reduced.
- There would be no opportunity for politicians to give special consideration to special interests.
- Government budgets and reports would be more intelligible for the layman.
- Equal treatment of rich and poor would reduce the tension between them.
- Equal treatment of corporations and individuals would become practical.
- Lower personal taxes would encourage the creation of new businesses.
- Equal treatment of domestic and foreign corporations would minimize the advantage they now have over domestic businesses.
- The use of tax havens like the Cayman Islands to facilitate global commerce becomes unnecessary.
- The system allows true capitalism. Since taxes would be equal for all products and services, competition would be based on merit, marketing skill, and demand.

The special interests will scream in horror at this proposal, but I believe the American people will see the merit in it. If democracy is to survive, we must reduce the level of helplessness, fear and frustration felt by many people in their dealings with government. Ultimately, these feelings lead to anarchy. Let's rebuild the people's confidence in our political system and in our politicians. Let's remove from their hands the tools of their own destruction and ours.

All of the data in this chapter is taken from official sources. Much of it is not in easily useable form, but it is verifiable. I believe the conclusions they lead us to are inescapable. Let's review them.

1. Personal income is an inadequate tax base to meet our needs unless one is willing to tolerate much higher progressive income tax rates.

2. Income taxes represent about half of all taxes collected at all levels of government.

3. The remaining taxes are hidden in the cost of products and services.

4. When all forms of taxation are considered, the bottom half of income earners pay substantially more in taxes than the top half.

5. Various tax reform proposals (Fair Tax, National Sales Tax, and Value Added Tax) do not tax investment income, so they disproportionately tax the bottom half.

6. Progressive income tax rates punish success.

7. Corporate revenues are a much larger potential tax base than personal income.

8. Corporate profits are an inadequate tax base and are not easily verifiable.

9. Basing taxes on the basis of country of registration or location of facilities is illogical as corporations are increasingly global in scope.

10. All tax reforms and tax cuts enacted and proposed to date have disproportionately benefitted the highest earners.

11. The complexity and inequities of the current system breed distrust and fear of government.

12. The proposed Gross Revenues Tax (GRT) is a combination of a tax on consumption and revenues, and will be eminently fair if applied at all levels of government—federal, state, and local.

13. The GRT has the potential to eliminate the national debt within one generation.

14. The GRT is defined as **a single flat rate income tax on gross receipts of all individuals, corporations, and organizations without exception, payable in the country and state from which money is received, with no exemptions, deductions, exclusions, or subsidies, and no place to hide**

Taxes are the price of civilization.

Oliver Wendell Holmes Jr. (1841- 1935), Associate Justice of the U.S. Supreme Court

Immigration Reform

Illegal immigration has been put forth as a problem primarily on our southern border. That is a gross oversimplification. The truth is that tens of millions of people enter this country legally on tourist, student, and work visas from nations all over the world by air, sea, and land. Many simply overstay their visas, and we have no effective system in place to identify, track, and remove them. Furthermore, citizens of more than two-dozen countries do not even need a visa to enter the United States. Several of the 9/11 highjackers came here legally. If we are serious about the war on terror, then solving this problem is every bit as important as securing our borders. An effective solution has to deal with all sources of illegal immigration.

Illegal immigration has nearly doubled our unemployment rate and stressed our health care and education budgets. The Latinos that cross our borders illegally are mostly Mexicans, but also include those from other Central and South American countries. Why are they streaming across our border? The answers are simple: they are looking for a better life, we love cheap products, our businesses love cheap labor, and the same politicians who inflame anti-immigrant sentiment refuse to put any constraints on businesses that hire illegal aliens.

While Mexico's top income tax rate is 28%, its effective rate of taxation on personal income is between 12 and 15 percent. Its revenues come from PeMex, its government owned oil company, at about 35%; remittances from Mexicans working abroad of 30%; and tourism contributes around 20%. Mexico is not a poor country. It exports oil, silver, and agricultural products. It has many foreign-owned automobile and other manufacturing plants, as well as domestic industries. Most of its banks are foreign owned. There is much wealth, but it does not trickle down to the common people. Unemployment is typically low, but underemployment can reach 50 percent. Wages are generally reported as averages that conceal huge inequalities. The minimum hourly wage is less than $1.00 per hour, and the standard workweek is 48 hours.

Mexico's economy, except for its oil industry, resembles RISC, the hypothetical country in the second chapter. Much of its manufacturing is in Free Trade Zones called maquiladoras, which give little back to the economy. About 3000 companies have maquila plants, most of them along the U.S. border. They employ more than one million workers, and represent nearly half of Mexico's exports. Under the program, foreign companies can set up plants, import all materials duty free, manufacture the products at low cost, then export them. All profits go to the foreign companies.

On January 1, 1994, we entered into the North American Free Trade Agreement (NAFTA), presumably to bolster the economies of Mexico, Canada, and the U.S. Prior to NAFTA, we exported more to Mexico than we imported. Since then, our trade imbalance has steadily increased to approximately $70 billion. Much of the imports are oil, which provides little benefit to Mexico's workforce. NAFTA may have increased the profits of some U.S. corporations, but it has done nothing to improve the lot of workers in either country.

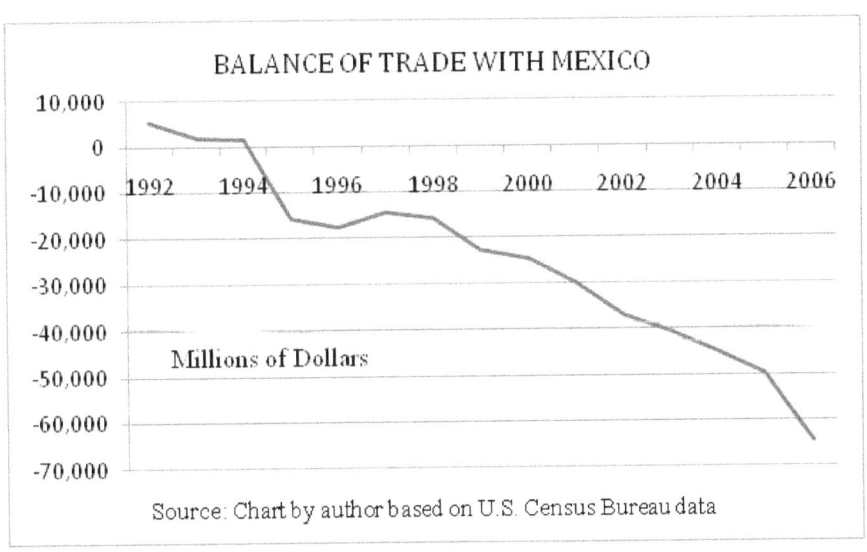

Mexico is our second largest foreign supplier of oil after Canada. Its natural resources should enable it to provide for its own people, but it does not. Instead of using its oil revenues to build a domestic consumer-based economy, Mexico has used them to reduce its tax base. With most of its revenues going to the government, PeMex has insufficient finances to fund exploration to replace its diminishing capacity. Cheap labor and very low taxes give its other domestic businesses good profits, but no incentive to expand in the absence of consumer demand. Cheap labor increases the profits of its foreign owned companies, but contributes little to its economy. Remittances from its citizens working in the U.S. give the government no incentive to stop the flow across the border.

Like much of the rest of the world, they have a mistaken understanding of the role of government, a utopian view of economics that has little basis in reality, and increasingly short-term thinking due to the excessive influence of corporate interests. We have used Mexico as an example, but its problems apply equally to dozens of other countries. I applaud those who gain their wealth by building steel mills, railroads, schools, hospitals, manufacturing plants, highways, and homes, and by producing the goods and services that enrich our lives. Much of today's wealth is gained by people who would rather let their money do all the work without creating the infrastructure, jobs, and technologies that will fuel future success. I call it **'lazy money'**. Much of it is made by betting against the success of those who risk their fortunes to build our tomorrows.

Most of us would gladly cross a border to secure a better life for ourselves and our families. I have watched Mexican children in rural areas walk many miles carrying buckets of water to their shantytowns, or their very expensive books to distant schools. Mexican railroads allowed their employees to build shantytowns beside railroad tracks where there is no water or sanitation. The employees don't earn enough to have real homes. One would have to have a heart of stone not to feel compassion for their people. Nonetheless, we cannot tolerate illegal immigration. Turning the United States' economy into Mexico's will not benefit our people or theirs. We should also not tolerate the politicization of this issue.

Arizona passed two laws dealing with immigration. The first allows police to ask proof of legal status if a person is suspected of being illegal. The second, if I understand it correctly, requires all schools to teach in the English language only. There are a number of possible objections to these laws. The first is that they do nothing to limit illegal immigration because they do not prevent employers from hiring illegal aliens. That tells me that the laws are less about stopping illegal immigration than they are about making it a hot button political issue. It effectively turned our attention away from the financial industry reform bill being discussed at the time.

The second objection is that immigration is the responsibility of the federal government, not states. Assuming that Arizona's police do catch some illegal aliens, what will they do with them? Do they have the authority to deport them? Even if they did, what would prevent them from coming across the border again? Would they simply put them in prisons? They already have too many prisoners living in tents. Who would support them? The federal government should have enforced its laws. Why hasn't it? The business community has thwarted every effort to do so because it loves cheap labor.

Another objection is that the laws may be unconstitutional, but that is a matter for the courts to decide. My objection is that it opens the door for harassment of legal immigrants while having no effect on illegal immigration. During the current recession, the number of illegal aliens in the United States has actually declined because of high unemployment, suggesting that the problem is best solved at the employer's door.

The last immigration bill debated in Congress raised a passionate public outcry, some in favor of amnesty and some vehemently opposed to it, but it would not do anything to stop illegal immigration and ultimately failed to pass. One idea being discussed is to have illegal immigrants pay a large fine to remain here. Where would someone at the earning level of most illegal immigrants get that kind of money anyway? That is usually accompanied by the suggestion of paying back taxes. Many of these workers have phony Social Security cards, and have been paying income and many other taxes throughout their stay here. How do we determine who did or did not pay taxes when we cannot even identify them? Another is to have all illegal aliens return to their home countries and reapply for admission. That would instantly shut down much of our economy. Many suggest denying medical and educational benefits to illegal immigrants. Those benefits are de-facto subsidies to the businessmen who hire them. The cost of cheap wages is passed on to the taxpayer. Another proposal was for a 'temporary guest worker' program that would flood this country with cheap labor even when citizens are experiencing declining wages and high unemployment.

The notion that illegal immigrants only take jobs Americans won't do is false. In my previous life as a senior executive in an international manufacturing company, our U.S. factories employed workers at relatively low pay. The workforce consisted of about one-third each African-Americans, Hispanics, and whites. Some of the whites were Polish immigrants here on two-year work visas or legal permanent residents. The Hispanics all had social security numbers, but on several occasions, more than one or two people had the same number. Although we never intentionally hired illegal immigrants, there is little doubt that some were. The jobs were difficult, fast paced factory work. An incentive system allowed workers to earn more by exceeding productivity standards. We never had any difficulty finding legal workers willing to do the jobs. Once properly trained, all three groups performed equally well. If a company provides proper training, supervision, discipline, and sound management, it will find legal workers willing to do most jobs.

I love this country. I am a legal immigrant and United States citizen. In my earliest years, my family and I experienced the brutal Soviet occupation of Eastern Poland, then barely survived two Nazi concentration camps, and endured four years in refugee camps. Our experiences gave us a different perspective than many Americans who tend to mythologize history. Let me share a few insights into the immigrant experience with you.

Most immigrants that arrived in the United States were indeed grateful. My family and I certainly were. America had helped free us from slavery under the Nazis. We entered the U.S. not at Ellis Island but New Orleans. Our first place of residence in the United States was in Perry County, Arkansas, the poorest county in all of the United States at that time. Fortunately for us, the surrounding community had many German-speaking people. My parents and siblings spoke German well. I spoke little German. The only way I could communicate with my teachers and classmates was to learn English.

Learning English was never a major consideration—survival was. Cities like New York, Chicago, Minneapolis, San Francisco, and others had schools that taught in Italian, Polish, German, Norwegian, Chinese and other languages until sometime after World War II. Ethnic communities within these cities provided a support structure well into the second and third generation. The children were usually the first to learn English. The parents learned only enough to get by in the workplace. Most adults could not afford to go to school to learn English. They were usually underpaid and worked long hours, often without a day off.

For the first six months, we worked without pay, except for room and board. We lived in a one-room log cabin with dirt floor. Most of our meals consisted of sweet potatoes and buttermilk. A compassionate doctor, himself a Polish immigrant back in the 1920s, helped us to break away from our sponsor. We rented a shack without electricity, gas, or running water, for $5 per month. It was on about four acres of land. Before we were able to grow any vegetables, we went without food for up to four days at a time. Kind neighbors, seeing our plight, reached out to help us. The pastor of our little church came with a twenty-five pound sack of flour. A neighbor brought some milk and eggs. By the end of summer, we were self-sufficient. When my father found a job, he was paid 27 cents an hour, half the minimum wage at the time. It took three years to save enough money for one train ticket out of Arkansas. When my dad arrived in Chicago, he slept on the floor in an apartment shared with two other families. Without the support of the community, we would have starved. Any success I have enjoyed since then is due in large measure to the welfare provided by the United Nations Relief Agency, Catholic Relief Services, our church, and good neighbors. God bless them all! A hand up is not a handout.

When we finally got to Chicago, my parents were grateful to be in a Polish neighborhood where they could have a relatively normal life. Most stores in our neighborhood had Polish-speaking help. Most places of employment had someone who could interpret. Our church had a service in Polish. Italian and German neighborhoods provided similar support to their residents. My parents learned English slowly, as do most adults, because the workplace made it necessary, especially when immigrants began to leave their ethnic communities in search of better opportunities. Their lack of English language skills in no way impaired their love for the United States of America. We should all be proud of our ethnic heritage, as well as being proud of being Americans. There is some beauty and value in every culture.

There is nothing wonderful about the hardships we endured and nothing bad about multilingual societies. Illegal immigration is a serious problem that needs to be solved, but it cannot be solved by the methods proposed to date. As long as businesses can hire illegal aliens with impunity, and we have no means of knowing who they are, they will continue to come, regardless of how tall the fences we build, whether we mandate English as the only official language, deny them education or health care, or deport them. Most of us would do exactly what they do if we lived under the same conditions they come from.

There are two ways to stop illegal immigration. The first is to continue the course we are on — keep cutting taxes for the rich, exporting good paying jobs, importing cheap labor, and increasing the national debt. That will ultimately make our economy just like that of the countries illegal immigrants came here to escape. They will have no reason to come here. The alternative is to enact real immigration reforms.

Before we can control illegal immigration, we must have some means of determining who the illegal immigrants and other aliens are. The time has come for a secure tamperproof positive identification card that contains a person's encrypted name and aliases, DNA, fingerprint, biometric, immigration status, citizenship, and place of origin data plus digital photo as well as a visible one, and a unique encryption key. The identifying data should be maintained on secure encrypted databases with restricted access. It may seem somewhat burdensome, but it will have benefits in many other areas such as prevention of terrorism, identity theft, Medicare fraud, and crime in general. Ultimately, the card could serve as a drivers' license, credit card, electronic signature, proof of insurance, medical authorization, professional certification, firearms carry permit, and a myriad of other uses. Identity theft would become extremely difficult. We will discuss some of the other potential applications in later chapters.

Imagine a card reader capable of displaying a photo and other needed information at immigration points, transportation ticket counters, wherever cell phones and other communication devices are sold, hospitals and doctors' offices, police stations, gun shops, currency exchanges, and banks. The cards should be interactive so that they can be updated automatically to include new data when they are used. Scanning the card should display the decrypted photo, name and address, telephone numbers, immigration status, and other data critical for the type of transaction being processed. The benefits to citizens would far outweigh any privacy concerns, especially since all critical data would always remain encrypted. We could issue an identity card to every arriving alien, and document their arrivals and departures. The database would maintain a record of their whereabouts, and notify authorities of overstays. Passports can be forged. The identity card cannot, and so can act as a passport as well. The database could be screened to find people with multiple identities. Stealing a card would do the thief no good because the thief's appearance and other characteristics would not match.

Let me put any privacy concerns you have to rest. If you are not an illegal alien, you have no privacy. For a few dollars, anyone can access your unlisted phone number, every address you have had, what schools you attended, your criminal record, known associates and relatives, credit history, social security number, what you read, what television programs you watch, where you eat, what your hobbies are, and much more. Insurance companies, credit card companies, cable companies, and many others maintain databases of this information. Most of it is available to affiliated firms, marketers, and anyone else willing to pay for it. Why do you think you get travel brochures after you have been on a cruise, or magazine subscription offers of interest to you? The politicians yielded to the special interests in this regard also. You should not have to opt out of anyone's privacy policy to keep your personal information confidential.

Student visas have been an area of concern for national security. Universities should be required to report aliens on student visas that drop out without reapplying in another school, in which case their visas should be revoked.

We must change the law on citizenship by birth. If Osama bin Laden's favorite daughter has a child born while visiting the United States, should that child be a United States citizen? I don't think so. A child born in the United States should be a citizen only if at least one parent is a citizen, or both parents are legal permanent residents who have not been convicted of a felony.

Once a positive identification system is in place, we should require every alien to register within six months, or leave the country. To ease the initial implementation burden, legal permanent resident aliens and citizens could be processed after the six month period. After the first six months, aliens who have not committed a felony or violated their visas should be allowed to remain in the United States, be given a two-year work visa and allowed to apply for permanent resident status. While this is amnesty of sorts, other provisions in this proposal will dramatically reduce the number of illegal aliens entering the country in the future. It is also the humane and reasonable thing to do. Legal migratory workers should be required to leave the country after each planting and harvest season.

After the first six months, we should immediately deport any unregistered aliens with their immediate families. Arrest and deportation orders for aliens who violate their visas or commit felonies should be issued automatically. Any deported alien who returns to this country illegally should be imprisoned for a mandatory minimum sentence of two years, and then deported again.

The next step, to be taken within the first twelve months, should be to require all employers to certify that all their employees are registered. All corporate officers and business owners, as well as the Human Resources Manager, should sign the certification. Thereafter, we should imprison the employers' Chief Executive Officer (or owner), Human Resources Manager, and any other manager or person who hires an alien without the proper identification. Monetary penalties for employers do not work. They are often far less than the savings from employing illegal aliens.

We must tie the number of legal immigrants allowed into the country to our real unemployment rate. No immigrants, permanent or on work visas, should be allowed in if the unemployment rate exceeds 4%, with the possible exception of a few political refugees. The current method of determining the unemployment rate is a farce. It does not account for undocumented work, partial employment, and the discouraged that have quit looking. We should require US employers to report their employment, hires, layoffs, terminations, hours worked, and wages by class of worker each month to get a true reading of unemployment and the employment picture on a timely basis. The report could be part of their monthly tax payment voucher, or easily submitted on the Internet.

We must really secure the borders. A fence in more densely populated urban border areas might help, but that would only require a small fraction of the 700 miles under construction. Elsewhere it would only waste money. All it takes to defeat a tall fence is a tall ladder or deep tunnel. Once this proposal is implemented and enforced, only the criminals and terrorists will have a reason to risk crossing our borders. Manpower and technology are the best ways to deal with those threats. Much of the criminal element can be eliminated by a sensible drug enforcement policy, an issue addressed in a later chapter.

The imprisonment of two US Border Patrol agents who shot and wounded a Mexican drug trafficker defies reason. While we may never know the details of why the criminal was given a pass for testifying against the Border Patrol agents who were apparently just doing their job, it raises serious questions about who is running our government.

Finally, all immigration and customs officials and their superiors must comply with all applicable laws or face termination, imprisonment, or impeachment. Let's let our politicians know that they work for us, not drug cartels and big business. English is and will continue to be the dominant language of the United States. There is no need to make it the official language by law, which would prohibit any dual-language official documents. Doing so only serves to increase the difficulty for all immigrants, including those here legally. The company I worked for had operations in Canada, England, and Germany, an office in Hong Kong, customers and suppliers in nearly sixty countries. In Canada, our product packaging, warranties, and other literature were printed in three languages: French-Canadian, English, and Spanish. It would not have made sense to try to sell our products to the large French-speaking consumer base if they could not read our product information. The same is true of Hispanics and other large consumer groups in the US.

Business is built on consumer demand, which, in turn, depends on disposable income. Henry Ford certainly understood this. He doubled the wages of his workers so they could afford to buy his cars. That attitude is missing in today's corporate climate. Corporate chief executive compensation has reached the level of obscenity while real incomes of workers have actually fallen and the stock prices of their companies have declined. Flooding the country with cheap foreign labor will ultimately make us the type of country immigrants came here to escape.

We can solve the illegal immigration problem, but we should do so with common sense and compassion.

Let's review the key points in this chapter.

1. Illegal immigrants come by various means from many nations, not just from our southern neighbors.
2. Our national security, including our economic security, depends on stopping illegal immigration.
3. Mexico's economic policies are a major contributor to illegal immigration here.
4. Illegal immigrants come here for jobs. We can only stop the flow by preventing employers from hiring them.
5. Fences have limited effect on illegal immigration.
6. Most proposals to stop illegal immigration are merely inflammatory political rhetoric and do not address the business community's role in perpetuating it.
7. The high cost of education and health care for illegal immigrants is a subsidy to employers who benefit from cheap labor without sharing in the cost of benefits.

8. Illegal immigrants do pay taxes here.
9. Before we can stop illegal immigration, we must have a positive means of identifying who they are, where they are, and what their immigration status is.
10. Providing illegal immigrants a path to legal status is the only way to get them to register.
11. Registration is the only way we can begin to enforce immigration laws.
12. Children born here of illegal immigrants and visitors should not automatically become citizens.
13. Immigration into the U.S. should be limited when unemployment, properly measured, exceeds four percent.

Remember, remember always, that all of us, and you and I especially, are descended from immigrations and revolutionists.

Franklin D. Roosevelt (1882-1945), President of the United States

Public Welfare

Let me share with you a few words from a wonderful document. *"We the People of the United States, in Order to form a more perfect Union, establish **Justice**, insure domestic Tranquility, provide for the common defence, promote the **general Welfare**, and secure the Blessings of Liberty to ourselves and our Posterity, do ordain and establish this **Constitution for the United States of America.** "*

What does 'establish justice' mean? If the framers wanted to limit it to 'criminal justice', they would have used words like 'rule of law'. Instead, they used the word in its fuller sense of fairness, impartiality, righteousness, and honesty. It implies social justice. The 'general welfare' part is also often misunderstood, and causes much division and animosity. Some believe that it is entirely a personal responsibility. Others want government to do everything for them. We should carefully consider whether welfare programs are necessary, why some are necessary, who they help, and who pays for them.

Much public welfare does nothing to promote the general welfare. Rent subsidies go to the landlords. Heating subsidies go to the gas or oil suppliers and utility companies, food stamps go to the supermarkets and food suppliers, Medicaid goes to health care providers. Since the subsidies do nothing to lift the recipients of welfare out of poverty, they doom them to a lifetime on the dole at the expense of those who actually pay taxes. We deprive the recipients of the dignity of being productive members of society.

In every society there are those who do not have the capacity to support themselves, either because of physical, mental, or intellectual limitations. Every society has to decide how to deal with them. Some rely on their families, some on charities, and others on government programs. There is a cost associated with all of these. Hitler's solution was to cut cost by disposing of 100,000 handicapped individuals. We have a moral obligation to care for those who truly cannot care for themselves, but it is not always easy to determine who they are. If you visit a homeless shelter, you will find that a surprising number are individuals and families that are just down on their luck. They are willing and able to work, but have no home address, no telephone, no computer, no transportation, no decent clothes, and no facilities for personal hygiene. No doubt some are responsible for their own problems, but many are victims of circumstances beyond their control who were thrown into poverty by unemployment, wage erosion, or medical costs. This can be seen in the following chart, which shows a dramatic increase in welfare cost as the current financial crisis developed.

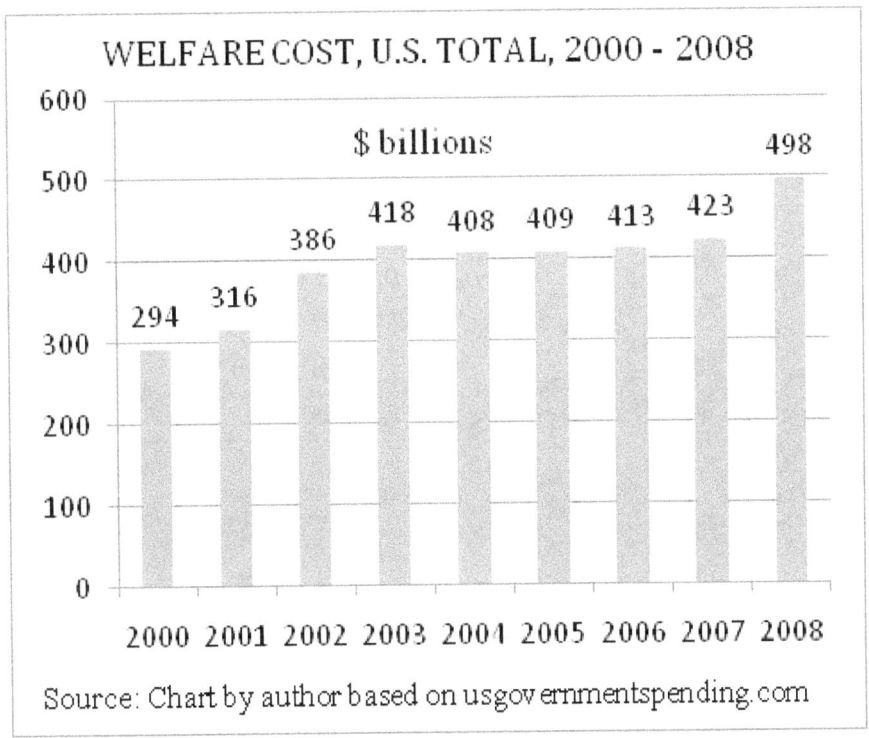

Over two of the last three decades, proponents of cheap labor fought against minimum wage increases while executive compensation skyrocketed. Wages must keep pace with inflation, or real wages and disposable income decline. Business and the general economy also decline. There are few businessmen today who have the foresight of Henry Ford. In 1914, the average wage in the auto industry was $2.34 for a nine hour day, or $0.26 per hour. Ford more than doubled his workers' wages to $5.00 for an eight hour day. Morale, productivity, and quality improved, while turnover and absenteeism decreased. His workers could then also afford to buy his cars. The most prosperous period in the last forty years followed substantial increases in the minimum wage. Between 1995 and 1997, oil prices and interest rates remained relatively stable, but the minimum wage was raised from $4.25 to $5.15 per hour. Surprisingly, inflation actually declined, unemployment dropped to the lowest level in decades, and we experienced budget surpluses for the first time since 1969. Some would argue that tax increases in 1993 were responsible for the surplus, but they are usually the same people who argue that tax increases kill jobs and lead to recessions. They cannot have it both ways.

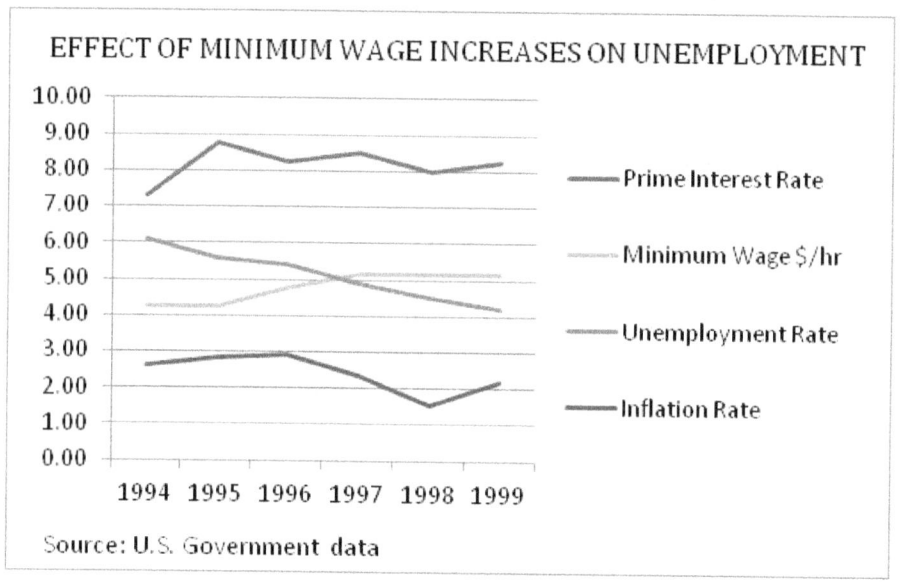

There can be no doubt that business benefitted during that period. The Hoover Institution at Stanford University published an **Essay in Public Policy** that stated, *"In 1997 the Fortune 500 corporations recorded best-ever earnings of $325 billion..."* Lifting people out of poverty is good for everyone. Would we not be better off if minimum wage adjustments occurred annually in proportion to the rate of inflation instead of being dependent on politicians?

Much of the decline in real wages since then is due to illegal immigration. There were an estimated 8.5 million illegal aliens living in the United States in 2000. By 2008, there were nearly 11.9 million, of which about 8.3 million were in the workforce. That is 5.4% of our workforce. They have driven down wages, increased unemployment, and stressed health care and education budgets. The previous administration's proposed solution was a 'guest worker program'. Could anyone not see that we already had too many uninvited guest workers? Unemployment has averaged 6.4% over the last forty years, yet every attempt at reforming immigration has failed. Why? Could it be the business community's myopic love of cheap labor?

We have already touched upon the role the Overseas Private Investment Corporation and high inflation in the early 1980s played in shipping jobs to foreign countries, but that is only part of the story. Many companies have set up foreign subsidiaries to avoid the high cost of employee health care benefits in the United States, and also to take advantage of favorable tax treatment. The resulting high rate of domestic unemployment has also had a detrimental effect on wages, increased poverty, and strained our welfare system.

There are companies that have been driven into bankruptcy by very high labor and benefit costs, but they are usually at the top of their industry's compensation range, General Motors being a prime example. When companies at the bottom of the compensation scale fail, it is usually due to mismanagement. Businesses must be able to control costs so they can compete. If their wages are too low, more people are thrown into poverty, their customer base erodes, and they must either downsize or go out of business. That is what is known as the 'prisoners' dilemma' in economic game theory. Since the concern of business is short-term profit, it does not typically concern itself with long term effects. The long term view must be taken by government. Government must establish a level playing field for economic competitors by establishing a minimum wage that allows an adequate number of its citizens to be active consumers and by controlling unemployment by adjusting workweek hours and limiting immigration. During the Great Depression, Franklin D. Roosevelt established a thirty hour workweek to provide some income to a greater number of workers. We must find ways to avoid the necessity for such measures, but the tool should be available. When the business community exerts disproportionate influence on government, government's view becomes increasingly short term. The result is recession, high unemployment, increased illegal immigration, and longer welfare rolls.

Why would businessmen resist workweek adjustments? For a given amount of work, a shorter workweek would require more workers, and more workers means higher costs for benefits. Health insurance premiums are already completely out of control. The Kaiser Family Foundation, as quoted in USA Today, reported that between 2000 and 2009 employer based insurance premiums increased from $6,438 to $13,375 per year for a family plan. Five years ago, before we qualified for Medicare, our privately purchased HMO annual premium was $19,816 for my wife and me. We can only speculate what it would be today. That insurance premium alone, excluding any out-of-pocket costs would represent 39.4% of the $50,303 median household income in 2008. Many businesses can no longer afford health insurance coverage for their employees. Between 2007 and 2008, 1.1 million people lost their employer based health insurance, and 13.2% of our population was living below the poverty level. Those at the median income level who lose their jobs are almost certain to lose their homes and health insurance. In a survey by Families USA reported in the February 10, 2009, issue of the L.A. Times, COBRA premiums in 41 states are more than three-fourths of those states' unemployment benefits. The recipients' only recourse is either Medicaid or the emergency room. Medicaid is obvious welfare. The emergency room is hidden welfare. Someone has to pay the hospital—either by government subsidies or by increased billing to insurance companies. Our health care and health insurance system creates welfare recipients—not the 'general welfare' our Constitution proposes.

It should be readily apparent that any subsidy to any person or entity is a tax on every other person. Subsidies are in fact welfare, but they are not limited to individuals. Many corporations including insurance and pharmaceutical companies receive them. The above cited Stanford University essay states that corporations received $100 billion in government subsidies in 1997. It goes on to say that the growth of subsidies parallels the growth of the Washington K Street lobbying industry. What the current subsidies are is anyone's guess since the number of registered lobbyists in Washington has increased dramatically with nearly 14,000 actively lobbying Congress for favored treatment.

A 2008 study by Management Information Services, Inc. of Washington, D.C., showed that federal energy subsidies from 1950 through 2006 totaled $725 billion in 2006 dollars. The oil and gas segment received 60% or $436 billion, and 60% of the total or $261 billion was in tax breaks. The Bush administration gave oil companies tax cuts variably reported as $12 - $18 billion even though the oil companies were experiencing record profits. Those figures deal only with direct subsidies. They do not take into account many indirect subsidies like the Strategic Petroleum Reserve (SPR) which contains more than 700 million barrels of crude oil stored in exhausted salt mines, and which is planned to double in size. More than half of it is the less desirable high sulfur content (sour) crude, which is generally sold for less than sweet crude. The SPR has been filled at full market price. This appears to be a multilevel subsidy that cannot be easily explained.

Washington Post article in December of 2006 stated that "just last year the government paid out about $15 billion [to farmers] in income support or price guarantees, which increasingly are going to the largest farms--those with annual sales of $500,000 or more." These subsidies flow through to food processors and distributors at the expense of taxpayers.

Cities and states are just as guilty of giving away our tax money as the federal government. While contemplating the construction of five distribution centers around the country, I investigated the tax incentives available in the various states. Most of the states were willing to underwrite low cost revenue bonds well in excess of what we needed to construct an appropriate facility. They would typically give a free ride on property and other taxes for a period of ten years, provide various incentives to employ locals, and sometimes offer free land. In most cases the level of incentives offered by the different states was proportional to their tax structures. Since every state offers similar deals, it is not about competition between states and communities, but an outright giveaway.

Wal-Mart Subsidy Watch by Good Jobs First, reports that Wal-Mart has received more than $1.2 billion in tax breaks, free land, infrastructure assistance, low cost financing, and outright grants from state and local governments. Does anyone really believe that Wal-Mart would quit building stores if they had to do it on its own? Wal-Mart is by no means alone in this. Most major retailers get similar breaks.

In the mid 1990s, Sunbeam Corporation, a well known consumer products manufacturer with twenty-six plants located mostly in small towns in the south, decided to construct a 725,000 square foot advanced manufacturing and distribution facility in Hattiesburg, Mississippi, a town of 46,000 people. The plant would employ about 1000 people. Sunbeam was reported to have received $30 million in direct incentives, although one of their executives told me it was much higher. I had been approached about managing their Hattiesburg operations. After surveying their operations and interviewing key managers and executives, I notified their management in Schaumburg, Illinois, that I was not interested because the entire project was so poorly planned and executed that there was no way to make it profitable and to achieve satisfactory customer service. About two months later, the top management was gone, and "Chainsaw" Al Dunlap took the helm as CEO. Two years later, he too was gone, and, not long after, Sunbeam was in bankruptcy. Its pursuit of cheap labor and Mississippi's need for economic development blinded all involved to issues of logistics, availability of skilled managers and technicians, and the need for local support of technologically demanding plastics injection molding operations.

In his book, *Free Lunch*, David Cay Johnston, New York Times Pulitzer Prize winning reporter, describes several corporate welfare schemes. All a business needs to do is threaten to move a business elsewhere to get the local government to roll over. We see it whenever professional sports teams want a new stadium built. George Steinbrenner, principal owner of the New York Yankees, got a stadium built on land taken from city parks in Brooklyn. In 1989, before he became President of the United States, George W. Bush, along with friends of his family, bought the Texas Rangers baseball team. When they threatened to move the team from Arlington Texas, the city raised the capital for building the new stadium by sales tax increases. The land for the stadium was either bought or seized from its owners who had to fight in court to get paid. In 1998, the team was sold. Bush got $14.9 million for his initial personal investment of $606,000. The story was reported by David Cay Johnston in his book, on CNN by Brooks Jackson on May 13, 1999, and several other sources. Why should taxpayers pay for stadiums when many cannot afford to attend the games?

Business facilities should be built with their owners' money in locations that best serve the interests of their businesses. Corporate interests can and do manipulate state and local governments. That may be why big money likes small government. The number of taxing authorities and the many forms of taxation in most jurisdictions makes transparency and accountability difficult to achieve. At the federal level, earmarks, the special requests tacked on to bills in Congress for projects within their states and districts, can also be used as corporate welfare.

We live in Colorado Springs, home of the Air Force Academy, Fort Carson Army Base, NORAD, and Peterson and Schriever Air Force Bases. Many of our close friends are retired career military officers. We honor their service and respect their patriotism. Some have been disabled due to their military service and deserve all the support we can provide. What they receive is compensation, not welfare. All military personnel make sacrifices in the form of frequent deployments and relocations, and many other ways. We thank them for their service. In return, they receive education benefits and a retirement plan unlike any other. After twenty years of service, while some are still in their thirties, they can retire and immediately receive a pension equivalent to 50% of their base pay. As an option, they can take 40% plus a $30,000 bonus. After they retire, many get hired by defense contractors, become civilian contractors to the Department of Defense (DOD), or start other second careers. Their pension increases each year by a cost of living allowance. If an officer remains in the military until age 65, he or she receives 100% of pay at time of retirement, and it continues to increase every year thereafter. In addition, retired military and their families receive health care at a small fraction of the cost to the general public. They can shop at the commissary and pay no sales tax. Other benefits include moving allowance, housing allowance, food allowance, clothing allowance, involuntary separation pay, flight pay, parachute duty pay, hazardous duty pay, and enlistment and reenlistment bonuses. Some of the benefits are non taxable. Their second career can last longer than their military career. That entitles them to receive their military pension, social security, plus any corporate pension. Military pensions cost taxpayers $50 billion in 2009. If military pensions resembled civilian pensions, perhaps the pension cost could be cut in half.

Other federal employees, including senators and congressmen, also have a retirement plan that far exceeds private sector plans. In addition, the government pays up to 75% of the premiums for post-retirement health care. Since retirement can be taken at age 57, or 50 under certain circumstances, long before Medicare eligibility, the cost can be substantial. In a December 11, 2009, article, *USA Today* said that between December of 2007 and June 2009, the number of civilian employees in the DOD who earn more than $150,000 per year increased from 1868 to 10,100. At the same time, the number of Transportation Department employees earning over $170,000 per year increased from 1 (one) to 1690. About 19% of civil servants now make more than $100,000 per year. The impact on future pension costs is yet to be realized. I suspect these runaway salary increases may have been politically motivated. They have pushed the average federal worker's pay to $71,206 compared to $40,331 in the private sector. Federal employees' pensions cost the taxpayers $68 billion in 2009.

By contrast, in the 20 years between 1985 and 2005, the number of private employers offering pensions declined from 112,208 to 28,769. Between 2006 and 2008, contributions to non-government pension plans were reduced by half. Most private pensions cannot be accessed before age 65, and withdrawals from one's IRA retirement account before age 59½ are subject to a 10% penalty. General Motors' post employment health care and pension costs, which are probably smaller than the governments', have driven it into bankruptcy. It will do the same to our country if we do not reestablish some balance, perhaps by unifying and standardizing social security, military, and federal civilian retirement plans. Retirement plans are a necessity for most people. It is only the excess that can be considered welfare.

That leaves us with one remaining category of welfare recipients: those unable to care for themselves. Most prominent in this category are veterans with disabilities. Their care is a moral obligation that must be honored. Nobel Prize winning economist, Joseph E. Stiglitz, and Linda J. Bilmes, a Harvard University expert in government finance, in their book, *The Three Trillion Dollar War*, say that about 3.5 million veterans (plus their survivors) received $34.5 billion in disability benefits in 2005, plus $1 billion in disability retirement benefits. The numbers are certainly much higher now. The injuries from the Iraq and Afghanistan wars are such that many of the veterans may be unemployable and will require lifelong support and care. It is unlikely anyone would argue against providing those benefits to them. A capitalist society can and should be compassionate. It should also consider war as a last resort.

Compassion is sometimes lacking in the business community. To cite one example from Illinois, sheltered workshops affiliated with mental hospitals, religious institutions, and social service organizations, provided simple assembly and packaging services to industry at very low cost. I used a number of such workshops in the 1970s and saw firsthand what great satisfaction it gave to the handicapped workers to be able to perform these relatively simple tasks, and to earn a few dollars through their own efforts. Contract manufacturers complained to the state that sheltered workshops were undercutting their prices, and depriving them of business. The state responded to their demands by requiring the workshops to charge for overhead as well as labor. Because their overhead was sometimes greater than that of low cost manufacturers and their productivity generally lower, the use of workshops dropped off.

We hear much about post traumatic stress disorder among the military, but fail to recognize that other forms of stress (financial, emotional, or job related) can also lead to mental problems. In 1970, there were approximately 400,000 people in mental institutions in the United States. Over the succeeding two years, that number was reduced to less than half. By 1986, there were only about 100,000.

The government concluded they were not a danger to society so most were released. I often wondered what happened to them. When I got involved with a program serving the homeless, I found that, in addition to those down on their luck and handicapped people, nearly 40% of the homeless had psychological problems like schizophrenia, bipolar disorder, depression, and substance abuse. With proper treatment, most could have led normal lives. Instead, many wound up in homeless shelters and prisons. In recent years, 28% of prison inmates have been receiving treatment for various mental disorders.

Following World War II in Germany, the refuse of concentration camps and forced labor, starved and bewildered, was dumped into refugee camps. My family and I were sent to Wildflecken, now an American military base. It had been a Nazi stormtrooper training camp housing up to 7,800 soldiers. By that winter, it held 25,600 refugees, many of them young people with nothing to do and little to eat. The first rations to arrive were powdered eggs and contaminated powdered milk years out of date. The young people rioted and smashed the camp's telephone switchboard, its only contact with the outside world on which they were dependent for aid. Frustration and inactivity drove them to commit this and other utterly irrational acts.

The effect of stress can be seen in experience of one of the homeless people. Melissa was a very intelligent and attractive thirty-one year old computer systems programmer. She had worked for a major bank in downtown Chicago. The bank was undergoing a complete systems change. That required an enormous effort to learn the new systems while working up to eighty hours per week implementing them. They were eighty percent done with the conversion when management decided in favor of a totally different system. When her superiors refused to listen to her pleas for help, Melissa had a nervous breakdown. She quickly exhausted her savings, was evicted from her apartment, and began to live out of her van. As winter approached, she was forced into homeless shelters. She could not work again in any job where there was any kind of stress. She found a job as a cashier at an all night gas station, working three hours a night on the midnight shift. The shelters were only open from 7 PM to 7 AM. That left little time for sleeping. The challenge was to stay warm all day, so she, like all the others, moved from library to train station to various stores, then to a shelter for the night. The shelters provide a very necessary service and the people who work there are to be commended, but they stop far short of providing remedial help or professional care in any form. Melissa could neither heal herself, nor care for herself.

The plight of the mentally ill is exemplified by another woman I befriended. Ruth was a manic-depressive. When I met her about twenty-eight years ago, she was thirty-three years of age. She had two small children, ages two and five. Her husband, also a manic-depressive, had just left her, and she was being evicted. She appealed to our church for help. I rented a trailer and, along with some friends, helped to relocate Ruth to a small apartment in the city of Chicago. Ruth had been a legal secretary before her illness worsened. I helped her prepare a resume and coached her on interviewing. After some jobs that lasted anywhere from a few days to a few weeks, she landed a job as a receptionist in a law firm. It lasted nearly two years until she began asking the firm's clients for large sums of money. Her explanation was, "You have plenty and I need it, so give it to me." She lost her job, her apartment, and then her children. She became unemployable, but succeeded in getting Social Security Disability payments. Although she never gave up trying to return to self-sufficiency, her low income and frequent lapses into delusional or belligerent behavior made that virtually impossible. Ruth would contact me whenever she became desperate. I would take her to a shelter, they would help her find an inexpensive apartment and get her some furnishings, and within a few weeks she would be evicted. The stress drove her to ever more bizarre behavior. The police would take her to a hospital psych ward. Hospitals were authorized to keep an indigent patient for up to three weeks. She would then be transferred to a mental hospital for another three weeks. By the time she was released, her condition was somewhat better, she would have received her disability check, and the cycle would start all over again. Over the eighteen years preceding our move out of the area, we helped to move Ruth many times. Her many hospital stays have cost the taxpayers a fortune — far more than it would cost to provide a room in a facility providing housing, employment and medical oversight. It is extremely difficult to get someone committed to a mental hospital involuntarily. Manic depressives alternate between a sense of euphoria and deep depression. During euphoric periods, they feel they don't need the medication. They may refuse to take, or quit taking, their medication because of unpleasant side effects, or they cannot afford it.

There is a bidirectional relationship between income and health. A November 26, 2007, Gallup Poll by Frank Newport shows that only 27% of those earning under $20,000 consider themselves in excellent mental health compared to 58% for those earning over $75,000. The relationship was quantified in a 2004 discussion paper by Dr. Audra T. Wenzlow with others at the Institute for Research on Poverty at the University of Wisconsin in Madison. Their research shows that the incidence of poor health is several times higher among those in the bottom 40% of income than among those in the top 10%. See it at *http://www.irp.wisc.edu/publications/dps/pdfs/dp128704.pdf.* A study reported in the *British Journal of Psychiatry* showed similar correlation. An article in the June 2005 issue of the *New England Psychologist* cited a large-scale, seven-year study by Christopher G. Hudson, Ph.D., chairperson of the School of Social Work at Salem State College. He studied 34,000 patient records which indicated that poverty, acting through economic stressors such as unemployment and lack of affordable housing, is more likely to precede mental illness than the reverse. Low income workers are less likely to have health insurance. Even with health insurance, they cannot afford the co-pays. Their financial problems lead to stress disorders. Stress disorders lead to physical ailments. Mental and physical ailments lead to further reduced income. Insurance policies may not cover mental disorders. The cost of their care must be passed on to those with health insurance and to taxpayers to cover the cost of Medicaid and Medicare. Health care will be addressed in a separate chapter. The key point of this chapter is that our economic and social policies create the need for welfare, but offer no way to end it.

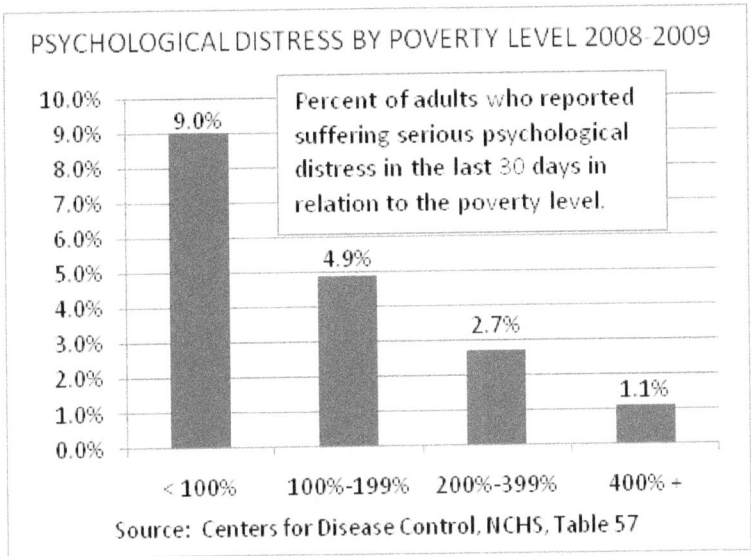

PSYCHOLOGICAL DISTRESS BY POVERTY LEVEL 2008-2009

Percent of adults who reported suffering serious psychological distress in the last 30 days in relation to the poverty level.

Source: Centers for Disease Control, NCHS, Table 57

The chart below tracks the psychological distress level of those in poverty against the unemployment rate over several years. The correlation is immediately apparent. The distress level rises with unemployment, but falls up to a year later than unemployment.

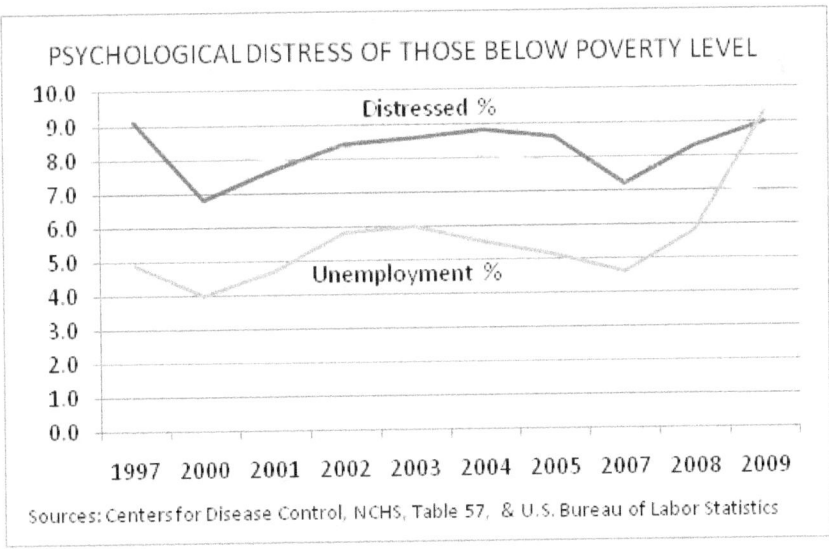

PSYCHOLOGICAL DISTRESS OF THOSE BELOW POVERTY LEVEL

Sources: Centers for Disease Control, NCHS, Table 57, & U.S. Bureau of Labor Statistics

There is a tendency to attribute the problem of unemployability to laziness and easy welfare. That may be true in some cases, but is a gross oversimplification. People are not born equal in intelligence, temperament, or health. Cultural factors, disintegration of families, and lack of education also play a role. Some who fall below the norm can function reasonably well in society, but others require significant support. If the family lacks the resources, the burden falls on the taxpayer. During periods of high unemployment, natural selection decreases the chances for marginal workers to be hired. The export of relatively unskilled jobs compounds the problem. When we drive through a depressed neighborhood and see dozens of young people hanging around instead of working or attending school, the assumption is that they want to be there. When unemployment among young people in some communities is between 30 and 50%, they are there because they have nowhere else to go. They could be in school, but if getting a high school diploma does not significantly improve your chances of employment, why bother going to school? High unemployment and poverty are the breeding grounds for crime, addiction, as well as physical and mental illness. People without work cannot develop a good work ethic. The best welfare is the opportunity to work for a living wage.

Where do we get the jobs? The technologies that fueled our economic growth and provided jobs have the potential to undo much of the progress that was made. Scanners in grocery stores and automated checkouts have reduced the need for checkers. Online shopping is reducing retail employment. Email is reducing the need for postal workers. Automated telephone attendants have replaced most telephone receptionists. One person can now farm 1,200 acres of land where his predecessor, using a horse to plow, might do 20. Robots perform many of the manufacturing tasks previously performed by humans in automobile assembly, electronic assembly, telecommunications, tool and die making, and many other occupations. At the same time that employment in each of these segments was shrinking, real incomes were declining and forcing more people to work multiple jobs to stay afloat financially. Much of the demand for talent is in technical fields where the high rate of change requires constant reeducation and retraining. The relative ineffectiveness of elementary and secondary education, and the outrageous cost of higher education puts the most needed skills out of reach for many. Instead of developing talent within our borders, we drain talent from foreign countries, as we have done to supply our doctor shortage. That undermines the development of healthy economies in other countries.

A well-educated workforce, whatever the cost, is essential for our long-term economic survival. Educated people are the source of innovation, and each innovation brings new economic opportunities. Well-compensated skilled professionals provide employment for the nanny, housekeeper, lawn service, window washer, dog walker, etc. Their services free up time for professionals to pursue career advancement and leisure time activities. It is a symbiotic relationship benefiting all parties.

As technology improves efficiency in every field of endeavor, the greatest growth opportunities will be in medicine and other human services. Caring for those who cannot care for themselves (the aged, handicapped, children, and the indigent) is the moral thing to do, and, in the long run, best for the economy. Any discussion of the subject always comes back to cost. Eliminating every form of welfare except this will actually reduce cost. That will not in and of itself establish a sound economy and full employment, but it will certainly help. If you understood the chapter on Fair Tax, then you know we can afford it.

We cannot have it all one way. We have proven that we cannot have high unemployment and simultaneously low welfare cost. We cannot have full employment unless we reduce work hours or provide alternative jobs to those willing to work. We cannot reduce work hours unless we fix the cost of health care. Even with full employment, wages must be maintained above a realistic poverty threshold to keep people off welfare. Although unemployment compensation is called an insurance program, endless extensions of unemployment benefits quickly exhaust the funds and drain tax revenues. That money gets spent quickly, so it does have a stimulative effect on the economy, but leaves only debt behind and political wrangling over the extensions. It would be far better to provide alternate employment.

During the Great Depression, work hours were cut to 30 per week, and even that was inadequate to achieve full employment in the absence of consumer demand. The Franklin D. Roosevelt Administration created the Civilian Conservation Corps (CCC) and the

Works Progress Administration (WPA) to put people to work. Many of the national parks and monuments we enjoy today are the product of those programs, as are many dams, bridges, and highways. It is time to start thinking of ways to replace welfare with jobs for able workers, not as reactions to crises but as means of preventing them.

We should begin by recognizing that unemployment of four or more percent is unacceptable. Unemployment compensation should not be a welfare program but insurance against involuntary unemployment. Its benefit payments should be limited to three months, after which the recipient should be given a job. The type of job does not matter as long as it provides some benefit to society. For example, they could assist at soup kitchens and homeless shelters, deliver meals to homebound seniors and disabled persons, pick up litter along highways, separate trash at recycling centers, work at public libraries, etc. Such a program can be run much like a day-labor operation.

How should we deal with families with small children. Prior to 1997, welfare was provided under a program called AFDC (Aid to Families with Dependent Children). It was often abused. In 1997, the Clinton Administration implemented TANF (Temporary Assistance to Needy Families). Among its provisions was a requirement that a recipient go to work within two years of receiving benefits and limited lifetime benefits to five years. United States Department of Health and Human Services (HHS) data shows that by 2007, the number of recipients had dropped from more than twelve million to less than four million. The program worked well as long as employment opportunities existed. With unemployment high over the last three years, many families will lose their benefits and be thrown into desperation. The need for an ongoing public works program (let's call it PWP) should be obvious.

For a PWP to work there must be provision for child day care for poor parents who do not have a family member or friend that can take care of their children. I believe benefits under TANF for poor families should extend until a child reaches thirty months (2 ½ years) of age. By that time, a child should have been toilet trained and be ready to engage in early learning. Since the cost of commercial day care is out of reach, a community based non-profit day care center should be provided. It could employ some parents plus professional staff. A portion of the parents' wages should be used to compensate those employed there.

Benefits under the current system are inadequate to give recipients a way out of poverty. One of the myths that circulate over the Internet is that many welfare recipients are getting rich on welfare. The following chart, based on HHS data should help to dispel that notion. In 2006, the average monthly benefit per recipient was only $154, much lower in real dollars than it was 30 years earlier.

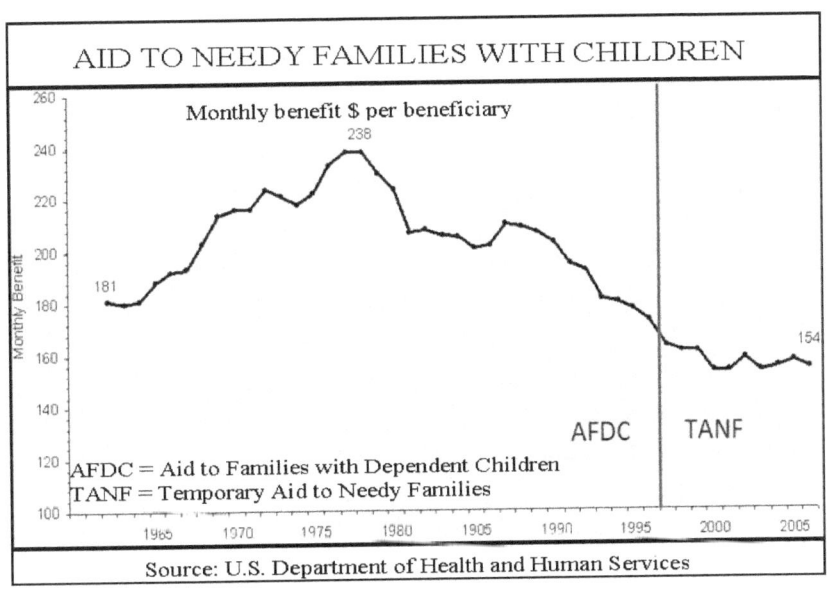

Economic systems should provide employment opportunities sufficient to ultimately bring them out of poverty. True capitalism recognizes that most business is based on consumer demand, consumer demand is based on disposable income, and that disposable income is based on a living wage. We can end most welfare if we choose to. We can invest our money where it can produce jobs at a living wage, which will increase demand for our products and services, or we can continue to pump it into the FIRE sector, which produces nothing.

The key points in this chapter:

1. Assistance to the poor does nothing to lift recipients out of poverty.
2. Most recipients of welfare are willing and able to work.
3. Declining wages and high unemployment create welfare recipients.
4. Irrational immigration policies, illegal immigration, and lack of enforcement are a major factor in wage erosion.
5. Export of jobs to foreign countries increases domestic poverty and welfare.
6. The best form of welfare is work for a living wage.
7. Poverty causes mental and physical disorders that drive up welfare costs.
8. Our system of health care and health insurance is a source of overt and hidden welfare.
9. Corporate welfare is far costlier than assistance to the poor.
10. The cost of military and other federal employee retirement and health care plans has risen to the level of welfare.
11. We have a moral obligation to care for those who cannot care for themselves.
12. Providing that care will be the biggest source of employment in the future.
13. Affordable education is essential for the innovation that will continue to fuel our economy.
14. Well paid professionals provide service employment opportunities for the less skilled, thereby reducing the need for welfare.
15. Welfare programs must be replaced with work program.

People from both political parties have long recognized that welfare without work creates negative incentives that lead to permanent poverty. It robs people of self-esteem.

Mitt Romney, 2012 U.S. Presidential candidate

Free Market Economics

We have been told repeatedly that economics is very complicated. I am not an economist, but I will try to demystify several cherished notions about economics. We will examine whether markets can indeed be free; if they are free, for whom they are free; whether they promote competition; and whether free markets are inherently efficient and self-correcting as some economists claim.

At various points in our history, economic activity was driven by agriculture, industry, services, and information. Now it is dominated by the FIRE sector (finance, insurance, and real estate), which represents about forty percent of our economy. It is a fitting acronym for a sector that nearly burned down the economy of the entire world. Before we look at what happened, let's consider what we should expect from the FIRE sector.

The core function of financial systems is to provide the financing for activities that create needed infrastructure, products, and services, and protection for our money. The role of government is to provide the necessary regulation and oversight to limit financial systems to these objectives – the creation of real value. When we build a home, buy stock in a business, or start a business, we create real value for ourselves and for those employed in making it happen. In recent times, the system has been perverted so that money can be made by the destruction of value using derivatives. A derivative is a financial instrument that has no value of its own, but a bet that the price of some asset (stock, currency, or commodity) or group of assets will move in a particular way. Derivatives can take many forms: contracts to buy or sell an asset at a certain price within a certain time frame, even if one does not own the asset or intend to take possession; swaps, which are essentially insurance policies that will pay off if an investment fails; or outright bets that the stock market, group of stocks or bonds, other investment vehicles, or even some economic indicator will perform in a certain way. It is now possible to make money by destroying a company by selling its stock that the seller does not own, thereby driving down its market capitalization. One can do the same thing by buying futures contracts for a commodity or currency that one does not intend to take possession of, thereby driving up the price and reselling them. Of course, these tactics only work when one has enough money to cause market swings. Most of us are not in that league.

Financial systems must be based on trust. When we put our money into a bank, we expect that it will be there when we need it. We expect it to retain its value, so it must earn interest sufficient to offset inflation. We expect the bank to lend some of the money out to responsible borrowers at a reasonable fixed rate of interest that will assure repayment. It should require borrowers to have sufficient down payments to protect our investment against decline in value of the borrower's property. The bank must have sufficient capital on hand to meet its obligations to us under most circumstances. To protect against it engaging in risky behavior, it must retain a significant portion of the loans it grants, preferably as much as 20%, and the retained portion must have the same aggregate risk as the loans it sells. The bank is acting as our agent, and must have our best interest in mind. It must not be allowed to gamble with our money in the stock market, hedge funds, commodities futures trading, or derivatives of any sort. If we choose to invest our money where it is exposed to risk, we are free to do so ourselves. It was precisely to protect depositors from such activities that the Glass Steagall Act was enacted during the Great Depression. It created a firewall between commercial banks and investment banks.

What should we expect from investment banks? First and foremost, they must act in our best interest and protect our property rights. For example, when I buy a stock or other security for my account, even though they hold it for me, they must not be allowed to lend it to another investor for a short sale, nor should they be able to sell it short for their own account. In a short sale, the seller sells what he does not own, but borrows it from others' accounts. The seller does so in anticipation that the price of that particular security will fall. If the sale is large enough, it drives down the price and the value of my investment. The seller can then buy the security at the lower price, pocket the difference, and return the stock to the lender and to my account. The argument some might make is that buying back the security increases the price of it and, consequently, there is no harm and no foul. My answer is that it is my security and I am the only one who has the right to benefit from it. With the precarious situation in the financial markets today, and many investors using computer software to make trades automatically without human intervention, a sizeable sale can precipitate an avalanche of sell-offs that can affect the value of my investments for an extended period of time. A trader's reported typographical error precipitated just such a cascade in May of 2010. The damage it can cause was demonstrated in the 1990s when George Soros broke the Bank of England by short selling $10 billion worth of British pound sterling.

Investment banks should also not trade for their own account. They are, in fact, acting as our agents. We pay them a commission on trades or a management fee. If they advise us to buy a certain security, they should only benefit further if we benefit. Reportedly, Goldman Sachs, a global investment banking firm was being investigated for allegedly advising customers to buy certain securities while themselves short selling them. They agreed to a fine of $550 million, a small fraction of their profits, without admitting guilt. I consider that type of behavior fraud. It is quite likely that other firms acted in the same way. Similar activities contributed to the stock market crash of 1929 that started the Great Depression. Commercial banks were using depositors' money to invest in risky issues. Poorly secured loans were issued to companies in which banks had invested, and the banks' clients were advised to invest in the debtor companies. Any financial industry reform must deal with short sales and proprietary trading. Investment banks should probably not have access to loans from either the Federal Reserve or commercial banks since that would put public and private depositors' money at risk. Limiting their access would reduce the amount of leverage an investment bank could carry, and it might just prevent bubbles from forming that could upset the economy. According to news reports, the industry had hired about 3500 lobbyists and spent a fortune to defeat meaningful reform. It remains to be seen whether the recently passed financial industry reform bill will curb any of these abusive practices.

Insurance companies are actually banks. We put our money into a pool in anticipation that it will be available if and when misfortune strikes some of us. Insurance companies must have adequate reserves and sufficient liquidity to quickly respond when a calamity occurs. Its reserves must be considerably higher than those of commercial banks in order to meet the needs of regional catastrophes like hurricane Katrina. Its investment activities should be limited to commercial banking. Under no circumstances should insurance companies own investment banks or engage in their activities. It is our money held for our benefit and must not be exposed to undue risk.

In 1999, Congress passed the Gramm-Leach-Bliley Act, repealing the Glass-Steagall Act and further deregulating the banking industry. The lines between commercial banks, investment banks, and insurance companies blurred, and some banks grew so large that the failure of one or two could bring down the entire economy. Reinstating something akin to the Glass Steagall Act was proposed and should have been enacted, but financial industry pressure forced it to be dropped in favor of giving government the tools to take over failing banks and resolve them—essentially to dismantle them and sell off the pieces. The logical question is "to whom?" Only insurance companies and big banks have sufficient resources to do that. Would that not only make them bigger and ultimately lead to a repeat of the current bailout in the future?

At the same time as Congress passed the Glass Steagall Act in 1933, it created the Federal Deposit Insurance Corporation (FDIC) to protect depositors against bank failures. When the current financial industry reform bill was being discussed, a self-insurance program like FDIC was proposed for investment banks. Opponents argued that it would encourage them to take greater risks that would ultimately increase failures. They succeeded in having that proposal quashed. Their arguments were utter nonsense. The truth is they would rather have taxpayers bail them out than give up the tiniest portion of their profits. They cannot explain why the number of bank failures declined from 4000 in 1933 to 57 in 1934 under newly imposed regulation, and why bank failures increased under deregulation in the 1980s and again in 2007-2010. In fact, most domestic financial crises in more than a century were precipitated by failures in unregulated segments of the financial sector: trusts in 1907, investment banks in 1929-1933, deregulated savings and loans in the 1980s, and the shadow banking system (money market) in the current crisis.

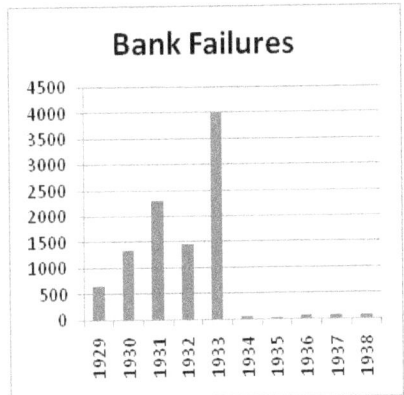
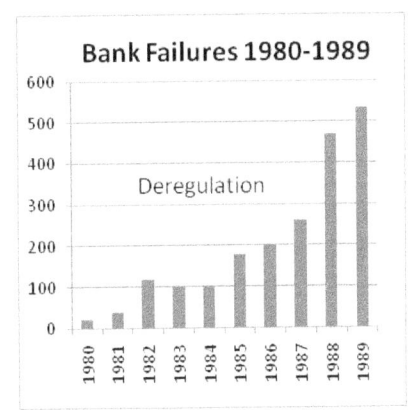

One must question why the financial industry would fight to preserve policies that lead to financial crises and bank failures. They knew that the government would be forced to bail them out. The biggest banks always survive. In a crisis, they gobble up weaker banks, thereby increasing their market share. By 2005, several economists were expressing concern that the economy was in serious danger. A clue that the financial industry also knew is that it succeeded in getting Congress to pass changes to bankruptcy laws they euphemistically called the Bankruptcy Abuse Prevention and Consumer Protection Act, which made it more difficult to file bankruptcy, increased the cost, and limited the amount of relief it could provide just as defaults and foreclosures were about to explode. We know of people who have abused bankruptcy law, but we must keep in mind that more than 50% of all bankruptcies were caused by exorbitant health care costs, and that ever more people are now uninsured and underinsured. The health care reforms recently enacted may have some effect in the short term, but the most meaningful provisions do not take effect for years.

A few years ago, the default rate on credit card debt was only 1.5%. It is now nearly 10%. Cheap money in the early 2000s allowed credit card issuers to lower their standards and, unrestrained by limits on interest rates, they could allow higher default rates and make even greater profits. College kids with no income were solicited on college campuses. Multiple credit cards were issued to individuals and families. In the face of declining wages and increasing credit card debt, the banks began to pile on fees and increase interest rates as high as 30%. A late payment to any one creditor could allow all creditors to jack up their interest rates to that debtor.

The mortgage crisis had its roots in several rounds of regulation and deregulation. In 1977, Congress passed the Community Reinvestment Act (CRA) to reduce discriminatory credit practices against low-income neighborhoods, a practice known as redlining. The Act encouraged regulated financial institutions to meet the credit needs of the local communities in which they are chartered, **consistent with safe and sound operation**. The CRA was largely ignored over the next fifteen years. In 1982, the Reagan Administration enacted the Depository Institutions Act that removed interest rate ceilings and limits on loan to value ratios. It also gave banks greater flexibility to invest in riskier ventures. Over the next six years more than 1300 banks failed. A $600 billion government bailout prevented an even greater crisis. In 1993, the Clinton Administration began to enforce the CRA to encourage home ownership in poorer communities. In 2002, the Bush administration signed the Single-Family Affordable Housing Tax Credit Act which gave nearly $2.4 billion in tax credits over the next five years to builders and investors who would build affordable single-family homes in distressed areas. That was followed in 2003 by the American Dream Down-payment Act that committed $200 million per year over four years that offered up to $10,000 of assistance to low income families to help them buy a home. Under normal circumstances this would have been a blessing, but it came at a time of decreasing wages, increasing living costs, and unbridled behavior by banks. The Federal Reserve kept interest rates very low to the banks to avoid slipping back into the 2001-2003 recession. With their money cost extremely low, and no restrictions on what they could charge consumers, mortgage lenders promoted variable rate and other sub-prime mortgages to entice home buyers, essentially transferring all risk to the home buyers enticed by the low entry cost. The banks obviously knew that interest rates could only go up. They were willing to tolerate a higher level of foreclosures, so they lowered the standards for granting loans. Home prices were rising rapidly, so the risk may have seemed reasonable. To further insulate them from risk, they created credit default swaps (CDSs), essentially insurance policies to protect the banks against collapse of the mortgage backed securities market. If the market did collapse, the government would have no choice but to bail them out. Thus began the greatest bank robbery ever, not of banks but of American taxpayers by banks.

For a fuller treatment of this topic, I highly recommend *How Markets Fail: The Logic of Economic Calamities,* by John Cassidy. In it, he shows sub-prime mortgage originations increased to $173.3 billion in 2001. Between 2002 and 2006, lenders originated more than $2.2 trillion in sub-prime mortgages. The peak came in 2005 with $625 billion. Other books worth reading for a better understanding of the financial crisis include *Crisis Economics* by Nouriel Roubini and Stephen Mihm, *The Return of Depression Economics* by Paul Krugman, and *Freefall* by Joseph E. Stiglitz.

As incomes declined, living costs escalated, credit card debt mounted, and unemployment increased, home prices collapsed in a perfect storm of foreclosures. In 2008, Lehman Brothers and Bear Stearns, two large investment banks, collapsed along with 25 other banks including Washington Mutual, the nation's largest mortgage lender with assets of $300 billion. Since then more than 200 additional banks have failed, and 700 more are estimated to be in danger of failing. Fearing another Great Depression, the Bush administration enacted the Troubled Assets Relief Program (TARP) to pour taxpayer money into the banking system. Part of it has since been repaid, but the bailout would not have been necessary if a FDIC-like program were in place for all financial institutions.

TARP was enacted in the hope that banks would resume lending and renegotiate many of the toxic mortgage loans that created the crisis. Instead, much of the money went for huge bonuses to their executives, and foreclosures continued unabated. According to an Associated Press report dated December 21, 2008, banks that received bailout money paid out nearly $1.6 billion in bonuses. One must ask how any responsible bank executive could allow his bank to issue junk loans like NINJA loans to people with no income, no job, and no assets; along with 100% no-recourse loans that would allow borrowers to walk away from their loans if property values declined, 'interest only' loans that would never be paid off, and variable rate loans with very low teaser rates guaranteed to be unaffordable as soon as the teaser rates expired. The answers are simple: perverse incentives and negative competition.

Perverse incentives are those that reward one for doing the wrong thing. Negative competition results when short term benefits take precedence over longer term success. Consider this hypothetical example: three fishing corporations (one with one boat, one with two boats, and one with three) fishing on one lake to supply fish to surrounding states. Each corporation has a proportional share of the fish market in the area. The larger one decides to add a boat. In the absence of additional demand, the oversupply of fish will force prices down and potentially drive the smaller operator out of business. The larger one, whose fixed costs are lower, will gain market share. Fear of losing market share will force the other two to add boats. They will continue to do so until the lake is fished out. If there is sufficient demand, they will all benefit for a while. In the end, all will fail. If any survive, it will usually be the largest one, and it will be only a shadow of its former self. In a race to the bottom, nobody wins. Only government can prevent the collapse of that industry by regulating the number of fishing operations on the lake and setting take limits. After all, the fishing companies all acted in a way that was reasonable under the circumstances. It is called the 'prisoner's dilemma' in which one can lose regardless of whether one expands or fails to expand. There are many real world examples of this phenomenon: auto makers expanding their models in the face of an oversupply, or a drugstore, supermarket, bank branch, or coffee shop on nearly every corner. The perverse incentive in some of these cases is state and local government subsidies that fuel the unneeded expansion.

That is exactly what happened in the mortgage meltdown. The Federal Reserve dropped interest rates to refuel the economy after the 2001-2003 recession, and kept them low far too long. Banks had access to cheap money, and deregulation allowed them to charge their customers whatever they wanted. The perverse incentive was that riskier loans brought higher returns. Cheap money meant the risk to banks was low, so they could tolerate higher default rates. Investors would also take advantage of cheap money to buy up the loans packaged as securities. Availability of easy-to-get mortgages increased the number of home buyers. Increased demand for homes drove prices ever higher. Bank after bank got into the junk loan business to protect their market share and benefit from the higher returns. Thus began the race to the bottom. As long as home prices continued to rise, the risk seemed reasonable. Many homeowners refinanced their homes, taking money out of their equity, partly to offset declining wages and dramatically increased costs for energy, education, and health care. As disposable income declined and debt mounted, foreclosures increased at an alarming rate. Home prices plummeted, home construction stopped, and the economy went into freefall.

One is less likely to take risks when one has one's own 'skin in the game'. A few decades ago, you went to your local bank for a home loan,. The bank would hold your mortgage for the duration of the loan. There was a limit to how many loans it could do without depleting its capital reserves, so most banks tended to be small. If it gave a loan to someone with a poor credit history, it bore the entire risk. Since the bank owner was often directly involved, the risk also became a personal one. With the growth of mega banks with a branch every few blocks in a city, all that has changed. Bank branches operate with relatively unskilled help. One now goes to a mortgage broker who may work with many banks. The broker is paid a fee for arranging the loan, checking credit, and preparing all necessary paperwork. Once the loan is approved, the broker is out of the picture. There is no risk to the broker—no skin in the game. The lending bank may never see the borrower. Its underwriters, working at a computer in a remote location, check the deal for compliance with management direction. The loan is then sold to an investment bank. The lending bank has no further responsibility and no skin in the game. The borrower sends payments to a servicer whose only responsibility is to process the payments on behalf of the bank. The investment bank packages the loan with others into a bond for sale to investors. The risk level of the bond is rated by a rating agency. The rating agency is paid by the seller, so it has no incentive to downgrade the bond. The investor, who may be a pension fund, hedge fund, individual investor, or even the bank that originated the loan, assumes all risk at that point. The borrower and the investor are the only ones who have any skin in the game. To all other parties concerned in these transactions, maximizing their returns by taking on higher risk seemed the reasonable thing to do. Any bank that failed to do junk loans would certainly lose market share as investors pursued higher returns elsewhere.

The downside of securitizing mortgage loans is that it makes them more difficult to restructure, but there are some benefits as well. It is possible that economic difficulties in an area served by a neighborhood bank could bring the bank down. By selling its loans and buying mortgage backed securities, it can buy into mortgages from around the country, which would be safer under normal circumstances. What happened in the last few years were not normal circumstances. A tidal wave of refinancing by existing homeowners and massive influx of new buyers lured by low initial interest rates and interest only loans was met by declining wages and much higher costs for gasoline, health care, and higher education. A virtual stampede of defaults nationwide was inevitable. Home prices fell precipitously. Highly leveraged banks, those operating with high debt to capital ratios, found the value of their assets shrinking below their liabilities. With the entire financial system imploding, the Bush Administration moved to bail out the banks by creating TARP.

Prior to the collapse, the banks felt safe. They had protected themselves against a collapse in the value of mortgage backed securities (MBSs) and collateralized debt obligations (CDOs) by creating credit default swaps (CDSs), essentially insurance policies that would pay the bank if their MBSs or CDOs lost value. They could not lose. What a deal! When you start a business, you can get insurance against various calamities, but no insurance company will insure you against business failure due to your own ineptitude or business conditions. So, why can banks get that kind of protection? Is it not because insurance companies are heavily involved in banking, and there is no firewall between them? Another reason is that there are only so many ways insurance companies can raise reliable revenues, and executive compensation is often tied to revenue growth. Given the unlikelihood of a general collapse of the market, the risk might have seemed reasonable if one could overlook the perverse incentives. American International Group (AIG), one of the world's largest insurance companies, was the largest issuer of CDSs. When the market collapsed, its capital was inadequate to meet its obligations. Collapse of AIG would have brought down the banks that were its counterparties, including many foreign banks that had bought our junk MBSs. With a worldwide depression looming, first the Bush Administration then the Obama Administration extended more than $182 billion of credit to AIG. AIG paid off its counterparties in full. The banks were rescued, and much of the money they received went into executive bonuses. One would have expected the banks to renegotiate homeowners' loans. Once they had been rescued, they felt no obligation to the masses of homeowners losing their homes. Very few loans were renegotiated, and foreclosures continue unabated.

In 1938, the government established the Federal Home Mortgage Association commonly called Fannie Mae. Its purpose was to make home mortgages available to low income families by guaranteeing repayment of the loans. Home ownership increased significantly. In 1968, Fannie Mae was converted to a stockholder owned enterprise. By 1970, it was completely privatized. Its purpose was to buy loans from banks, package them as securities, and sell them to investors on the open market. In 1970, the Federal Home Loan Mortgage Corporation, commonly called Freddie Mac, was created. It too was a stockholder-owned corporation. Both are called government sponsored enterprises (GSEs), although they are **not government agencies** and the **government does not guarantee the loans**. In 1968, the Government National Mortgage Association, commonly called Ginnie Mae, was established. It is wholly owned by the federal government. It does not purchase or originate loans, and it does not issue, sell, or purchase securities. It guarantees timely mortgage payments on loans insured by federal agencies. Lending institutions participating in its program and the loans they issue must meet standards set by Ginnie Mae, as a result of which it was not party to the mortgage meltdown. The lenders benefit because they can get higher prices for their securitized mortgages backed by government guarantees. Fannie Mae and Freddie Mac were required to buy loans that conformed to government established standards. They were losing market share to competing banks, which were offering higher returns on sub-prime (nonconforming) securitized mortgages. In 2004, in response to shareholder pressure, they lowered their standards to make them more competitive. Fannie and Freddie moved into the sub-prime market and found themselves in the same dire circumstances as many banks. In September of 2008, they were taken over by the federal government, and placed under the conservatorship of the Federal Housing Finance Agency.

There were many ways that TARP money could have been used that would have rescued the banks **and** prevented many foreclosures. Joseph E. Stiglitz, Nobel prize winner in economics, outlines a number of them in his book *Freefall*. I prefer simpler solutions if they can be found—perhaps like the following. Once Fannie and Freddie were nationalized, the government could have given the TARP funds to Fannie and Freddie to purchase the junk loans from the banks at a deep discount, possibly 70% of principal. The banks would have the option of accepting, being thrown into receivership, or struggling through if their pockets were deep enough. AIG could then have been required to pay 30% of the credit default swaps to Fannie and Freddie. All the loans could then have been converted to 30 year fixed rate loans at 4½% interest. Any borrower who could not afford the home under those circumstances would be foreclosed. Everyone would share the pain, and there would be no justification for huge executive bonuses.

Some investment banks set up shadow companies to keep the so-called toxic assets off their balance sheets. It allowed them to escape the notice of regulators since the banks' financials appeared sound. Among these shadow companies were hedge funds. Hedge funds typically serve investors with deep pockets who can afford to take on added risk to maximize their returns. They offer a broad range of investment types including stocks, currencies, commodities, debt, and various kinds of derivatives. They hedge risk by options, derivatives, and short selling. They are typically heavily leveraged with debt to capital ratios approximately thirty to one. Hedge fund ownership by an investment bank may seem like a logical extension of their business, but it exposes our investments to unwarranted risk. They get to gamble with our money for free. That is not what 'free market' should mean.

Hedge fund managers typically charge a management fee of about 2% of the assets under management plus a bonus that could be 15 to 50% of the fund's profits. Is there any mystery as to why banks get involved in them? To prevent future crises, something akin to the Glass Steagall Act must be reinstituted to create a firewall between commercial banks, investment banks, hedge funds, and insurance companies.

There may be some good consumer protections in the Financial Industry Reform Act, but it stops far short of preventing future financial crises. You can see that our expectations of the financial industry are reasonable. They have not been realized because of the enormous influence of financial industry money in politics. That money is used not to promote free markets and competition but to stifle it. What competition there was in the finance sector was negative competition—a race to the bottom. Only government intervention, however poorly planned and executed, prevented another even-greater depression. The notion that the market is efficient or that it is self-correcting or that it is concerned with long term prosperity ignores reality. Where labor unions once exercised their power to improve wages and working conditions, we now have a new kind of union: the industry association. It exercises its economic power through lobbyists to buy favorable treatment from government and set anti-competitive guidelines for its members. How else can one explain that virtually all the banks raised their interest rates while their money cost was so low, introduced myriad fees to consumers, and reset their customer agreements in similarly barbarous terms? This coherence of action and prices is seen in energy, pharmaceuticals, insurance, and other industries. Their influence even extends to the Supreme Court. The recent decision to allow corporations and associations to spend unlimited amounts on political campaigns on the basis of freedom of speech is a further insult to common sense. Corporations may be legal entities, but they are not persons. Our nation was founded on the principle of one man, one vote. The political contribution that I make gives me one voice. The chief executive of a corporation can contribute personally, through his company, through his industry association, and through the lobbyists he hires. His money gives him many voices. Preventing corporations and organizations, including labor unions, from making political contributions and funding political advertisements in no way prevents them from speaking to issues to the public on talk shows, news programs, and other media and venues. Another example of the Supreme Court kowtowing to business is the issue of privacy. A number of cases have been decided on the basis of the right to privacy, yet the court allows businesses to use my confidential information for their gain free of charge. If it is truly a right, I should not have to opt out of their unprivacy policy. They could do what real capitalists do: compensate me for the right to use my private information (my asset).

The very people who claim they derive their economic philosophy from Adam Smith as stated in his 1776 work, commonly called *"The Wealth of Nations"*, fail to notice his warnings about monopolies, free trade, subsidies, price fixing, labor unions, and trade associations. He writes: ***"We rarely hear, it has been said, of the combinations of masters, though frequently of those of workmen. But whoever imagines, upon this account, that masters rarely combine, is as ignorant of the world as of the subject. Masters are always and everywhere in a sort of tacit, but constant and uniform, combination, not to raise the wages of labour above their actual rate...Masters, too, sometimes enter into particular combinations to sink the wages of labour even below this rate. These are always conducted with the utmost silence and secrecy till the moment of execution; and when the workmen yield, as they sometimes do without resistance, though severely felt by them, they are never heard of by other people. In contrast, when workers combine, the masters..never cease to call aloud for the assistance of the civil magistrate, and the rigorous execution of those laws which have been enacted with so much severity against the combination of servants, labourers, and journeymen."*** Careful reading of his work shows a concern for the poor, fair wages, and the general welfare.

Economics courses tell us that prices are set through competition among suppliers based on the law of supply and demand. Yet for many of the most important commodities this is simply untrue. Those prices are set by commodities markets, not individual producers. Take oil as an example. What is the last time you saw a significant difference in the price of gasoline between one brand and another? Isn't the free market supposed to promote competition? What makes gasoline worth $2.50 per gallon one year, and $4.50 the next when there is no meaningful change in the real supply or cost of production, or even large change in demand? None of those can account for oil going from $64.20 per barrel average annual price in 2007 to $126.33 in 2008. Commodity prices are based more on perceptions of supply and demand than on actual supply and demand—not supply and demand of oil but oil futures contracts. Oil companies are huge global enterprises with many subsidiaries around the world. They are highly compartmentalized into functional groups like exploration, production, transportation, refining, distribution, and retail. With so much computerized automatic trading taking place, any one of those subsidiaries can trigger a feedback loop by buying futures contracts. The oil company would in effect be buying oil from itself to drive up the cost for others. That sets up another feedback loop that devastates the economy. Prices of nearly everything increase, people's disposable incomes drop, the Federal Reserve responds to the inflation by raising interest rates, and the country is thrown into recession. The money supply shrinks for everyone but the oil companies.

Feedback loops also occur in other commodities, but for different reasons. Farm subsidies cost American taxpayers as much as $30 billion per year. They go disproportionately to the largest farm corporations. The largest subsidies are to growers of corn, cotton, wheat, rice, and soybeans. The subsidies are intended to support prices of these and other commodities to allow farmers to make a living and to keep food prices low. Part of the reason may also be to support exports of these products in competition with foreign countries that heavily subsidize their agricultural products. Subsidies encourage increased production, which, in turn, lowers prices. Lower prices encourage more production to take advantage of greater subsidies. About 40 % of the calories consumed by us come from corn. The use of corn to produce ethanol for automotive fuel has increased the demand for corn, the acreage devoted to it, the subsidies, and, consequently, the cost of food products as more acreage is devoted to corn. Ethanol producers also receive a 51 cent per gallon subsidy. Competition from cheaper sugar cane based ethanol has been restricted by a 54 cent per gallon tariff on imports from Brazil. The ethanol subsidies defeat the purpose of farm subsidies—one subsidy reduces food cost and the other raises it. Another unintended consequence of these subsidies is that farmers in Africa and other underdeveloped regions of the world, whose governments cannot afford to subsidize and whose primitive farming methods mean higher cost, cannot make a living. I would rather pay the full value of the food I buy to the farmer rather than have my tax money used to subsidize food processors and ethanol producers. It is difficult to find any business category where special interests have not obtained tax breaks, subsidies, relaxation of rules, imposition of import quotas and tariffs on competing imports, government contracts, and other special favors.

As this is being written, angry protesters in several Middle-Eastern countries (Tunisia, Egypt, Jordan, Yemen, Libya, and Syria) are attempting to remove their current autocratic governments in favor of elected ones. One of the dominant complaints is dramatic increases in food prices fueled by speculators buying up food commodity futures contracts. The Franklin D. Roosevelt Administration imposed position limits on commodity futures during the Great Depression to keep food prices in check. In essence, that limited the number of contracts that could be held to the available supply of a commodity. During the 1990's, pressure from the financial industry caused position limits to be deregulated in the Financial Services Modernization Act of 1999 and the Commodity Futures Modernization Act of 2000. The latter bill exempted swaps from being regulated by the SEC, in essence treating them as commodities. It was passed at the insistence of Senator Phil Gramm (R-TX), the Chair of the Senate Banking Committee, after contentious debate. Between those years, oil prices increased by more than 65%.

Much of the money sucked out of the housing market and general economy has gone into commodity futures, driving prices up sharply. The mechanics of commodities futures trading are beyond my limited understanding. I believe it is now possible to buy futures contracts far in excess of available supply during any one time period. The increased demand drives prices upward, but the contracts will never be executed because there is inadequate supply during the timeframe of the contract. The speculator can then sell the commodity or current futures contract at the higher price without actually taking possession of the highest priced commodity. A proposed Dodd-Frank bill is currently under consideration to impose stricter position limits of 25% of available supply in the spot (current at the time) trades and 10% on future trades. As this paragraph is being updated, a popular uprising in Libya is attempting to overthrown their dictator, Muammar el-Qaddafi, causing oil prices to jump up suddenly. There must be some way to limit the ability of speculators to jack up prices by creating artificial demand. Perhaps requiring futures contracts to be exercised at the contract price as soon as supplies are available would prevent the worst abuses. Futures contracts might then become real demand, not speculation.

The United States was founded on the principle that people should have a voice in their own government. The government must work for our welfare, not lord over us. Therefore, we don't need kings. But, that is exactly what we have—not hereditary royalty, but lords of finance. When I buy shares in a public company, I become a part owner—a partner—and should have a right to participate in decisions about the hiring and compensation of executives hired to run it for me, and the board members selected to represent my interests. That might put a stop to obscene golden parachutes and bonuses for executives who fail to protect my investments. Corporate executives should be compensated on the basis of performance. The very people who deprived millions of people of their homes and nearly destroyed our economy were actually rewarded for doing so. The following chart shows the top ten companies that received TARP money and the compensation of their executives in 2007 just as their companies were about to hit the wall. Does anyone really think they deserved huge bonuses?

"Curst greed of gold, what crimes thy tyrant power has caused"
Virgil (70 BC–19 BC), ancient Roman poet

COMPANY	TARP FUNDS	CEO	2007 PAY
Citigroup	$50 Billion	Charles O. Prince	$25,520,621
Bank of America	$45 Billion	Kenneth D. Lewis	$23,646,455
American International Group	$40 Billion	Martin J. Sullivan	$13,960,382
JPMorgan Chase	$25 Billion	James Dimon	$28,887,532
Wells Fargo	$25 Billion	John Stumpf	$14,797,458
General Motors	$14.3 Billion	G. Richard Wagoner	$19,761,874
Goldman Sachs	$10 Billion	Lloyd C. Blankfein	$53,966,198
Morgan Stanley	$10 Billion	John J. Mack	$41,790,854
PNC Financial Services Group	$7.6 Billion	James E. Rohr	$18,623,679
U.S. Bancorp	$6.7 Billion	Richard K. Davis	$6,473,874

There are numerous examples of how our failure to regulate and enforce regulations upon financial markets damages our economy, how subsidies feed back upon themselves to create further subsidies, and how the financing of political campaigns is changing us from a democracy to a corporatocracy or oligarchy ruled by wealthy elites. They benefit from boom and bust cycles, during which they, having very deep pockets, can expand market share by buying or merging with weaker competitors. For example, between 2007 and 2008, Bank of America absorbed Merrill Lynch, U.S. Trust, and La Salle Bank. J.P. Morgan Chase & Co. absorbed Bear Stearns and Washington Mutual. Between 1930 and 2008, between the two, they absorbed 88 banking firms. In the process, they became too big for them to be allowed to fail.

Under normal circumstances, corporations can grow at a rate of one to three percent per year. They can exceed that rate by creating innovative high-demand products (iPhone, iPod, iPad, Toyota Prius, flat screen televisions, etc.), expanding into underserved markets, or by mergers and acquisitions. The first two options are difficult and time consuming, but they increase total economic activity. Mergers and acquisitions are quicker, but they do not expand the overall economy. For example, if Ford and General Motors were to merge, it would not increase the total number of cars sold. In fact, they might reduce their combined staffs and the number of dealerships and factories.

Furthermore, for two years following the merger, it would be difficult to determine true profitability of the resulting entity because of write-downs and write-ups of assets, accelerated depreciation, and other tax reduction measures. It is lunacy to reward their executives before true profitability and long-term viability can be determined. It is easy to build a house of cards, but it may not stand long when the wind begins to blow. How wise is it to build a coffee shop, or a bank branch, or a drug store, or an investment firm's retail storefront office, on every corner? Just as in the hypothetical example above of the three fishing corporations, they will continue to expand until there are no more corners available, they begin to lose money, or they run out of financing. The market does not always get it right.

The drive for short term benefit has decimated our manufacturing base, reduced the demand for domestic technical talent, and deprived our young people of opportunity for meaningful employment. Some defend the export of manufacturing technology and jobs. Dick Morris, in his book 'Outrage', claims that we could not have the standard of living we have now if we did not have access to low cost products and services from other countries. In a recent advertisement, Wal-Mart claimed it is saving the average family around $2600 per year. That would be remarkable if the average family's disposable income had not declined by more than that, but it has. We would benefit far more from good education, health care, employment and retirement security, and reduced stress levels than we do from the latest gizmos that we mistake for a good standard of living.

We are part of an increasingly global economy. National debt, balance of trade, and investment potential are all affected by currency exchange rates and speculation in currencies. The Federal Reserve has just announced a $600 billion increase in the money supply to stimulate the economy and prevent deflation. This constitutes a devaluation of the dollar. On the one hand, it means that our debts will be repaid with cheaper dollars, and foreign countries will find our exports less expensive. On the other hand, foreign imports will become more expensive, and our trading partners and currency speculators may opt to dump dollars in favor of other currencies, even selling dollars short. That would further devalue the dollar in yet another feedback loop.

Other countries caught in that trap were forced to buy back their currencies to protect their value, increase interest rates to unprecedented levels to attract foreign capital, and cut spending. Those that did so were thrown into deeper recessions with high unemployment, declining wages, budget deficits, and increased debt. In the last two decades, even before the current recession, financial crises have occurred in many countries including Argentina, Mexico, Thailand, Indonesia, and Japan. At the heart of them are flawed government policies, speculative perversion of the free market system, and weakened consumers. For a detailed treatment of these financial crises, I highly recommend *The Return of Depression Economics and the Crisis of 2008* by Paul Krugman, recipient of the 2008 Nobel prize in economics.

There are many contradictions in the economic philosophies we have been fed. Contrary to the belief that cheap labor is good for an economy, it reduces consumer demand, increases the need for public welfare, reduces the tax base, increases budget deficits and ultimately debt. Tax cuts, because of our progressive tax system, invariably give the greatest benefit to the already wealthy. They also increase deficits and debt, but do not significantly increase consumer demand. As this is being written, the bipartisan Deficit Commission has released an early list of suggestions including extending the Bush tax cuts, reducing Medicare and Social Security spending, and tinkering with various provisions in the tax code. None of this can have any beneficial effect on the current recession. It is merely political theater.

Proponents of small government believe that government should not be involved in any activity that could be performed by private business. Government is seen as grossly inefficient. Yet, as in the case of Fannie Mae prior to its privatization, some government enterprises are more efficient than the private sector. For example, Medicare administrative costs are about one-third those of private insurers. The Veterans Administration has lower per-patient costs than most other medical systems. In 2004, Sallie Mae, which was founded to provide affordable college loans, was privatized as SLMC Corp. It recorded an astounding 37% profit that year while interest rates on college loans shot upward. Education is the driver of innovation, and innovation is a key driver of our economy. This gift to the banking industry made college education much less affordable, and was certainly not in the national interest. The financial industry as a whole was experiencing record profits up to the current meltdown, yet they were not satisfied. They acted in concert to impose outrageous fees and interest rates on consumers. The free market that is supposed to take care of all this by providing competition has obviously failed to do so. The free market is not free; someone always pays, and it is US. One way to restore some common sense without micromanaging the banking industry would be to require banks to pay to depositors one-third the combined rate of interest and fees it collects from debtors. For example, if a bank collects 9% in interest and fees on unpaid balances, it would be required to pay depositors 3% interest on their combined deposits. The alternative is to reinstate anti-usury laws that limit the amount of interest banks can charge. Remember that they are using our money.

Over the last several chapters, we have seen how deregulation of (or failure to properly regulate) financial institutions, huge tax cuts, wage erosion, our system of taxation, government subsidies, energy and international trade policies, political contributions by special interests, the growth of "lazy money", runaway prices in key sectors, and overconcentration of wealth have combined to create the boom and bust cycles that threaten to undo the American Dream. The current economic crisis and the Great Depression had these same characteristics in common. The upward flow of wealth has done nothing to expand domestic productive economic activity. Instead, it has gone into expanding foreign operations, mergers and acquisitions that do not generate additional economic activity, hedge funds, and speculation. It is a worldwide problem, at the heart of which is the excessive influence of corporate and financial elites. Low corporate tax rates relative to their revenues leave an inadequate tax base to balance national budgets. That forces their governments to run deficits or increase the tax rates of individuals to punitive levels. The resulting debt can almost never be repaid, with interest payments absorbing ever more of their budgets. Exorbitant individual tax rates on higher income individuals leaves them clamoring for reduced social programs. It is easy to forget that many of the social programs were necessitated by high unemployment, low wages, and socialization of the cost of financial failures in what should have been a competitive free market, but which has squashed it instead.

You may be tempted to think that I am proposing redistribution of wealth, but that would be totally incorrect. You may recall that my proposed tax system has much lower rates for all individuals. The current tax system punishes success and rewards losses. It encourages debt, speculation, exporting of jobs, price gouging, and outrageous executive compensation packages in pursuit of revenue growth. It creates bubbles because there is no mechanism to restrain unwarranted expansion. Taxing all corporate revenues can provide that restraint. Taxing on the basis of source of revenues will also slow down the flight of business out of home countries. Prices will be whatever the market can bear when all parties are playing by the same rules. When an industry doubles its prices, it will also double its taxes. The higher prices will restrain revenue growth. The money taken out of the public's disposable income will be returned to the public in lower taxes. Lower individual taxes will foster the formation of new businesses and enable consumers. Those corporations that are most efficient in the use of money, materials, labor, and services will experience higher profits and will get to keep the profits they make. Perhaps Wall Street will begin to reward them on the basis of real performance.

As more nations enter the world economy, the resulting productive capacity will far exceed worldwide demand for consumer goods. Economic systems based solely on the production of things will fail in the long term. Expansion of health and human services along with innovation in energy, materials science, agriculture, clean water and other environmental issues, transportation, and other infrastructure development – all those things we are currently resisting – are precisely what we must address for the future well-being of society.

The function of financial systems should be to create wealth. No one should gain by destroying the wealth of others. I reject the notion that there must be winners and losers. We should all have the opportunity to win to varying degrees based on our abilities and effort. That does not mean that every business deserves to succeed, or that everyone deserves to own a house, car, or luxury goods. However, everyone should have the opportunity to earn a wage sufficient to provide for the basic necessities of life: food, clothing, shelter, and health care. That is what our founding fathers must have meant in the Declaration of Independence when they stated that *"We hold these Truths to be self-evident, that **all Men are created equal, that they are endowed by their Creator with certain unalienable Rights, that among these are Life, Liberty and the pursuit of Happiness."*?

The free market is supposed to lead to prosperity. Prices, quality, and innovation are supposed to be driven by competition. I find little evidence for competition in financial services, energy, pharmaceuticals, health insurance, food, or any number of other industries, although, among them, there is much competition for government subsidies, tax breaks, and favorable regulation. The benefits they receive are through collusion and not competition. When most banks have access to virtually free money, how can they all justify a 30% interest rate on many credit card balances? That is more than some loan sharks charge. The 'invisible hand' of the free market that should create jobs and wealth instead is picking our pockets with the help of our elected representatives. How is it that they have convinced so many of us that we are a democratic society with a free market economy when we resemble neither?

When Adam Smith wrote The Wealth of Nations, most goods were made by hand and sold in local shops. Agricultural products were the most frequently traded commodities. Most trades were spot trades (simultaneously executed on the spot). There were no derivatives. Credit and banking were primitive. Prices were set by producers. Transportation was slow and difficult. Words like capitalism and economics did not exist. Still, much of what he wrote is as true today as it was more than two centuries ago. What passes for capitalism today bears little resemblance to what he envisioned. Changing our system of taxation, ending public and corporate welfare, ending illegal immigration, minimizing the effect of money in politics, and making other changes outlined in this book will not be easy. It will require the full cooperation of our representatives in state and federal governments. I am hopeful that there are people of good will in Congress who would like to see democracy and capitalism reborn.

Government of the People, by the People, and for the People

That was the great American dream, and it remains a dream. The founding fathers wanted a country run not by kings, military or religious leaders, or the very rich alone, but by people like you and me working through people we choose to represent our interests and the common good. What a noble idea! Many thousands of colonial rebels laid down their lives so we could create a new kind of society where each of us could have a voice in determining our own destiny. They framed a document that contained the building blocks of that society. What would they think if they saw us now?

We have endured some of the longest political campaigns in history. The 2008 presidential campaign lasted nearly two years. The campaigns were each raising more than $50 million per month, saturating the air waves with television commercials bashing each other's opponents with innuendo, half-truths, and outright lies. Even after numerous debates and countless speeches throughout the country, we were left confused and ill-informed. In the meanwhile, our business remains undone. Where do you think all that money for these very expensive campaigns comes from?

	ACTIVE LOBBYISTS	TOTAL SPENDING
1998	10,404	$1.44 Billion
1999	12,943	$1.44 Billion
2000	12,541	$1.56 Billion
2001	11,845	$1.64 Billion
2002	12,131	$1.82 Billion
2003	12,923	$2.04 Billion
2004	13,158	$2.17 Billion
2005	14,070	$2.43 Billion
2006	14,516	$2.62 Billion
2007	14,869	$2.85 Billion
2008	14,216	$3.30 Billion
2009	13,664	$3.49 Billion
2010	12,488	$2.61 Billion
Source: Center for Responsible Politics based on Senate Office of Public Records Data		

You will notice in the above chart that the number of active lobbyists swells as presidential elections approach. In 2009, there were 13,664 registered lobbyists who actively lobbied 535 members of Congress (100 senators and 435 representatives), funneling $3.49 billion to their coffers. That is an average of $6.5 million for each of the politicians. Lobbyists all work for special interests that expect something in return for their patrons' money. Is it any wonder that their interests come before ours?

It will never change until we reform our system of financing political campaigns. The Supreme Court has made that a virtual impossibility by their recent decision to allow corporations, associations, and various special interest groups to spend unlimited amounts on political campaigns. Reaching that decision on the basis of freedom of speech, and allowing their contributions to remain anonymous, is an insult to common sense. Corporations may be legal entities, but they are not persons. Money is not speech. Our nation was founded on the principle of one man one vote, not one dollar one vote. The political contribution that I make gives me one voice. The chief executive of a corporation can contribute personally, through his company, through his industry association, and through the lobbyists he hires. His money gives him many voices. Preventing corporations and organizations, including labor unions, from making political contributions and funding political advertisements in no way prevents them from speaking to issues to the public on talk shows, news programs, and other media and venues.

There are many tax-exempt non-profit organizations that are not regulated by the Federal Election Commission. 527 organizations were originally formed under the United States tax code 26 U.S.C. § 527 as issues oriented advocacy groups. They are not allowed to coordinate their activities with election campaigns. An examination of their activities and advertising during recent campaigns shows that many are, in fact, entirely political. You have undoubtedly heard of MoveOn.org, Swift Boat Veterans for Truth, College Republican National Committee, and Club for Growth. 501(C)(3) organizations are non-profits that are usually charitable in nature, but may advocate for certain positions with political overtones and may engage in limited lobbying. 501(C)(4) organizations are generally called social welfare organizations. They can spend unlimited amounts on lobbying and political activity while remaining tax exempt. Among this class are the National Rifle Association and American Civil Liberties Union, and many other well-known organizations. The proliferation of these groups and the resulting barrage of political advertising during the 2010 mid-term election leads one to ask where all the money is coming from. On the surface, these groups appear to be grass-roots popular movements, but the positions they promote appear to be carefully orchestrated by special interests. They should never be allowed to advertise for or against any political candidate, contribute money to political campaigns or parties, or promote party platforms in any way. I repeat: one man one vote, not one dollar one vote. Whether it is possible to completely eliminate abuses in this area is open to question, but we must try.

Restricting the ability of special interest groups to contribute to political campaigns will have two benefits: it will reduce the duration of campaigns and the cost. There is no reason for a campaign not to be completed within one calendar year. During the campaign, I believe our senators, congressmen, and other federal officials who are candidates should be required to spend at least two days a week in Washington, D.C. or other duty post performing the duties for which we pay them. It should allow them time to understand the issues they are voting on. State and local government officials should be subject to the same requirement. Hopefully that will yield a return on our money because something worthwhile may be getting done during the campaign. Senators and congressmen serve the people of their states. It is the citizens of their states that should finance their campaigns and decide their election, but not groups, individuals, or entities from outside their states' borders. The same should be true for national elections; they must be financed only by contributions of individual citizens of the United States, not organizations or foreign entities.

A political campaign should in fact be an extended job interview with us as the decision makers. Businesses require us to submit a resume to be considered for a position. Candidates for public office should be required to submit resumes detailing their employment histories, voting records (if any), education, accomplishments, conflicts of interest, involvement in criminal and civil legal cases, and other pertinent information. We are the hiring authority. They will work for us, and should be held to the same standard as we when we apply for jobs. Imagine a job interview in which a candidate only speaks of his opponents weaknesses instead of his or her own strengths and qualifications, or whose friends and relatives do so. That candidate would never get hired. Yet we continually hire politicians who themselves and through their supporters conduct smear campaigns filled with half-truths and outright lies. What does that say about us as stewards of our nation.

One of the proposals that surfaces from time to time is term limits. At the beginning of the Clinton Administration, the Republican minority promoted the idea of term limits for senators and congressmen. When they came into the majority, term limits came off the table. That notion has resurfaced as a suggestion that politicians be limited to a single term. The operative idea being that they would not need campaign financing since they could not be reelected, and so would not be beholden to special interests. One need only look at the number of politicians who become lobbyists after leaving office to realize that promises of employment are as powerful an inducement to sell one's vote as campaign contributions. Politicians are, after all, just like the rest of us – they want secure employment. On the positive side of this proposal is the fact that eliminating the need for campaigning would increase the time available for doing the nation's business, but it comes at a very high price: lack of experience. Government is complicated. We ask our politicians to consider and vote on national security, defense, commerce, energy, education, and a myriad other critical issues. It can take a long time to develop expertise in these matters. We should correct the flaws in the system that prevent them from doing an effective job, not replace them with amateurs. Stability and continuity are vital for smooth functioning of government. I have watched repeatedly as corporations fell for the **miracle man theory of management,** hired a genius Whiz Kid to run their company, then paid the price in often irreversible mistakes.

If we allow for seniority, then we must live with reelection campaigns. Restricting the money available for campaigns should shorten the campaign cycle. Currently, a newly elected president, spends nearly one year working under his predecessors budget and priorities, one year on his own agenda, then two years campaigning for the next election. It should not be a surprise that so little gets done. Even if the campaign cycle were cut in half, that still only leaves fifty percent of the term available for constructive effort. At the very least, the president's term should equal the six year term of senators, but preferably eight years. A two year term for congressmen is equally inadequate and should be doubled. When the founders prepared the constitution, senators and congressmen were part time employees of a very small government faced with much smaller challenges. These short terms in office are an anachronism.

Some people chafe at the pay and benefits our politicians receive. Actually, their salaries are paltry when you consider that many of them maintain two homes, one in the capitol and one in their home region. The cost of maintaining two homes and traveling between them can be very high. Their positions require other expenses that many of us do not have. That is why people of moderate means find it difficult to run for office even if they are very qualified.   In return for higher wages, they must not be allowed to receive gifts, meals, transportation, or entertainment from any other source except family members, and only if their family members are not lobbyists or employees of lobby firms. Violation of the rules should be punished with mandatory prison sentences and removal from office. If we want honest people in government, we must be willing to pay them enough so it is possible for them to remain honest, and deal harshly with them if they don't. A good starting point would be to pay senators at the top one percent income threshold, and the top two percent for congressmen. Presidents should receive double the salary of senators.

How do we communicate to them that they work for us? In the private sector, employees get performance reviews, and their supervisors decide if they get wage increases and how much. Politicians should not be able to vote their own pay increases any more than any one of us. We have seen the ridiculous top executive compensation packages in the corporate world. Do you think they would exist if shareholders got to vote on executive compensation? The only reason that has not happened in Congress is that salaries are not their primary source of income. Cut off the lobbyists, and you will see salaries rise quickly. In a sense, we do review our politicians' performance when we vote to reelect them. Automatic annual cost of living increases based on the Consumer Price Index should eliminate the need for them to vote themselves salary increases. At the end of their term, their constituents can decide whether they have performed well enough to keep their jobs. As for their benefits, they should not exceed those the rest of us receive.

In both the 2000 and 2004 elections, voting irregularities with punch card ballots and electronic machines created some concern about accuracy of vote counts. The voter has no means of ascertaining that the vote has not been tampered with or the machines hacked. Democracy depends on every person's vote counting. That requires positive identification of voters and means of verifying their vote. Most of us cannot remember how we voted on every issue and for every position. We should receive a printout of our vote from the voting machine. Our votes should be transmitted electronically to the Federal Election Commission to serve as a crosscheck. Then a postcard documenting our vote, coded for privacy, should be sent us in the mail. That would allow us to compare the vote we cast to the vote as it was counted.

We tend to value most highly those representatives who **bring home the most bacon** (pork) to our states. They do so by requesting money for various projects in their home states by attaching the requests, called **earmarks**, to various bills going through congress. In many cases, the earmarks are attached to bills having nothing at all to do with subject matter of the bills. This makes it virtually impossible to establish fiscal responsibility. Many of the projects are not bid competitively, may be intended to benefit political supporters, or may not be needed at all. It is long past time to establish a proper budgeting process. States should submit their requests to Congress in priority order categorized (transportation, education, health care, research, etc.) for easy incorporation into a master budget. All such projects should be competitively bid and be approved by the voters of their state. I am relatively certain the voters would not approve a study of the sex life of ants (low value), or the building of a parking garage in Provo, Utah, (a purely local matter). The federal government should only support state expenditures that promote the wellbeing of its citizens, facilitate interstate commerce, and are in the national interest. Except for responding to disasters beyond the capability of individual states, the federal government should not otherwise be involved in strictly local matters. How much any one state gets should never be based upon the clout wielded by its representatives, but by the state's needs. Perhaps a simple formula might be used to determine need. For example, the amount allocated for assistance to states times the sum of one-half the percentage of the nation's population plus one-half the percentage of the nation's land area. Imagine how much simpler legislation would be without the pork. Issues might then be resolved on the basis of merit, not political considerations. The states would each get their highest priorities met without driving the nation into deficit spending.

As an alternative, several politicians have proposed giving the President a line item veto. On the surface it may seem like a good idea, but it could be dangerous. A very partisan president could gut any bill proposed by an opposing party. That could severely damage our multi-party system. It could tilt the balance of power between the branches of government too far in favor of the executive branch. Disallowing unrelated earmarks in legislation would serve the same purpose without the downsides.

Not all earmarks are for state priorities. Federal budgets should be prepared in similar fashion, starting with a list of binding priorities approved by the voters. Provisions can always be made for emergency requests, but they must be kept to a minimum. There are times, such as now, when the government must stimulate the economy to prevent it from falling into depression. That mandates deficit spending, but it must never become a way of life. When a corporation loses money, the shareholders are forced to put in more money or lose their investment in bankruptcy. The same should be true of government. It must either raise taxes or cut spending, or both. Deficits increase debt so more of our tax money goes for payment of interest. During the 1980s and

1990s, interest on the national debt absorbed up to 18.4% of our national revenues. In 2007, we paid $430 billion in interest on the national debt. That is more than $3700 per household, or 7.4% of the median household income of $50,233. It is shocking that so few of us recognize the seriousness of this problem. The very politicians that railed against deficit spending and increased debt proposed extending the previous administrations' tax cuts that drove up the deficits and debt. They also proposed drastic cuts in government spending, which is the only thing keeping our economy from tanking. These are political positions devoid of any understanding of economics. Once again, I refer you to the proposed Gross Revenues Tax system that meets all the nation's needs at a low tax rate without running deficits.

Have you ever wondered why most countries, states, and municipalities are so indebted? Financiers love government debt because they know we cannot let them default. It is one of the safest investments. In the case of municipal bonds, we even give the holder tax free income. Many states issue industrial revenue bonds, essentially loans at very low interest, to aid corporations in expanding their operations. One former client was able to get $6 million for a planned expansion which actually cost about $2 million. The remainder was invested for several years at a profit. We often hear cries of "get government out of business". I would modify that somewhat to "get business out of government."

It might seem that enacting these reforms would significantly reduce the power of our senators and congressmen, but the lobbyists and their patrons are the ones whose power would be most greatly diminished. Getting the citizenry involved in much of the decision making is the right thing to do. Some have expressed concern that most people are not smart enough to make those decisions. Perhaps they would be if our legislators had a vested interest in educating us instead of keeping us dumb. With the growth of the Internet and smart phones, it is becoming possible to involve citizens directly in the decision making process, perhaps by a quarterly or semi-annual vote on various critical bills. With the lobbyists out of the picture, their patrons will have to argue their cases in the public forum.

It is difficult to have intelligent debate on any issue with the current overconcentration of media ownership. The major news networks rarely present more than a cursory glance at opposing viewpoints without preventing opponents from expressing their views by talking over them or resorting to ridicule. Imagine how much we could learn if debates had multiple opposing moderators questioning multiple opposing experts on critical issues within their disciplines. If each viewpoint was accompanied by supporting facts and evidence, we might finally understand how the economy really works, which health care systems work the best, whether global warming threatens the future of our planet, etc., etc.

I believe in democracy and capitalism, the kind where everyone has an equal voice and gets to play on a level playing field. That is why we must urgently reregulate the financial industry, rethink our system of taxation, and reform how we finance the political process. It will never happen if we continue to allow special interests to buy votes to get favorable treatment from the government. We must restore competition among oil companies, banks, insurance companies, pharmaceutical companies, energy producers, defense contractors, and other industries. They will not easily surrender the privileges they have bought. Only a massive public outcry by an informed citizenry can bring about the change we need. Now, let me borrow a few words from one of our greatest presidents, Abraham Lincoln. **"...we here highly resolve that these dead [who shed their blood for our freedom] shall not have died in vain — that this nation, under God, shall have a new birth of freedom — and that government of the people, by the people, for the people, shall not perish from the earth.**

"One wanders to the left, another to the right. Both are equally in error, but, are seduced by different delusions."

Horace (65 BC-8BC), ancient Roman poet

Retirement Security

My wife and I were having lunch with friends at a local restaurant after church one Sunday about three years ago when our conversation turned to politics. One presidential candidate had spoken of eliminating entitlements. A couple in an adjoining booth, about our age, decided to join the conversation. The man said, "We ought to get rid of entitlements." I asked him, "So, you want to quit getting a Social Security check?" He quickly responded, "No." I followed up with, "Then, you must want to give up Medicare, and buy your own health insurance?" Again he responded, "No." That led me to ask, "So, exactly which entitlements do you want to get rid of?" The puzzled look on his face told me he had fallen for the political rhetoric without understanding the implications. To many people, entitlements are what everyone else gets. Hardly anyone wants to lose their Social Security or Medicare. That has forced some politicians to redefine 'getting rid of entitlements' to its exact opposite, 'saving Social Security.' That leads to another question: "Why does Social Security need saving?"

We have all heard that the problem is an aging population – people living longer – and that is certainly true, but it is only part of the story. The Social Security Trust Fund (SSTF), unlike your bank account, does not actually contain any money. The FICA taxes you and your employer pay are used to buy special government bonds from the U.S. Treasury, essentially IOUs that pay interest. They are resold to the treasury in order to provide Social Security and disability payments to current retirees and beneficiaries. In 2009, the SSTF bought $1,049 billion and sold $950 billion of these special bonds. As of 2008, the SSTF contained approximately $2.4 trillion of these IOUs. The interest the SSTF earns is not in cash, but in more IOUs purchased with your FICA payments, making less and less of your FICA available for payment of benefits. The money used to purchase the bonds goes into the U.S. Treasury's general fund, and is spent like any other tax money. The bonds are backed by the full faith and credit of the federal government, which simply means that you and your descendants are guaranteeing to pay any taxes necessary to meet current benefit requirements plus interest on the SSTF. The bonds are considered assets. They are valued at face value, which would only be correct if the government were solvent, but not when we are running enormous budget deficits. Of course, the government could print the money to redeem the IOUs, but that would devalue the dollar and make your personal savings worth less. It is the worst possible investment. Instead of paying us interest on our money, it charges us interest. Think about where the interest comes from. Does anyone not see the feedback loop in the system?

All its faults notwithstanding, Social Security is an essential safety net for the majority of people whose incomes leave no room for retirement savings. The following chart shows that 30.6% of all households have incomes under $30,000, the approximate poverty level. Once the householders reach 75 years of age, 58.1% fall in that bracket. The median household income for older seniors is barely more than their Social Security benefit.

Source: U.S. Census Bureau 2009 Current Population Survey					
Age of Householder	Number of Households	% of Total Households	Number With Gross Income Under $30,000	% of Households	Median Household Income
All Ages	117,538,000	100.0%	35,985,000	30.6%	$ 49,777
65-74	13,164,000	11.2%	5,091,000	38.7%	$ 38,895
75 & Older	12,106,000	10.3%	7,035,000	58.1%	$ 25,693

Most of us get a free ride through early life on the backs of our parents. They provide the necessities of life, education, and protection often into our twenties. We have a moral obligation to repay their toil when they are no longer able to work or lack the resources to care for themselves. In some Asian societies, extended families live together. The grandparents who can no longer work care for the children and help around the house until they are no longer able to do so. Even then, they are respected, honored, and cared for. Sadly, our me-centered society with its serial divorces has broken those familial bonds. A child may have multiple step-parents and many step-grandparents. That makes the Asian model impracticable here.

On a trip to Rome about thirty years ago, as my wife and I exited St. Peter's Basilica, we were confronted by a woman begging. She was very thin, frail, and might have been close to ninety years old. She stretched out her hand and said, "Per favore" (please). Sensing a kind of desperation in her voice, I placed a $20 bill in her hand. She said, "Molte grazie" (Thank you very much). When she looked down at her hand, she broke into tears, took my hand and kissed it. Tears came to my eyes also. She repeated, "Grazie, grazie, grazie." Something inside me groaned as I thought, "This could be my mother. Is this what I would want for her?" My parents have been gone for many years. They were able to live out their last few years with dignity because of the safety net Social Security provided. They were both hard working and extremely frugal. They did not own a home until the last decade of their lives, and it was little more than a shack, but it brought them great joy. They never owned a car, took only brief vacations to visit family, never attended entertainment events, and never had a credit card. Dad received a small pension of about $100 per month. They never bought anything they could not afford, and saved every penny they could. They were fortunate to live out their working lives in Chicago which had a very good public transportation system and essential services. Their employer provided health insurance covered most of their health care cost until they were eligible for Medicare.

Many employers are dropping health insurance and retirement plans for their employees. They are simply not affordable when competing with foreign companies that do not provide such benefits, or domestic businesses that exploit illegal aliens. Let's determine whether it is possible for most families to afford private health insurance and retirement plans. In 2009, the median household income was $49,777. According to a Washington Post Article in October of 2010, health insurance premiums averaged $13,770 (ours were $19,816 five years ago). We will examine health care in greater detail in a later chapter. For now, let's estimate what it might cost to provide some retirement. Average life expectancy in the United States is about 78 years for all races and sexes. With a current retirement age of 65 years, that leaves 13 years of retirement. Without Medicare or Social Security, a retired couple with no car or mortgage payments might get by on $30,000 per year, of which $13,770 would go for health insurance. The remaining

$16, 230 would assure them of continued poverty. Thirteen years at $30,000 each means that they would have to save $390,000 over a 40 year working life -- that is $9,750 per year in current dollars. After deducting health insurance, only $26,257 remains for living expenses. That is below the poverty level for most families or households. You can forget about owning a home or a car, getting a college education, having a nutritious diet, taking vacations, or attending sporting or entertainment events. Here it is in table form:

HYPOTHETICAL RETIREMENT SAVINGS PLAN				
Retirement savings	$390,000		Household Income	$49,777
Retirement years	13		Working years	40
Annual budget	$30,000		Retirement savings	$9,750
Health insurance	$13,770		Health insurance	$13,770
Everything else	$16,230		Everything else	$26,257
2009 current dollars, median household, ignoring inflation and interest earned				

Under the current tax system and cost structures in health care and education, if there were no Social Security or Medicare, more than 50% of U.S. households would be living in abject poverty, and America would be a third world country. Think about these numbers. If you want to quibble, you can substitute any reasonable retirement age and any reasonable cost of living with the same outcome. Without some government sponsored health care and retirement program, that outcome is inescapable. We must decide whether the American Dream is only for the wealthiest few or if there is some way we can all participate to some degree.

It is time to face reality. The Social Security Trust Fund will never be solvent as long as we pretend it is earning interest. Wherever we put our retirement funds, Social Security or private accounts, they must earn interest higher than the rate of inflation. That interest must come from investors' pockets, not ours. But where can we put it? The financial industry has already proven they cannot be trusted. The logical choice would be commercial banks if there were a firewall between commercial banks and investment banks to prevent them from gambling with our money. Since the deposits are protected by the Federal Deposit Insurance Corporation (FDIC) at bank expense, they would be secure.

We must quit pretending that Social Security is an insurance program. It is a tax! If it were an insurance program, the money would be invested for our benefit and not transferred to the sinkhole of the general fund. Since it is a tax, it ought to apply to all income and not be limited. We must also quit pretending that the lower income half of our population pays no tax. Look at any of the income numbers in this book and you will realize that the bottom half does not earn enough to pay more. As it is, they pay a disproportionate share of employment taxes and the hidden federal, state, and local taxes of all kinds listed in the chapter on Fair Tax. Without radical tax reform, the majority of people will never have retirement security. Implementing the gross revenues tax (GRT) will increase the disposable income of most Americans sufficiently to refuel the economy and provide a path out of poverty.

We must recognize the sacred cows in our midst. One of my Hindu friends, who imports products from India, attended a trade show with me at which Indian leather goods were shown. I asked him, "If cows are considered sacred in India, where do they get all the leather?" He replied with a wry smile, "Cows die." It seems they are only sacred while they live. Our sacred cows are the various special retirement plans for select groups like federal employees (including our senators and congressmen), career military personnel, state public employees, and railroad employees. It is time to merge them into a new and better Social Security system with a consistent retirement age and benefit structure. Only the truly disabled should be able to collect retirement and health care benefits before the designated retirement age. To ease the transition of military into civilian life, they should receive severance pay similar to private sector employees, usually about two weeks per year of service. Just as in the case of the GRT tax reform, such a change would have to be made over a transition period of ten years or so. The savings in administrative and benefits cost would be many billions of dollars.

What should this new retirement package look like? All contributions to it should be taken from our taxes. All withdrawals from it should be free of tax, much like a Roth IRA. Ideally, it should have two components. The first should be a personal retirement savings account based on a mandatory contribution of approximately 2% by individuals and corporations with the corporate contributions distributed to individual accounts in proportion to individual earnings. That would allow a higher benefit to higher earners to avoid catastrophic downsizing of lifestyles upon retirement. The second should be based on an equivalent 2% contribution by individuals and corporations with the contributions placed in a shared pool that would pay an equal benefit to all participants, it being based on the principle that one's obligation to society should be proportional to the benefits one receives from it. The minimum combined benefit to any participant must at least equal a realistic poverty level. Both funds must be invested in secure interest bearing accounts. But, where?

The stock market may offer a higher rate of return in the long term, but the short-term downside risk is unacceptably high, and an investment in stocks can lead to government ownership of corporations. Government investment in corporate bonds can easily be abused by both government and corporations. That also applies to investment banks. Loans to states and municipalities must be repaid with taxpayer money so they increase the tax burden. Loans to foreign countries are too often written off or at least written down. That leaves us with one relatively safe choice: mortgages and collateralized debt managed by commercial banks which must be protected by a Glass-Steagall-like firewall, FDIC insured, and closely regulated. The funds would have to be maintained in a way that would prevent them from becoming comingled with non-SSTF funds.

One possibility would be to have banks bid for fixed term contracts, essentially certificates of deposit (CDs) with the SSTF as depositor, that would pay a guaranteed minimum rate of interest on the retirement funds on condition that the funds be lent out as mortgages and other collateralized loans conforming to acceptable standards as described in the chapter on Free Market Economics. Participating banks would be required to hold the loans (not securitize them) and to credit the SSTF accounts with at least one-third of the interest and fees from loan repayments plus the guaranteed rate on that portion of the deposits that was not lent out. Prior to expiration of the term of the CDs, the banks could rebid to continue managing the funds or transfer the accumulated funds to the SSTF along with the open loans. The resulting funds and loans should then be offered to other bidders under the same conditions. Any bank wishing to participate must be solvent and must not be affiliated with investment banks, insurance companies, or hedge funds. To prevent monopolization, banks should not be allowed to hold SSTF funds exceeding 20% of their assets, and contracts should be awarded to banks from all states. Having the banks pay interest on the money not lent out should encourage them to lend the money as quickly and responsibly as possible. Having the loans held by the banks should serve to stabilize the housing market and make it possible to restructure loans if necessary.

Nothing in the recommended program prevents anyone from having an employer provided 401K, or personal IRA, except that contributions made by employers and employees should not be tax deductible, be limited to a total of 10% of income , and not be taxed when withdrawn after retirement. Interest on personal savings accounts in banks and credit unions should also not be taxed because most savings accounts do not earn enough interest to offset inflation. However, capital gains should be taxed at the standard rate.

You will notice that the recommendations in this book are part of an integrated plan where all the incentives are toward wealth accumulation with very simple, clear, and enforceable rules. They are private sector solutions for the most part with little opportunity for government micromanagement. The most important function of government is to provide a secure environment and a level playing field for its citizens. That is why we should consolidate the various retirement plans into one serving the needs of all its citizens. There is no reason for military personnel and other federal employees to receive retirement and health care benefits earlier than the statutory retirement age or in excess of what most taxpayers get. The administrative costs for the several federal plans and state plans and the excessive benefits put an undue burden on taxpayers.

If you compare my proposal to those currently being offered as a means of saving Social Security (SS), you will see its merits. Some propose cutting benefits. What's the last time any of us tried living on $1100 per month? Perhaps while we were living with our parents? After forty to forty-five years of working to support our families and our country, do we not deserve better? Of course, if health permits, we can supplement our incomes by working as greeters at Wal-Mart. There just aren't enough Wal-Mart stores to go around to save our retirement.

One proposal being put forth is to push the eligibility date back to age seventy or beyond. What is the last time any of us looked for a job beyond the age of fifty or sixty? Some senators and congressmen seem to be able to work into their nineties, but that is rarely the case in the private world. Corporate restructuring often results in the replacement of better paid senior employees with less costly younger ones. Several of my highly qualified associates between fifty and sixty years of age have been unemployed for as long as three years during times of relatively moderate unemployment. A few were forced to sell their homes or deplete their savings and retirement accounts to finance survival. Ultimately, they accepted positions far below their capabilities at a fraction of their former incomes. They rarely qualify for welfare. We do have a law against age discrimination, but it is difficult to enforce.

Another proposal would privatize SS. We already have IRA's, 401-K's, and similar plans. Expanding them under the current tax system would only give another tax break to those with money to set aside. Most people do not have the resources to do so or the knowledge of investment options. They could lose their entire retirement fund, either through their own or others' ineptitude, or by the actions of unscrupulous advisers. The burden would then fall back on taxpayers.

Another suggestion was to allow the SSTF to invest a portion of the SS fund in the stock market and corporate bonds. The problem is that it puts enormous power in the hands of those who decide where the money should be placed. Huge sums would be spent to influence investment decisions. The placement of the funds could be used as a competitive weapon between brokerage firms, fund managers, and corporations. The Enron, Tyco, WorldCom, and Madoff scandals would pale in comparison to what could result. It has only been two years since the stock market lost more than half its value, and it is still far from where it was three years ago. Does anyone want to take that roller coaster ride again? I do not.

So what is responsible for the disappearance of private sector retirement plans? They make our corporations noncompetitive in a global market. Our international trade policies only make matters worse. The growth of derivatives has enabled obscene fortunes to be made with lazy money that produces nothing. That stratifies the economy. With so much trapped in the FIRE sector, less is available to the general economy. The result is lower tax revenues and perpetual debt that makes a public sector solution untenable. Without a radical change in our system of taxation, retirement security for the majority cannot be achieved by private or public means. If we find the courage to fix the tax system, there will be no deficits and we will be able to fulfill our moral obligation to our parents and to our future selves.

The question isn't at what age I want to retire, it's at what income.

George Foreman

Quality Health Care

The United States have the best medical schools, the best trained doctors, excellent nurses, the best hospitals, the largest number of health care facilities, the most sophisticated medical equipment and more of it, shorter waiting times for many procedures, higher survival rates from many diseases, and spends more by half on health care per capita than any other country. By any measure, it ought to have the healthiest people in the world.

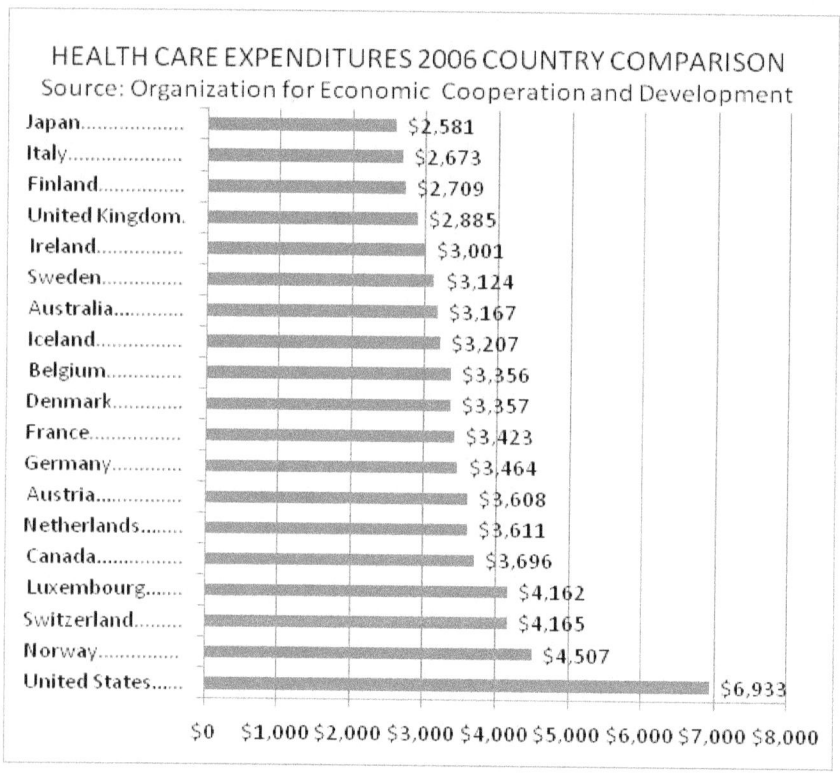

HEALTH CARE EXPENDITURES 2006 COUNTRY COMPARISON
Source: Organization for Economic Cooperation and Development

Japan	$2,581
Italy	$2,673
Finland	$2,709
United Kingdom	$2,885
Ireland	$3,001
Sweden	$3,124
Australia	$3,167
Iceland	$3,207
Belgium	$3,356
Denmark	$3,357
France	$3,423
Germany	$3,464
Austria	$3,608
Netherlands	$3,611
Canada	$3,696
Luxembourg	$4,162
Switzerland	$4,165
Norway	$4,507
United States	$6,933

$0 $1,000 $2,000 $3,000 $4,000 $5,000 $6,000 $7,000 $8,000

All of the above nations, except the US, have universal health care. Many are single payer systems administered by their governments. Their doctors and hospitals may be in the private sector, so they may not be entirely socialized. We often hear that their tax rates are outlandish. When we add our personal health care costs to our taxes, many of which are hidden in the cost of products and services, our overall costs are probably higher. What are we getting for the extra spending on health care? The CIA World Factbook 2010 shows the United States 46th in infant mortality and 48th in life expectancy at birth, behind some countries we have never heard of. The world's highest level of satisfaction with their health care system is in France, which spends less than half per person than we do. Japan spends the least among the nineteen shown, yet it has the best results. We, who spend by far the most, have some of the highest rates of obesity, diabetes, heart disease, cancer, and other ailments. There is an obvious disconnect between the cost of our health care and the results. The debate about health care reform has become so highly politicized that it is virtually impossible to determine what the facts are and what reforms would bring down cost and improve results. I am not a health care professional, but I will try to make some sense of this issue.

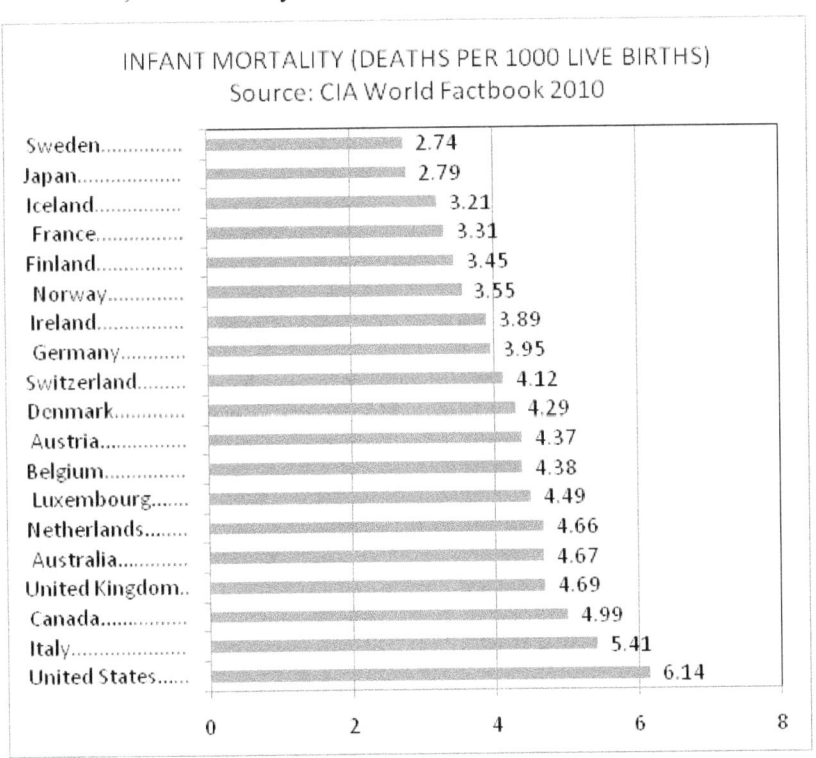

INFANT MORTALITY (DEATHS PER 1000 LIVE BIRTHS)
Source: CIA World Factbook 2010

Sweden	2.74
Japan	2.79
Iceland	3.21
France	3.31
Finland	3.45
Norway	3.55
Ireland	3.89
Germany	3.95
Switzerland	4.12
Denmark	4.29
Austria	4.37
Belgium	4.38
Luxembourg	4.49
Netherlands	4.66
Australia	4.67
United Kingdom	4.69
Canada	4.99
Italy	5.41
United States	6.14

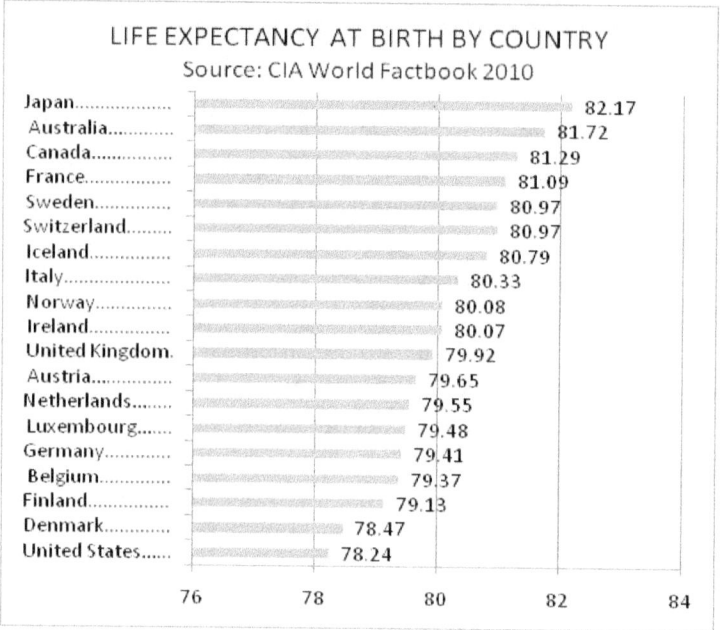

No doubt some of the differences are due to lifestyle. We are less physically active, eat more highly processed foods laden with preservatives, and consume tremendous quantities of sugars, sodas, and cheeses. Many of us live on a deep fried fast food diet devoid of fruits and vegetables. Our refrigerators are huge by comparison to those in other countries. Most foreign families shop each day for fresh meats, breads, fruits, and vegetables. They eat a broader variety of foods, which provide more of the essential nutrients. We have sacrificed quality for convenience. Our Food and Drug Administration has not adequately regulated and enforced food quality standards. We need a radical reeducation on nutrition and its effect on health, but that is beyond the scope of this chapter.

Our health care system is in crisis, both in cost and quality of outcomes. Politicians speak of the health care crisis, but most are unwilling to face the wrath of the special interests to do something about it. The health care reform bill that passed is, at best, a crude compromise. Before we can fix the problem, we have to face a few facts.

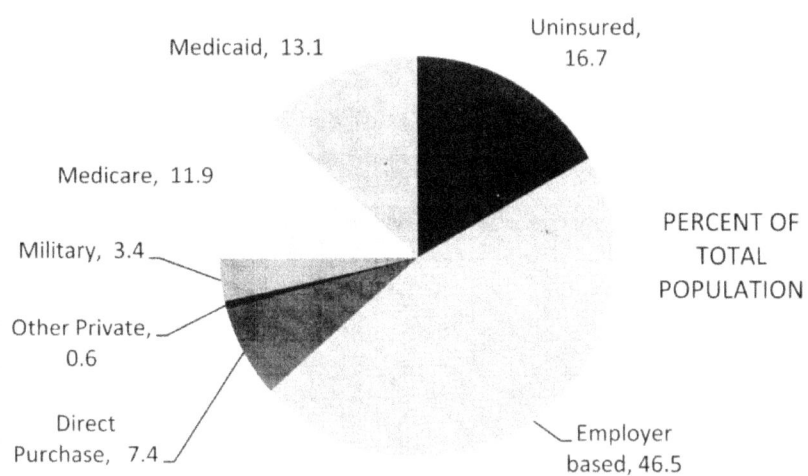

INSURED AND UNINSURED POPULATION 2009

Medicaid, 13.1

Uninsured, 16.7

Medicare, 11.9

Military, 3.4

Other Private, 0.6

Direct Purchase, 7.4

Employer based, 46.5

PERCENT OF TOTAL POPULATION

Source: U.S. Census Bureau Current Population Survey 2010

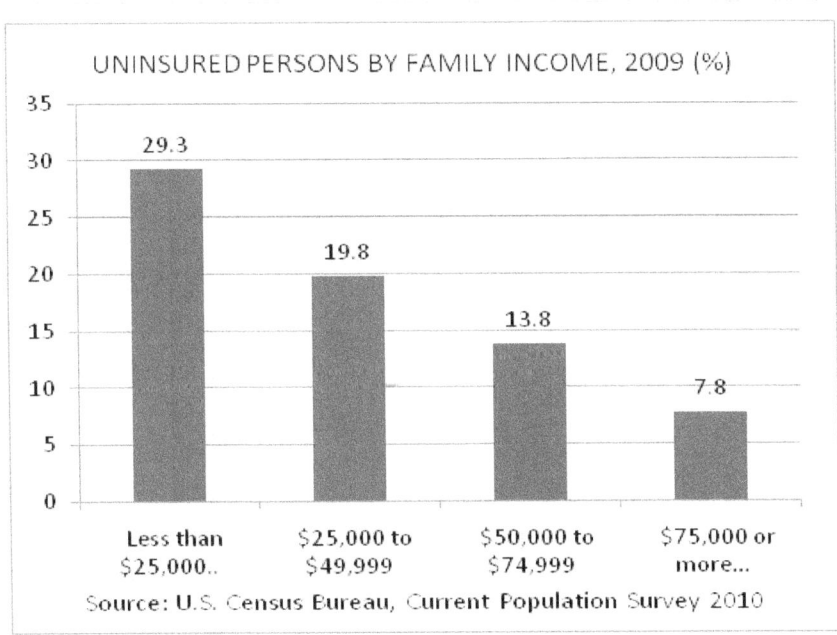

UNINSURED PERSONS BY FAMILY INCOME, 2009 (%)

Less than $25,000..	$25,000 to $49,999	$50,000 to $74,999	$75,000 or more...
29.3	19.8	13.8	7.8

Source: U.S. Census Bureau, Current Population Survey 2010

With health insurance premiums averaging $13,770 ($6.62 per hour for a full time worker), many businesses cannot afford health insurance for their employees, so they are reducing their share of health insurance premiums or dropping health insurance entirely. Between 2007 and 2008, 1.1 million people lost their employer based health insurance. There are now fifty million people without health insurance in the United States. More than half of all bankruptcies are due to medical expenses. Eighty percent of those filing bankruptcy because of medical expenses have health insurance. The 2005 bankruptcy reform act severely limits the amount of relief a family can receive.

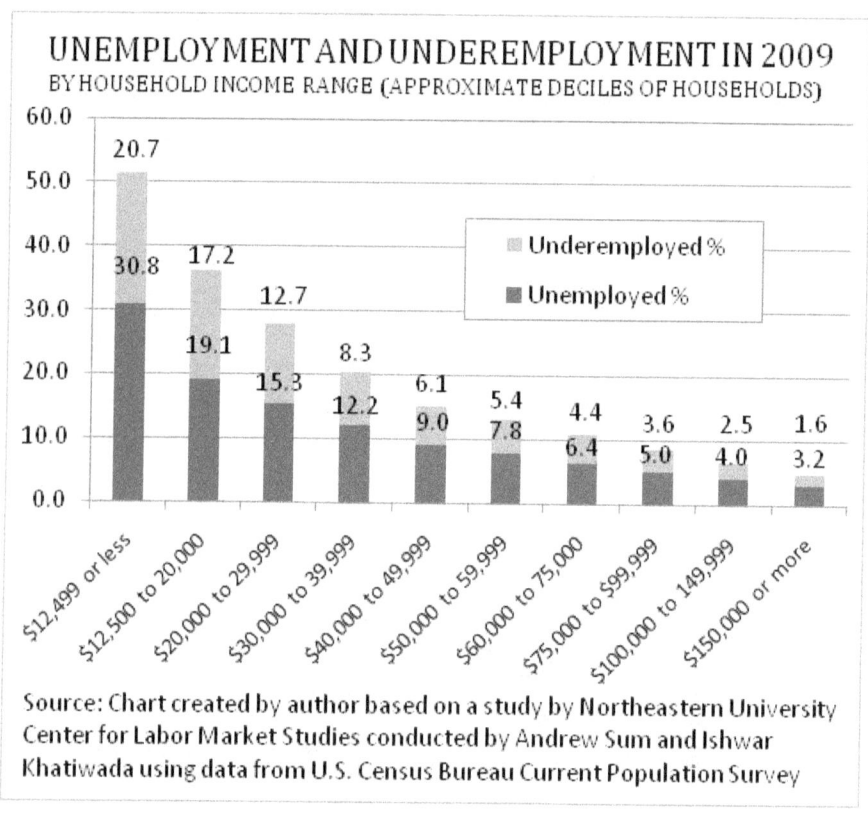

Source: Chart created by author based on a study by Northeastern University Center for Labor Market Studies conducted by Andrew Sum and Ishwar Khatiwada using data from U.S. Census Bureau Current Population Survey

This chart also explains why unemployment remains high during the current recovery. Many businesses are increasing hours for the underemployed rather than hiring new workers. Health insurance premiums are a disincentive to add new workers. All of this suggests that wage erosion and the export of jobs are contributing factors to the health care crisis. The unemployed can continue their health insurance under COBRA, but, as shown in a previous chapter, Cobra premiums exceed 75% of unemployment compensation benefits in 41 of 50 states.

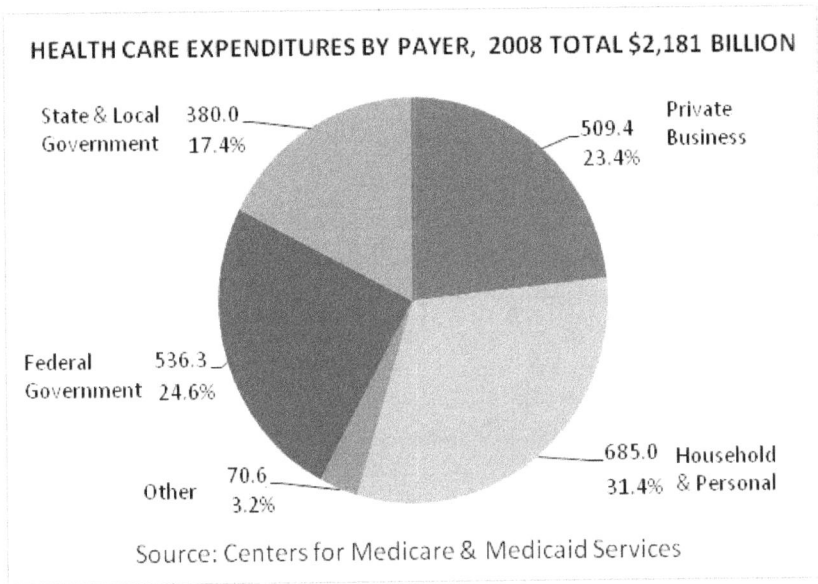

HEALTH CARE EXPENDITURES BY PAYER, 2008 TOTAL $2,181 BILLION

State & Local 380.0
Government   17.4%

Private Business 509.4 23.4%

Federal   536.3
Government   24.6%

Household & Personal 685.0 31.4%

Other   70.6
        3.2%

Source: Centers for Medicare & Medicaid Services

In spite of all the hoopla about government health care, we already have government run health care. Medicare provides coverage for people over 65 and those with certain disabilities and chronic illnesses. Medicaid covers the indigent. Tricare covers current and retired military and their families. The Veterans Administration provides health care for veterans. Employer provided insurance covers 46.5% of the population (see chart above), but paid only 23.4% of health care expenses in 2008. Employees pay the remainder. Corporations pay about 16% of the income taxes. That means that private citizens pay for 84% of government health care. Private business pays 30.1% of total health care cost, private citizens pay 66.7%, and all other payers pay 3.2%.

Employer provided health insurance may work for some people, but it is not affordable, lacks portability, makes employers non-competitive, and does not cover everyone. Add in time off benefits and a retirement plan, and you can readily see why businesses are dropping such benefits, and why illegal immigrants and foreign companies have an unfair competitive advantage. They enjoy the benefits of our market without any responsibility for its upkeep. It also explains in part why our domestic corporations have set up operations in other countries

instead of here. The next question to be answered is on whom all that
money is being spent.

2008 Spending for Health Care				
Demographic	Participants (Millions)	Percent with Expenses	Spending (Billions)	Amount per Beneficiary
Medicare, 85 + [1]	4.2	98.0	$ 56.1	$ 13,399
Medicare, 75-84 [1]	9.6		$ 97.9	$ 10,206
Medicare, Under 65 [1]	6.4		$ 54.2	$ 8,523
Veterans [2]	5.3		$ 38.3	$ 7,235
Medicare, 65-74 [1]	15.2		$ 92.9	$ 6,119
Private Insurance [4]	171.9		$ 509.4	$ 5,891
Medicaid [3]	56.8		$ 294.2	$ 5,180
Uninsured [5]	46.3	57.2	$ 46.9	$ 2,057
1. Centers for Medicare and Medicaid Services, Tables 143, 145				
2. Veterans Administration				
3. Centers for Disease Control and Prevention (CDC), Table 145				
4. CDC, Tables 137, 134, 123. Amount includes out-of-pocket.				
5. US Census Bureau, Tables 151, 132. Amount includes only those with expenses.				

Before we attempt to analyze the above table, be aware that health
care data is scattered over many spreadsheets that are derived from hard
data or population surveys, may contain inconsistencies, and are
organized in a way that defies easy analysis. Nevertheless, I believe
the above sufficient to prove a number of points. It has been widely
reported that half of all medical expense occurs in the last year of life,
and that approximately 30% of all expenses occur in the last two
months of life. After age 75, health care costs increase sharply. They
are also high for those under 65 who are disabled or have severe
chronic illnesses. Active duty military, veterans, and their families may
also experience higher expenses. Not surprisingly, all of the groups
whose health care is costliest are covered by government run health
insurance. As powerful as the health insurance industry is, and as
opposed to government run health care as they are, why did they allow
it? They defeated every attempt at a public option. When they could
not defeat the health care reform legislation immediately, they
succeeded in getting the effective dates of the most important
provisions pushed back three years to 2014, after the next presidential
election, and are now militating to have it repealed. It is my belief that

the reason we have Medicare, Medicaid, Tricare, and Veterans Administration health care is because the insurance companies saw no opportunity for profit there. They allowed the cost to be pushed onto individual taxpayers. We gripe about government run health care but offer no alternative. If insurance companies had to insure these high risk groups under the current private health care system, premiums would probably be double what they are now and almost no one could afford them. No one argues that the health care system is not broken, but nothing has been done to reduce cost or improve the system.

Insurance premiums would be less overall if young healthy people were required to have health insurance. After all, aren't we required to have auto insurance? My friends argue that we are only required to have liability insurance. My response is that no bank will lend you money to buy a vehicle unless you insure it against damage or loss. When an uninsured young person suffers an accidental injury or illness, the expense for his medical care typically becomes my liability as a taxpayer. I want the same protection a bank gets. My friends come back with, "Why should I pay for health insurance to reduce the cost for others when I have no physical needs?" My answer is, "Not yet, but you will. You are not reducing the cost for others, but for yourself in the future." As the above statistics show, we will all ultimately and almost without exception become those high maintenance individuals. We can make our retirement and our own health care more secure by paying it forward.

Our health care is spread over many federal, state, and local agencies, each with its own administration. In the aggregate, the administrative costs are staggering. Every doctor's office has at least one person to deal with the patient records and one person to negotiate the maze of insurance regulations. Many employers have benefits administrators in their human resources departments to assist insurance companies. According to numerous published reports, Medicare administrative costs are 3%, although they are 1.4% in the CMS (Centers for Medicare and Medicaid Services) report for 2008. Administrative costs for private employer based insurance are 17%, and even higher for privately purchased plans. These figures are disputed by Robert A. Book, Ph.D., in an article dated June 25,2009, on the Heritage Foundation website. He claims Medicare's administrative costs are as high as 6% and that, because Medicare recipients cost far more per person than those privately insured, the per-person administrative cost is actually lower for private insurers. He calls the published figures 'fuzzy math'. Both the 3% figure and his are an incorrect measure of efficiency. Medicare recipients, on a per person basis, have many more visits to doctors, emergency rooms, labs, and imaging centers. They are hospitalized more frequently, for longer stays, and have more expensive procedures. Each of these events is a claim that must be processed. The relative efficiency of administration can be determined by comparing the administrative cost per claim of public and private insurers, not the per person administrative cost nor the percentage of administrative cost to health care payments.

HEALTH CARE USAGE BY AGE					
Age	Percent with Hospital Stays in 2008	No. of Stays per Person 2007	Length of Stay Days 2007	Ambulatory Care Visits per Person 2008 [1]	Average Claims per Person
1-17	2.60	0.27	4.7	2.8	3.07
18-24	5.40	0.27	3.2		3.07
25-44	6.80	0.34	3.8	3.2	3.54
45-54	6.90	0.47	4.9	5.8	6.27
55-64	9.20	0.74	5.3		6.62
65-74	14.20	1.33	5.4	7.3	8.63
75-84	19.20	2.27	5.7	8.6	10.87
85+	27.40	3.01	5.6		11.61
Source: Centers for Disease Contro, Tables 98, 99, 102, 164					
1. Last available year shown for each table. Age brackets in Table 164 differ, so some brackets are combined. In combined age brackets, average cxlaims would be even higher for the older populations.					

Medicare's average claim is probably larger than that of private insurers. By the 'per claim' standard, Medicare is more efficient, but not by the margin claimed. Dr. Book's article states: "*In 2005, Medicare's administrative costs were $509 per primary beneficiary, compared to private-sector administrative costs of $453.*" If we estimate the number of annual claims per beneficiary to be 6 for the privately insured and 10 for Medicare recipients, the relative efficiency is as follows:

ADMINISTRATIVE EFFICIENCY		
Insurer	Private	Medicare
2005 cost per beneficiary	$453	$509
Claims per beneficiary	6	10
Cost per claim	$75.50	$50.90

Here is how Medicare spends our money:

Medicare Data for Calendar Year 2008					
	Part A	Part B	Part D	Total	Percent
Total income	$230.8	$200.6	$49.4	$480.8	
Total expenditures	**$235.6**	**$183.3**	**$49.3**	**$468.1**	**100.0**
Benefits	**$232.3**	**$180.3**	**$49.0**	**$461.6**	**98.6**
Hospital	$130.5	$26.8	—	$157.3	33.6
Skilled nursing facility	$24.2	—	—	$24.2	5.2
Home health care	$6.6	$10.0	—	$16.6	3.5
Physician fee schedule services	—	$60.8	—	$60.8	13.0
Private health plans (Part C)	**$50.6**	**$47.6**	**—**	**$98.2**	**21.0**
Prescription drugs	**—**	**—**	**$49.0**	**$49.0**	**10.5**
Other	$20.6	$35.2	—	$55.8	11.9
Administrative expenses	**$3.3**	**$3.0**	**$0.3**	**$6.5**	**1.4**
Enrollment (millions)					
Aged	37.5	35.2	n/a	36.9	
Disabled	7.4	6.6	n/a	7.2	
Total	44.9	41.7	32.3	44.1	
Average benefit per enrollee	**$5,179**	**$4,322**	**$1,517**	**$11,018**	
Notes: 1. Totals do not necessarily equal the sums of rounded components.					
2. "n/a" indicates data are not available.					
Source: 2009 Annual Report Medicare Board of Trustees, Table II.B1.					

Medicare total costs could be reduced significantly by eliminating payments to other insurance companies under Medicare Advantage (Part C) and by negotiating prescription drug prices under Part D. Medicare is insurance. It should not be subsidizing other insurance companies or pharmaceutical companies. Medicare Advantage (Part C) was started in 2003 to move Medicare enrollees to private health plans, typically HMOs, subsidized by payments to participating insurers by Medicare. In 2010, these subsidies amounted to $14 billion. The *Patient Protection and Affordable Care Act* of 2010 will eliminate the subsidies over the next several years. Can anyone figure out why one insurance company (Medicare) would pay another insurance company to be an intermediary between itself and its enrollees? Economist Paul Krugman in a September 4, 2010, article in the New York Times titled *Health Policy Malpractice* states: *"According to the Independent Medicare Payment Advisory Commission, Medicare Advantage plans cost the government 11 percent more per person than traditional Medicare. Oh, and mortality rates in these plans are 40 percent higher than those of elderly veterans covered by the V.A."* Why are we paying more for less?

The Department of Veterans Affairs (VA) is a government run health care system. It has been praised as one of the most cost effective providers of quality health care. There is no easy way for me to determine the makeup of the population using its services or the statistics related to its use, but I believe that they are probably similar to those for Medicare and Medicaid. The VA uses a comprehensive computerized team oriented system to treat its patients. Patients may be in the system longer, so their records are more complete and available to all practitioners. The VA does not have unlimited funds, so it negotiates prices with its suppliers and must function within a budget. One is tempted to think that there is a lot of fraud and lack of enforcement in Medicare, and undoubtedly there is some, but the more significant cause may be the 'fee for service' system – the more services they provide, the more they get paid. There is little incentive for the doctor, hospital, or insurer to provide less service or to charge less. Any cost controls are directed to increased profit internally, not to lower cost for the patient.

Medicare Part D prescription drug plan was enacted on January 1 of 2006 to provide drug coverage to Medicare recipients. In 2008, it cost taxpayers $49 billion. According to Families USA in an April 2007 study (*www.familiesusa.org/assets/pdfs/rhetoric-vs-reality.PDF*), the median cost difference between what the VA pays for the top 20 drugs prescribed for seniors and what Part D pays is 58% of Part D prices.

The VA negotiates prices with pharmaceutical companies; Medicare cannot. If that difference holds true across all drugs, then it should easily be possible to cut $28.2 billion from this gift to the pharmaceutical industry. Here are the figures:

Drug Name	Strength	Dose Form	Lowest VA Price Per Year	Lowest Part D Price	Percent Difference
PRICES FOR TOP 20 DRUGS PRESCRIBED FOR SENIORS VA VERSUS TOP PART D INSURERS, NOVEMBER 2006					
Actonel	35 mg	tab	$372.24	$763.56	105%
Aricept	10 mg	tab	$1,058.69	$1,561.44	47%
Celebrex	200 mg	cap	$632.09	$946.44	50%
Fosamax	70 mg	tab	$250.32	$763.56	205%
furosemide	40 mg	tab	$7.81	$15.24	95%
Lipitor	10 mg	tab	$520.49	$785.40	51%
Lipitor	20 mg	tab	$782.44	$1,120.32	43%
metoprolol tartrate	50 mg	cap	$10.84	$16.20	50%
Nexium	40 mg	cap	$848.45	$1,433.16	69%
Norvasc	5 mg	tab	$315.84	$486.48	54%
Norvasc	10 mg	tab	$448.88	$667.56	49%
Plavix	75 mg	tab	$989.36	$1,323.24	34%
Prevacid	30 mg	cap DR	$332.71	$1,444.32	334%
Protonix	40 mg	tab	$214.52	$1,148.40	435%
Toprol XL	50 mg	tab	$167.22	$263.16	57%
Toprol XL	100 mg	tab	$250.06	$395.52	58%
Xalatan	0.01%	sol	$427.08	$582.96	36%
Zocor [1]	20 mg	tab	$127.44	$1,485.96	1066%
Zocor [1]	40 mg	tab	$191.16	$1,485.96	677%
Zoloft [1]	50 mg	tab	$465.91	$819.96	76%
Median Price Difference			**$352.48**	**$802.68**	**58%**
1. Prices listed are for brand name drugs.					
Source: Families USA (www.familiesusa.org/assets/pdfs/rhetoric-vs-reality.PDF)					

Much of health care cost is expended during the last few months of life. A few years ago, our son David, age 32, was in an intensive care unit with end stage renal disease. His kidneys had been removed two years earlier because of recurring infections. He had been on dialysis for six years waiting for a transplant. When his heart valves calcified, he developed thyroid cancer, and he could not withstand chemotherapy, he was taken off the list. He was in a coma and on a ventilator. His nephrologist, a kindly man, asked us what our wishes were. Our answer was, "What would we be bringing him back to?" We told the doctor that we had discussed end of life issues with David months earlier, and that we would let David make the decision if he was able, otherwise we were prepared to let him go. After a few minutes of prayer, we returned to David's room to find him awake and aware. His condition stabilized, so nurses removed the ventilator tube. After visiting with his siblings and us, he suffered another seizure then his heart began to fail. Another doctor insisted on putting him back on the ventilator. We refused saying, "Ask David what he wants." The doctor asked, "Do you want to be put back on the ventilator?" David motioned with his hand indicating "No!" The doctor asked, "Do you know you could die?" David nodded "Yes." A short while later, David was gone. The counseling we had given him, and his faith in God, gave him peace and comfort. In an adjacent room, an eighty-six year old man with a terminal illness was going into cardiac arrest. Several members of his family were in the room. They demanded that every possible means be used to resuscitate him. Perhaps they thought that their 'pro life' religious beliefs would be violated if they let him go. Where is the line between 'pro life' and 'pro torture?' This man's family very much needed end-of-life counseling.

There was a provision in the recently enacted health care bill to have insurers pay for voluntary end of life counseling for terminally ill patients and their families. It was struck out because politicians, fueled by money from insurance company lobbyists, turned it into a discussion of 'death panels'. This was a provision that would have saved insurance companies money and given their clients peace of mind. Why did they oppose the bill? Because it came with other provisions that would have cost them money. They have a perverse incentive in that theirs is a 'cost plus' business – the more they pay the more they can charge you. The bill would require them to pay out benefits to a fixed percentage of premiums. David's medical bills amounted to $985,000 in the last two years of his life. Medicare and private insurance paid most of it. We were fortunate to be able to pay the premiums and co-pays. Many families would have lost their homes and their life savings. My father died of lung cancer that had spread throughout his body. He chose to die at home with his family around him, with only a minimum of pain killers because he treasured every lucid moment with us. Several of our friends chose hospice care rather than continue pointless treatment.

David was born with birth defects that made him uninsurable under a preexisting condition clause. This was before Medicaid and Medicare, but we would not have qualified for either. Out of pocket expenses ruined us financially. It took eleven years to dig our way out of debt. In the end, David was insured under my COBRA policy. Why was Medicare involved at all? Apparently, insurance companies succeeded in pawning off dialysis patients onto taxpayers because dialysis is expensive, and people can be on dialysis for many years. They only want to insure low risk clients. That may also be why employers are avoiding hiring people in the 55 to 64 age group. It drives up their premiums. We must ask ourselves how we were persuaded that health insurance industry reform is unnecessary. To be clear, I am not a proponent of government owned and operated health care – that is socialism. Medical care under Medicare is provided by the private sector. It merely insures those that private insurers either cannot or will not cover.

Another demographic that needs to be examined is Medicaid recipients. Medicaid is a program administered by individual states under broad federal guidelines to provide health care, including prescription drugs and dental, and nursing home care to low income families and people with certain disabilities who are citizens or permanent resident aliens. **It does not cover illegal aliens**. The federal government provides more than half of the necessary funding. Many states contract the care out to health maintenance organizations or private insurance companies, with the states paying the premiums. Some states require copayments. States also administer a program providing health care to children of working poor families, called CHIP (Children's Health Insurance Program), which, according to the Kaiser Family Foundation cost $10.05 billion in 2008. This table shows, in descending order, where the money is being spent:

MEDICAID SPENDING BY TYPE OF SERVICE 2008					
Type of Service	Recipients (Millions)	Percent of all recipients	Spending (Billions)	Percent of all spending	Spending per recipient
Capitated care [1]	37.74	64.8	$ 67.67	23.0	$ 1,791
Nursing facility	1.63	2.8	$ 47.37	16.1	$ 29,493
Inpatient hospital	5.24	9.0	$ 36.78	12.5	$ 7,070
Unknown service type	12.4	21.3	$ 35.30	12.0	$ 2,836
Personal support	6.35	10.9	$ 24.42	8.3	$ 3,865
Prescribed drugs	24.34	41.8	$ 23.24	7.9	$ 957
Mentally retarded intermediate care facility [2]	0.12	0.2	$ 12.36	4.2	$ 123,501
Outpatient hospital	14.68	25.2	$ 10.89	3.7	$ 734
Physician	21.55	37.0	$ 10.30	3.5	$ 485
Clinic	11.71	20.1	$ 8.83	3.0	$ 765
Home health	1.11	1.9	$ 6.47	2.2	$ 5,684
Dental	9.66	16.6	$ 3.82	1.3	$ 390
Laboratory and radiological	15.49	26.6	$ 2.94	1.0	$ 188
Mental health facility	0.12	0.2	$ 2.35	0.8	$ 21,848
Other practitioner	5.13	8.8	$ 0.88	0.3	$ 171
Primary care case management	8.74	15.0	$ 0.29	0.1	$ 32
Source: Centers for Medicare and Medicaid Services, Table 146					
1. Care contracted to a health maintenance organization on a fixed price per beneficiary.					
2. Percent of recipients and spending per recipient are as they appear in CMMS Table 146.					

This table raises more questions than it answers. There is no way that any HMO (see note 1) can provide health care for a mere $1,791 to so many recipients. The logical conclusion is that it simply refers beneficiaries to other services that are billed separately. If so, then they are little more than very expensive case management organizations. The fact that 12% of Medicaid spending goes to unknown types of providers is not surprising since the data is drawn from 50 states and several territories as well as countless local health agencies. It is also difficult to imagine that $123,501 can be spent on each of 120,000 mentally retarded persons in one year. I believe that Medicaid is one area where centralization of control has the potential for saving a lot of money.

Medicaid beneficiaries are predominantly blind, disabled, seniors whose families cannot afford nursing home care, and poor families with dependent children.

Medicaid Recipients and Spending 2008					
Basis of Eligibility	No. of Recipients (Millions)	Percent of Total Recipients	Spending per Eligibility (Billions)	Percent of Total Spending	Spending per Recipient
Age 65 or older	4.1	7.1	$ 60.9	20.7	$ 14,766
Blind and disabled	8.6	14.8	$ 128.3	43.6	$ 14,839
Adults in families with dependent children	12.8	22.0	$ 37.4	12.7	$ 2,912
Children under age 21	27.8	47.8	$ 56.8	19.3	$ 2,036
Other	4.9	8.4	$ 11.5	3.9	$ 2,335
Total	**58.2**	**100.0**	**$ 294.2**	**100**	**$ 5,051**

Source: Centers for Medicare and Medicaid Services, Table 145

People below the poverty level have more than four times the health concerns than those with annual incomes exceeding $100,000. We realize that post traumatic stress disorder affects military personnel, but stop short of acknowledging that unemployment and poverty are major stressors that have a similar effect on civilians. Changes in policy that create jobs which pay a living wage are an excellent way to reduce health care cost. They provide access to better nutrition, recreational opportunity, and preventive care.

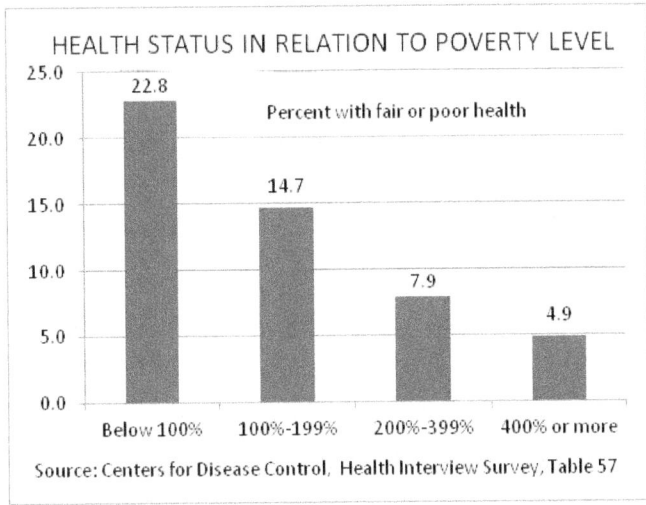

HEALTH STATUS IN RELATION TO POVERTY LEVEL

Percent with fair or poor health

Source: Centers for Disease Control, Health Interview Survey, Table 57

Another area where savings are easily possible is the Federal Employees Retirement System. Why do we need to allow federal employees, including members of the Senate and House of Representatives, to retire before the statutory retirement age? Why do we pay for three-fourths of their health insurance premiums during the eight to fifteen years between their retirement and Medicare eligibility? The vast majority of private sector employees must work to the statutory retirement age to keep their employer based health insurance. There are about eight million people covered by the Federal Employees Health Benefits Plan. The number of them that are retired, and the cost for their post-retirement health insurance is not easily available, but I suspect it is several billion dollars.

In the past ten years, there has been a significant expansion of military health care benefits under Tricare. The timeline for this cost expansion is shown in this chart from the Congressional Budget Office

TIMELINE FOR TRICARE EXPANSION

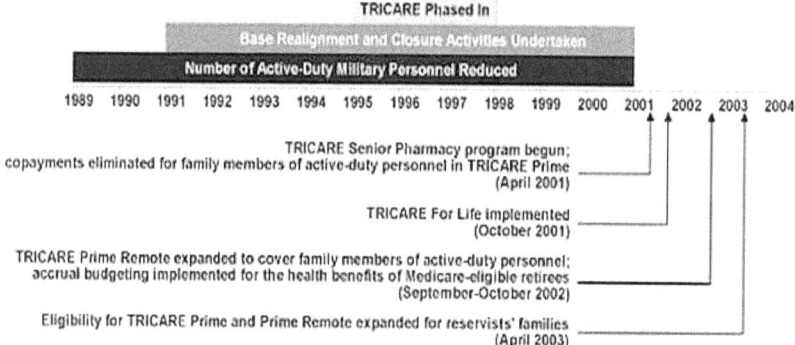

Tricare provides health care to active duty and retired career military personnel, some reserve components, and their families. Under Tricare, the country is divided into three regions (north, south, and west). One contractor, who bids for it on a fixed cost basis, administers the program in each region much like an insurance company. There are several plans available to each enrollee. In essence, they are the equivalents of HMO, PPO, and Medicare Supplemental Insurance. The cost of Tricare is covered by the

Department of Defense (DoD) budget. The Government
Accountability Office (GAO), shows health care spending by DoD
more than doubled from $17.4 billion in 2000 to $35.4 in 2005
(*http://www.gao.gov/cghome/d07766cg.pdf*). Tricare spending on prescription
drugs more than tripled from $1.6 billion to $5.4 billion.

The GAO report shows the factors responsible for the increases:

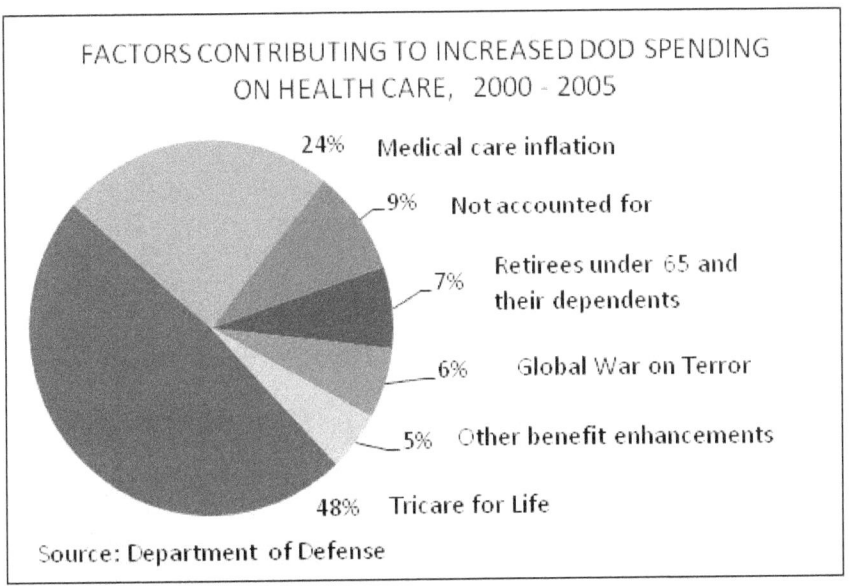

FACTORS CONTRIBUTING TO INCREASED DOD SPENDING
ON HEALTH CARE, 2000 - 2005

24% Medical care inflation

9% Not accounted for

7% Retirees under 65 and their dependents

6% Global War on Terror

5% Other benefit enhancements

48% Tricare for Life

Source: Department of Defense

Of the $18 billion increase, $8.6 billion went for Tricare for Life,
essentially a Medicare supplement insurance plan, $1.3 billion for
working age retirees and their dependents, and $3.8 billion for a
prescription drug plan, probably with the same gifts to the
pharmaceutical industry as Medicare Part D. It appears that at least $13
billion of this could be eliminated.

Tricare is nearly free for active duty personnel and their families,
as it should be. It should also be free to the occupationally disabled and
their families. However, most military retirees go on to second careers,
often with employers that offer health care coverage. They should be
ineligible for Tricare. Consider where the money is going now.

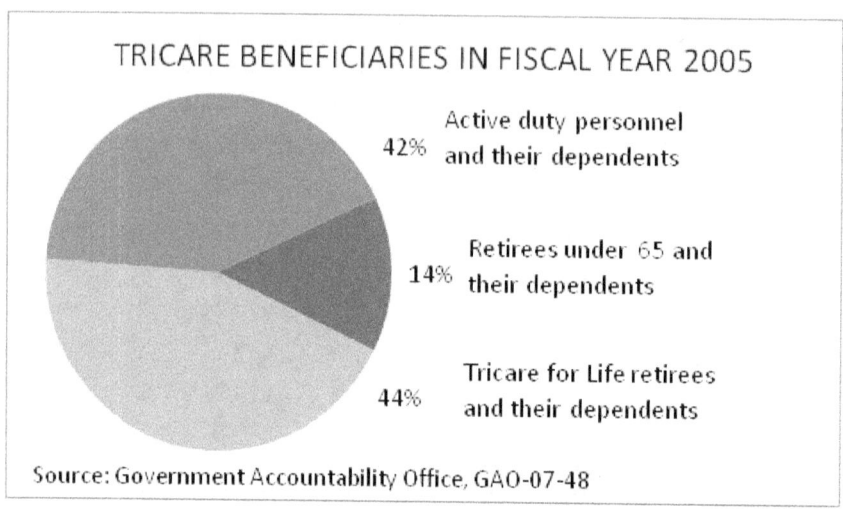

Civilians pay several times more for health care than military personnel. The most recent comparison I could find of out-of-pocket costs for Tricare to those of civilian counterparts dates back to 2002.

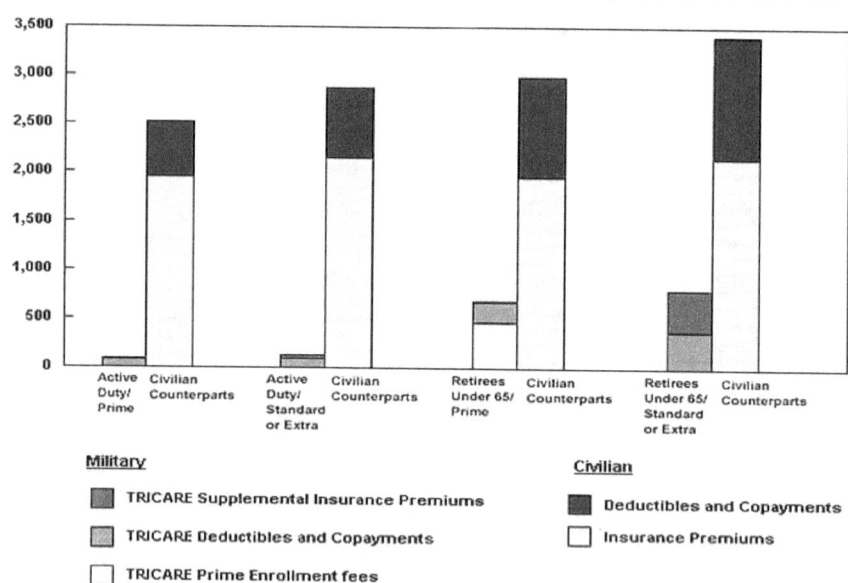

While Tricare spending has increased, beneficiaries' costs have remained unchanged or have been lowered over the last decade. For example:

- There is no enrollment fee (premium) for Tricare Standard or Extra.
- There has been no increase in enrollment fee for Tricare Prime since 1995.
- In 2001, the catastrophic cap (limit on beneficiary's costs) for under-65 retirees and dependents was lowered from $7,500 to $3,000.
- Tricare enrollment fees count toward the catastrophic cap, whereas premiums do not count toward out-of-pocket caps in other public and private plans.
- There has been no increase in Tricare deductibles since 1995.
- Tricare Prime copayments have been eliminated for dependents of active duty service members.
- Under-65 retirees and dependents paid 12% of their health care costs in FY 2005, down from 27% in FY 1996.

The GAO report also compared the Tricare out-of-pocket costs of Tricare versus the Federal Employees Health Benefits Plan (FEHBP) – including premiums, copayments, coinsurance, and deductibles – for a family of three in 2005.

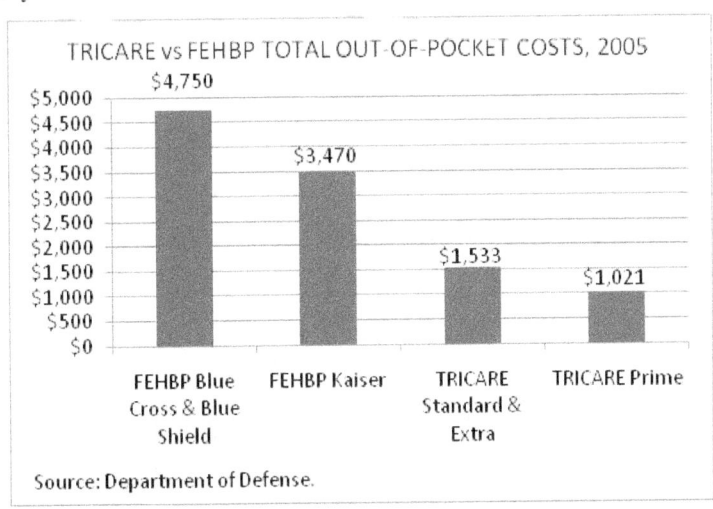

Source: Department of Defense.

There is one last point I would like to make about military retirees' disabilities. Many of our friends are retired military with varying degrees of disability. Some are the result of injuries received in the line of duty or exposure to hazardous substances, but many are simply chronic illnesses such as diabetes, heart disease, and other ailments unrelated to their military occupations. Their retirement pay is increased by the percentage of disability even when it does not impede their later employment or limit their lifestyles. No other plan, to my knowledge, pays people to be sick. Are we not already providing health care mostly at taxpayer expense?

Most discussions of health care reform bring up the subject of medical malpractice insurance as a major cost driver. The Congressional Budget Office (CBO) under both the previous and current administrations has studied the potential effects of tort reform on health care costs. A number of measures have been proposed to limit the cost of malpractice insurance. The CBO lists the following as typical:

- *A cap of $250,000 on awards for noneconomic damages;*
- *A cap on awards for punitive damages of $500,000 or two times the award for economic damages, whichever is greater;*
- *Modification of the "collateral source" rule to allow evidence of income from such sources as health and life insurance, workers' compensation, and automobile insurance to be introduced at trials or to require that such income be subtracted from awards decided by juries;*
- *A statute of limitations—one year for adults and three years for children—from the date of discovery of an injury; and*
- *Replacement of joint-and-several liability with a fair-share rule, under which a defendant in a lawsuit would be liable only for the percentage of the final award that was equal to his or her share of responsibility for the injury.*

CBO estimates: *"**the direct costs that providers will incur in 2009 for medical malpractice liability—which consist of malpractice insurance premiums together with settlements, awards, and administrative costs not covered by insurance—will total approximately $35 billion, or about 2 percent of total health care*** *expenditures. Therefore, lowering premiums for medical liability insurance by 10 percent would reduce total national health care expenditures by about 0.2 percent."* After considering several other cost factors, the report continues with: *"CBO now estimates, on the basis of an analysis incorporating the results of recent research, that if a package of proposals such as those described above was enacted, **it would reduce total national health care spending by about 0.5 percent** (about $11 billion in 2009). That figure is the sum of the direct reduction in spending of 0.2 percent from lower medical liability premiums, as discussed earlier, and an additional indirect reduction of 0.3 percent from slightly less utilization of health care services."* You can find this report at *http://www.cbo.gov/ftpdocs/106xx/doc10641/10-09-Tort_Reform.pdf.* The effect on the national budget would be measurable, but malpractice insurance costs are not the major driver in the cost of health care.

ESTIMATED EFFECT OF TORT REFORM			
(Billions of Dollars)	Changes in Mandatory Spending [a]	Changes in Revenues	Net Effect on the Deficit [b]
2010-2014	-10.3	3.2	-13.5
2010-2019	-41.0	13.0	-54.0

a. Includes Medicare, Medicaid, the Children's Health Insurance Program, and the Federal Employees Health Benefits program.

b. Negative numbers indicate a reduction in the deficit.

Source: Congressional Budget Office; Joint Committee on Taxation.

There is one caveat in the report: *"Because medical malpractice laws exist to allow patients to sue for damages that result from negligent health care, **imposing limits on that right might be expected to have a negative impact on health outcomes**. There is less evidence about the effects of tort reform on people's health, however, than about its effects on health care spending—because many studies of malpractice costs do not examine health outcomes."*

There is a perverse incentive for insurance companies in the health care/tort reform issue. They are 'cost plus' businesses. They are not playing with their own money but ours. The more health care costs, the more money they make. There is no serious competition in the industry, so there is nothing motivating them to reduce cost. Fear of law suits dictates much of how doctors treat patients' medical conditions and how many tests and treatments to administer. There are no easy answers to this problem. One approach that might have some benefit is to disallow insurance companies that offer health insurance from also offering malpractice insurance or belonging to the same industry associations. Another might be to mandate that law firms take malpractice law suits on a contingency basis and that their fees be limited to something like 10% on out-of-court settlements, 20% on compensatory damages, and 30% on punitive damages. That might discourage their pursuit of frivolous law suits. Any other potential solutions would probably be more intrusive and complex.

Another proposal that has been put forth to reduce health care cost is allowing people to buy insurance across state lines in order to foster competition. The states currently regulate insurance within their borders. It is difficult to envision how the proposal can be implemented without a standard set of regulations. Lacking such standardization, premiums would inevitably go up due to higher administrative costs. Presumably, a larger pool of enrollees should drive down administrative costs and, therefore, reduce premiums. It should also give insurance companies greater power in negotiating with providers. What is wrong with this scenario? First and foremost, it is not true. Since 1996 there have been about 400 mergers among health insurers; there are now 20% fewer. The economies of scale have increased insurance company profits, but they have not reduced premiums. According to the Kaiser Family Foundation in their *Employer Health Benefits 2008 Annual Survey*, health insurance premiums increased 120% between 1999 and 2007 while wages increased only 29%. Establishing a single nationwide set of regulations would merely open the door for the biggest players to squeeze out the smaller ones as they have done within individual states.

I was frustrated in my attempt to gather meaningful statistics on health insurance companies. Even the Government Accountability Office (GAO) had difficulty determining the level of competition and its effect. In its report on July 31, 2009, titled *Private Health Insurance: Research on Competition in the Insurance Industry*, GAO listed 41 studies on several aspects of insurance company competition. On each aspect, there were studies with diametrically opposing conclusions. The lack of transparency in health insurers' operations makes proper analysis difficult.

Health Care for America Now (HCAN) did a comprehensive study of health insurance competitiveness state by state in May of 2009 (*http://hcfan.3cdn.net/dadd15782e627e5b75_g9m6isltl.pdf*). The study was based on data from the American Medical Association. It shows that nearly all health insurance markets in the U.S. are highly concentrated. In the ten most concentrated states, two insurance companies control 80% or more of the market. In 24 of 50 states, one insurer controls 50% or more of the market, typically a Blue Cross Blue Shield Association member whose ownership is unknown to me, but I suspect it may be one of the top six health insurance companies in this table.

2000-2007 INSURANCE COMPANY PROFITS AND CEO COMPENSATION (Millions of Dollars)				
Company	2000 Net Profit	2007 Net Profit	Percent Change 2000-2007	Total 2007 CEO Compensation
UnitedHealth Group Inc.	$736	$4,654	532%	$13.2
WellPoint	$226	$3,345	1380%	$9.1
Aetna	$127	$1,831	1342%	$23.0
CIGNA Corp.	$987	$1,115	13%	$25.8
Humana Inc.	$90	$834	827%	$10.3
Coventry Health Care Inc.	$61	$626	926%	$14.9
Total	**$2,227**	**$12,405**	**457%**	**$96.3**
Source: Health Care for America Now, based on U.S. Securities and Exchange Commission filings.				

This raises an important question: "If insurers operating under the same rules within a state are not competing, what makes us believe that opening up the borders will make a difference?" The HCAN study describes some of the anticompetitive practices insurance companies employ to fix prices and stifle competition, and how your premium money is used. There is no mistaking the correlation between dramatic increases in premiums and insurance company corporate profits.

These six companies spent a staggering $51.3 billion of our premiums on repurchases of their own stock. Repurchases are used to improve earnings per share or return on equity, distribute excess cash to shareholders, acquire stock at low cost for employee stock options and stock purchase plans, hedge exposure to the exercise of employee stock options, reduce tax obligations, and change their debt to equity ratios. The benefit flows disproportionately to the CEOs and other shareholders directly out of policy holders' pockets..

Company	2003	2004	2005	2006	2007	2008	Total
UnitedHealth Group	$1,607	$3,446	$2,557	$ 2,345	$ 6,599	$2,684	$19,238
WellPoint	217	82	333	4,550	6,151	3,276	14,611
Aetna	445	1,493	1,650	2,323	1,696	1,788	9,394
CIGNA Corp.	-	676	1,618	2,765	1,185	378	6,622
Humana Inc.	44	67	2	26	27	106	273
Coventry Health Care	6	97	17	269	439	323	1,152
Total of All	**$2,319**	**$5,861**	**$6,177**	**$12,278**	**$16,097**	**$8,555**	**$51,290**

INSURANCE COMPANY REPURCHASES OF THEIR OWN STOCK (Millions of Dollars)

Source: Health Care for America Now
based on Securities and Exchange Commission, 10-K Annual Report filings

There are many myths about health care for the uninsured and how it is paid for. The Henry J. Kaiser Family Foundation (KFF) has published a number of studies and briefs on the issue of the uninsured through its Kaiser Commission on Medicaid and the Uninsured (KCMU). They are an invaluable resource for understanding various aspects of the health care issue such as health care for illegal immigrants. **Illegal immigrants are not eligible for Medicaid or SCHIP**, so their care must come either from employer based health insurance or emergency rooms. According to the Pew Hispanic Center, the percentage of uninsured in 2005 was 14% for U.S. citizens, 25% for legal immigrants, and 59% for illegal immigrants. Since hard numbers are hard to come by, we will make some estimates. Of the estimated 11.3 million illegal immigrants, approximately 6.7 million were uninsured at a total cost $12 billion for their health care. That is 0.6% of the $1,983 billion health care cost in 2005 – a far cry from some of the numbers that have been bandied about. The cost of caring for the

3.6 million legal uninsured immigrant non-citizens was $6.0 billion, or 0.3% of health care spending. The cost for 31.9 million uninsured citizens was $118 billion, or 6.0% of total spending. The total cost for all legal residents and citizens is $124 billion. These estimates correlate fairly closely with other studies I have read.

To offset the cost of providing care to Medicare, Medicaid, and indigent patients, more than 5,000 hospitals receive federal and state subsidies under the Disproportionate Share Hospital (DSH) payments program. They are an important source of hospital revenue, and typically represent more than half of a hospital's margin (profit), although most of the participating hospitals are registered as non-profits. Non-profits are exempt from income taxes. That exemption amounts to more than $12 billion. The DSH payments are according to a formula that takes the percentage of Medicare patient days to total patient days plus the percentage of Medicaid and indigent patient days to total patient days. There are also subsidies to hospitals and clinics in underserved areas according to a set of rules that seem sensible. Detailed recent figures are not readily available, but appear to be approximately $20 billion total from states and the federal government combined. The direct federal DSH payments were $6.1 billion in 2008. State payments were $15 billion in 1998, so we can assume they were at least that in recent years. More than half of state DSH spending is reimbursed by the federal government. Having more than fifty agencies involved in the process is not conducive to controlling costs. It is difficult to determine whether the money is going to the institutions providing most of the care.

A subsidy that is beyond the scope of this chapter is the Graduate Medical Education (GME) subsidy that compensates teaching hospitals for the cost of facilities, instructors, and resident student doctors. In 2008, GME subsidies cost taxpayers $9.7 billion according to the Congressional Budget Office.

The one question remaining is what the incremental cost would be to provide health care for all legal uninsured persons. In 2005, the cost was $4333 for each of the 84.7% of persons that had expenses. The cost for 35.4 million legal uninsured at $4333 would have been $153.5 billion. That would be an increase of $29.4 billion over the $124 billion estimated cost of health care shown above. Even if adjusted to 2011 levels, the incremental cost should not exceed $50 billion for all legal uninsured – that is the bad news. Now, here is the good news: **you are already paying for it!**

Prescription drug costs are completely out of control, as you could see in the drug cost comparison between VA and Medicare Part D above. I am a Type II diabetic with high blood pressure. Both are controlled with medication. One of the medications is known to increase the risk of heart attack. After suffering a mild heart attack four years ago, additional medications were prescribed. Medicare Part D quit paying after a total retail drug value of $2,450 (including co-pays) had been spent in any year, and resumed paying after a person has spent an additional $3,850 out of pocket, at which time catastrophic coverage would kick in. As of April of the following year, I was in the so-called 'doughnut hole', and paying full price for my medications while continuing to pay for the drug plan. In my travels, I often bought prescription drugs in Mexico, Canada, and Hong Kong. The drugs worked equally well as those purchased here, and the prices were often less than my co-pays. But, our government made that illegal. Ask yourself this question: "If free trade is desirable for all the foreign sourced consumer goods flooding this country, why it is not desirable for pharmaceuticals, especially since so many of the ingredients used in our medications are imported?" The Part D drug plan also prohibits our government from negotiating prices with the pharmaceutical companies, so the pharmaceutical companies are free to charge whatever they like, and they do. Is there any doubt that the 8,000 lobbyists they employ in Washington to funnel money to our politicians had a hand in crafting the legislation?

According to the Internal Revenue Service 2007 Corporation Source Book of Statistics of Income for the pharmaceutical industry (code 325410), its sales receipts in 2007 totaled $317.4 billion, in addition to which they received $10.7 billion in interest, $23.5 billion in royalties, $22.7 billion categorized as 'other receipts', and a few smaller entries for a total of $381.3 billion. That $22.7 billion figure is quite large for an 'other' category. There is no way of knowing whether the payments from Medicare are part of the sales receipts or 'other receipts'. You would think that such important information would be readily accessible to taxpayers. A similar situation exists in the deductions from income. The second largest category is 'other deductions' at $63.1 billion. The fourth largest, after salaries and wages, is advertising at $16.0 billion. There is no separate category for research and development, the category often cited as the reason for high pharmaceutical prices. The taxable income was $49.7 billion, or 15.7% of sales receipts. Compare that profit to that of Wal-Mart at 3.5% in 2007 ($12.2 billion on net sales of $345.0 billion). That puts pharmaceuticals in the same class as financial firms and oil companies, but very few other sectors.

IRS data shows that the pharmaceutical industry spent $16.0 billion on advertising in 2007. Several published sources estimated that $4.4-4.5 billion of that was spent on direct-to-consumer advertising. At that time, the U.S. was one of only two developed countries, along with New Zealand, that allowed consumer-direct advertising. All the ads tell us to ask our doctor if a particular drug is right for us. If the doctor makes the decision, why advertise to me? I have rarely been in a doctor's office for more than ten minutes without seeing a pharmaceutical sales representative, usually an attractive female. I have read that there are 96,000 pharmaceutical sales reps in the US, about one for every seven prescribing doctors, most earning more than $100,000. No other industry can afford to have such a high ratio of sales reps to customers, or pay so generously. They tell us that high drug prices pay for research to develop new lifesaving drugs, and to some degree they do, but they spend more on advertising than on research, and their profits are greater than their research and development costs. Furthermore, many of the new drugs are merely variations of existing drugs or combinations of existing drugs, the purpose being to get their patents extended or renewed. Is it any wonder that the average person now takes three times the medications prescribed just a few years ago? Is it a coincidence that private rooms at local upscale restaurants are frequently booked by pharmaceutical company representatives for private lunches with doctors, or that doctors are over-represented on cruises and other recreational junkets? In most industries, taking kickbacks is cause for termination.

Another explanation for drug overuse is side effect chain reaction. For example, one of the only medications that had some effect on my blood pressure caused constipation and water retention (edema). The doctor prescribed a stool softener and a diuretic (water pill). Diuretics typically deplete the potassium in the body, so a potassium supplement was prescribed. For my type II diabetes, he prescribed an insulin resistance lowering medication, which damages kidneys. Several of our friends with health issues were taking up to ten medications and were feeling sick much of the time. Upon being taken off most of the medications, they actually felt better. I replaced the stool softener with a high fiber diet and a psyllium fiber food supplement, a blood thinner with a diet full of leafy green vegetables, and very expensive cholesterol lowering statin drugs with Omega-3 fish oil capsules, and I feel great. A low carbohydrate diet and frequent exercise lowered my blood sugar levels with a minimum of medication. Doctors don't trust our self-discipline, so drugs are the easy way out.

When Anna Nicole Smith died, and a custody battle erupted over her baby daughter, it was revealed that the actress was addicted to prescription drugs. She managed to get prescriptions under several different names: her birth name, married name, actor name, etc. Her doctors continued to fill her prescriptions even after her addiction should have been obvious. During one of my mother's hospitalizations a few years ago, we examined her medicine cabinet, and found more than fifty different drugs prescribed by her doctor in the preceding few years. Some of them could have been deadly in combination. The doctor must have known her problems were not entirely physical, nevertheless he continued to prescribe remedies for every ailment she reported, and made sure she and many like her visited him every month. A positive identification system and central drug prescription database would alleviate much of the abuse.

One source of confusion over prescription drugs is that every manufacturer of a particular drug has a different name for it. I have been on so many different blood pressure medications over the years that I no longer remember their names, what class of drugs each was, and which ones had unpleasant side effects. On more than one occasion, my doctor prescribed a medication that turned out to be one I had taken previously under a different name, but which either did not work, or had the same side effects. I now check each drug prescribed for me online to make sure I understand what it is, what other medications and supplements it should not be taken with, and what side effects I should look for.

Many prescription drug commercials lead up to possible drug interactions or side effects of a drug by statements like "tell your doctor if you have any of these conditions." Should my doctor not know already? Therein lies one of the dilemmas of health care. Medicine is far more complicated than it used to be. No one doctor can know enough to treat every condition. Fifty years ago, our family doctor would come to our home when someone was too ill to take the bus to his office. Today, he is a 'primary care provider'. Although, in truth, he or she may be a secondary care provider, since I may see his nurse practitioner or physician's assistant several times before I see the doctor. That is probably just as well, as they usually have more time to dig into my two-inch thick file. Most visits are preceded by a lab test. Much of the visit is taken up with a comparison of lab results to previous ones. Invariably, the discussion turns to cholesterol levels. The recommendation is always for one of the cholesterol lowering statin drugs like Lipitor, Crestor, Zocor, or Tricor. All of them have been prescribed for me in the past, and all of them had unpleasant side effects, including severe muscle pain. I refuse to take them in spite of their insistence. When I do see the doctor, usually once a year, it is rarely for more than ten minutes. A quick feel around the body, a listen to the heart, a manual prostate check, a few keystrokes on his laptop computer, and he is off to another patient. He is a good doctor. I don't know how he makes any money in a one-doctor office with six employees. About forty percent of the work in that office is paperwork and negotiating with insurance companies. The point is that there is no doctor/patient relationship. He does not have time for it.

Anything out of the ordinary is referred to a specialist. For example, on one occasion, I experienced blood in my urine. I was referred to a urologist. The only appointment available was five weeks out. Another urologist in that group was available in two weeks. The bleeding had stopped, so I was not very concerned. I was relatively certain that I had burst a blood vessel lifting a three hundred pound weight. When I arrived at the urologist's office, I had to fill out and/or sign at least five pages of documents, including insurance information, two privacy policy papers, authorization to treat, agreement to pay any copayments, and medical history. That scenario is repeated every time I see any specialist. In most cases some test is required, then a follow-up visit to get the results or initiate treatment. On one visit to an orthopedist to explore the possibility of repairing a torn meniscus cartilage in the knee, after an x-ray and speaking with a physician's assistant, I saw the doctor for two minutes. He was intent on doing arthroscopic surgery that would not repair the cartilage. He never explained why. I never went back. Over the past few months, the vision in one eye has become blurred. I went to an optometrist. He referred me to an ophthalmologist who then referred me to a cornea specialist. There was a waiting period for an appointment with each specialist. Several pages of paperwork were required at each step. Each one duplicated the examination of the previous one. The specialists tend to work with others in their own discipline. Their offices may be miles apart. The very way their disciplines are organized results in poor communication between specialties and with the primary care provider. I may never see most of these doctors again, so there is little opportunity for a relationship to develop.

When anything appears to require immediate attention, I go to the emergency room. All the disciplines my situation may require are almost always available in short order. The communication chain is much shorter. They are working on the same page. Unfortunately, their records are often outdated – I may have seen several specialists or had prescriptions changed since my last visit. My primary care provider does not update the hospital's records, neither do specialists. Primary care providers no longer visit their patients in the hospital, so their only knowledge is based on relayed reports if any. Most of the mistakes I have witnessed or heard about are due to failures in communication. A central database accessible to all providers of medical care could potentially save thousands of lives annually. It would in effect allow all the providers to work as a team even when they are not all physically present. Several estimates published over the last two decades suggest that fully automating medical records could save about $75 billion per year.

The team approach and central database are part of the reason that the VA gets such high marks for quality of care over the last two decades. Enrollees may complain about the bureaucracy involved in getting signed up for VA medical care, but, based on published reports, report high levels of satisfaction with the care they receive. Keep in mind that veterans in the VA system may have received service related injuries, may be poorer than other military retirees, and so are more likely to be in ill health and require more treatment than most Medicare recipients. Furthermore, VA provides nursing home care whereas Medicare does not. How then can we justify paying so much more per enrollee for health care under Medicare. If our Medicare enrollees had access to the kind of care VA provides, the savings would be approximately $75 billion.

Medicare vs VA Healthy Care Costs (2008)			
Insurer	Participants (Millions)	Spending (Billions)	Amount per Beneficiary
Medicare Cost [1]	35.3	$ 301.1	$ 8,525
Medicaid Nursing Home [3]	1.0	$ 29.2	$ 826
Medicare Adjusted Cost	**35.3**	**$ 330.3**	**$ 9,351**
Veterans [2]	**5.3**	**$ 38.3**	**$ 7,235**
Estimated Savings VA over Medicare		**$**	**2,115**
1. Source: Centers for Medicare and Medicaid Services, Tables 143, 145			
2. Source: Veterans Administration			
3. Source: Centers for Medicare and Medicaid Services, Table 146			

The year before my wife and I became eligible for Medicare, our out-of-pocket health care expenses were about $34,000, including more than $19,800 per year for HMO health insurance premiums. Our eldest son was born with birth defects, and was uninsurable for several years. His medical expenses drove us deeply into debt. My position in senior management made it possible for us to pay it off in eleven years. He lived to the age of thirty-two. The medical bills in the last two years were $985,000, and that was fourteen years ago. Fortunately, insurance covered most of it. The co-pays probably exceeded the average family's income. How can a typical middle-class family manage to cope with such burdens? They cannot.

Our daughter, a registered nurse, was an operating room supervisor in a large hospital. During an operation in about 1994, discussion of national health care arose. The surgeon stated that he could not live on less than $600,000 per year. She promptly reminded him that the entire operating room staff did not earn that much, and they all still managed to live. Of course, none of them lived in a 16,000 square foot home with a six-car garage stuffed with three Ferraris, an SUV, and family cars. I doubt that many doctors make that much today. In any case, I do not begrudge them their success. They pay a high price for it in cost of education, long hours in their early careers, risk of making a mistake, and enduring often unjustified lawsuits. If you compare their earnings to those of insurance company executives and Wall Street traders, you will probably agree that doctors earn their keep.

One of the seemingly outrageous cost items our daughter talked about was a package of titanium screws and plates used in some surgeries to fix broken bones and correct some abnormalities. She said the package containing a few ounces of hardware costs about $20,000. I have no way of confirming the actual cost or the method of costing it. However, I have seen hospital bills with $23 aspirin tablets, a gross misapplication of activity based costing, which makes it possible to hide much hospital overhead. It makes it impossible to determine what we are actually paying for.

Medical technology is rapidly evolving. MRI machines, PET and CAT scanners, and other items of medical equipment are very expensive to buy and operate. Critics have argued that there are too many imaging systems in use, and that they are being overused. I have no way of knowing whether there are too many such machines, but I believe that they have greatly improved the quality of diagnoses. For anything other than a broken bone, I would much rather have an MRI than imaging by any x-ray device, partly because of wanting to avoid excessive radiation exposure and because I feel the results are more conclusive.

We all know that medical costs are crazy, but we have no easy way to determine why. What is obvious is that there is no incentive for anyone involved in providing health care to control cost. There is no competition among doctors, hospitals, medical equipment and drug suppliers, or insurance companies. Timely and accurate information is lacking. Those benefiting from government programs and subsidies have no incentive to change them. We pretend that ours is a free market system. In fact, we have privatized most of the profits and socialized much of the cost of health care. How can we simplify the health care system and reduce cost while retaining private ownership of health care?

There are a number of facts that are inescapable:

- Employer based health insurance makes United States firms noncompetitive in the global marketplace where people either have no health care or they have much less costly universal health care.

- Many employers are dropping health insurance for their employees or increasing employees' share of the cost beyond what many families can afford.

- Health care will never be affordable if insurance companies only insure low risk individuals. That forces the taxpayer to assume much of the burden.

- Insurance companies are among the most powerful financial entities, and they will resist the implementation of universal health care unless they remain major players in the system.

- Universal health care is only possible if health insurance is mandatory for all.

- Health care can only become affordable if insurers and providers are forced to compete.

- Wage erosion and runaway medical costs make individually paid health insurance out of reach for at least one-third of the population.

- Lack of transparency makes it difficult to get timely and accurate information about health care costs. Without it, we can only guess at potential savings.

- One area where potential savings are easily possible is in administration and standardization.
- Our choice going forward is a moral one: either make health care affordable for everyone or deny care to the many who cannot afford it – not exactly the equality and inalienable rights of *life, liberty, and the pursuit of happiness* that our founding fathers wrote so eloquently about.

Ask yourself this question: What makes it so good for Veterans, active duty and retired military personnel, Medicare beneficiaries, and Medicaid recipients to have socialized medicine, but so bad for everyone else? There is only one answer: political ideology. Take a poll and ask the beneficiaries of these programs whether they would like to give them up. The answer will be a resounding "No!". Yet, even the beneficiaries of these government run health care programs protest against government run health care and universal coverage. Perhaps it is because they realize that universal health care would level the playing field and bring their costs and benefits more in line with those of the remainder of American society.

I have already stated that I am neither a health care professional nor an economist. My skills are in management engineering. Much of my career involved reducing complexity, improving efficiency, and changing corporate cultures in the private sector. I believe in free market solutions, competition, and the government's role in enforcing free markets and competition when the private sector fails to do so. There is no easy way to enforce competition when provision of health care is scattered over so many state and federal agencies operating under varied sets of rules, so many insurance companies with different kinds of plans, and so much lobbyist money shaping every bill. There are some existing structures that seem to work well. Building on them, perhaps we can develop a system that preserves free enterprise and provides quality universal health care. As with my other proposals, implementation would require a transition over several years to minimize confusion and resolve any issues that might arise.

One change that has the greatest potential for reducing cost and improving quality is the creation of a central health care database. It would contain all insurance information, privacy preferences, living will statements, medical history, prescription data, identify all providers, contain all prescription data, record all costs, and submit the provider's bill for payment. It would eliminate the need for paper records at the provider's facility, the need to negotiate with insurance companies, and much of the billing and accounting process. With the records securely encrypted, privacy concerns should be minimal. Consolidating the administrative functions of the entire health care system should save a minimum of 15% of the health care bill. If implementation of the system had begun in 1998, by 2008 the savings could have been $327 billion per year. I use 2008 for most of the calculations in this chapter since that is the latest year for which most of the necessary data is available.

Imagine walking into your doctor's office, scanning your positive identification card (PID), and having your complete medical record available to him on his laptop computer. At the end of your visit, your record would be updated with any new findings and instructions, prescription changes, referrals, etc. Any laboratory results and MRI, CT, and other images would also be available during your visit. With today's peer-to-peer relational database technology and data mining capability, a fully redundant secure system is possible. Upon scanning the PID smart card, your photo and other personal identifying information would download to the doctor's laptop, your pharmacy's computer, or anywhere else where you would need to positively identify yourself. The scanning device could, if desired, incorporate a fingerprint or retina scanner as an added precaution. The doctor's charges would be automatically billed to the insurer without the insurer being able to tie the invoice back to you.

There are many advantages to such a system. Identity theft becomes extremely difficult. Insurance companies could not discriminate against you in any way. Medical mistakes should occur much less frequently. Any allergies you have would be immediately known to all providers. Hospitals would not have to determine what your wishes are in the event you are unable to communicate them. Statistical analyses of the database would make fraud easier to spot, aid in determining the effectiveness of treatments, and identify possible drug interactions and side effects. Complete medical cost data would be available on a timely basis. It would also make it easier to identify incompetent providers.

The system would rely on private sector insurers and providers, but a central administrative entity. For the sake of convenience, let's call it CHAP, the Central Health Administration Partnership. There would be no need for Medicare, Medicaid, and VA, all with their own administrative functions. Military hospitals and clinics would only serve active duty military personnel and their families, although, if the military system were completely compatible with the civilian system, there would be no reason why they could not receive their care wherever they want at taxpayer expense. All participants, military and civilian, would enjoy complete portability of their coverage. In many other respects, the system would function much like Tricare.

Once the database is operational, implementation could begin state by state, beginning with the smallest states, in order to work out any issues that may arise. All invoices would pass through to existing insurers with an up-charge added (perhaps 6%) to compensate for relieving insurers of their claims administration and related accounting function. Once sufficient data had been accumulated (perhaps one year), bid requests containing state by state data without personal identifying information would be put out to pharmaceutical companies, producers of medical supplies, and health care providers, including qualified foreign sources. In the event bids submitted are not sufficiently competitive, CHAP would have full authority to negotiate prices with sources. The bids and/or negotiated prices would be used for putting together a comprehensive health insurance plan including all necessary health care services (medical, psychiatric, dental, optical, and auditory) based on the average of the lowest bids (possibly 10% of bids received) for each equivalent product or service. State by state bid requests for this basic health care policy with one list of qualifying providers and one drug formulary, including cumulative data for each state, would then be sent out to insurance companies, including qualified foreign sources. The basic default policy would feature no caps, no copayments, no discrimination, and would not cover elective procedures. Only well-established insurers who are solvent, have sufficient liquidity, and whose quotes are in the lowest 25% of bidders should be qualified to provide default coverage.

This plan would in no way prevent us from having employer provided health insurance or individually purchased policies that might cover higher priced products and providers, either as substitutes or supplements to the basic default policy. All health insurance plans would use CHAP to process their claims and pay providers. All providers would have to be paid within sixty days in order to correct the defect in Medicare of having providers wait up to six months for a reduced payment. Several studies over the last twenty years by the Congressional Budget Office, the Government Accountability Office, and several other sources have shown that single payer systems offer substantial savings over the current system, with some estimates as high as 40% of health care cost. I used 15% in my estimate of savings above, but they would almost certainly be at least 25% when administrations in hospitals, clinics, doctors' offices, pharmacies, other providers, employer benefits departments, and state insurance regulatory agencies are factored in and prices are negotiated.

A CHAP center would be located in each state under one consistent set of rules. The largest cities might also have CHAP branches to provide redundancy to the state and central database, and to improve data access and transaction speeds. Participating insurers in each state would receive a monthly statement and payment of premiums with provider payments deducted. Everyone would be insured under their home state policy, but that policy would pay for services received while an enrollee is traveling or temporarily assigned outside that state. Since medical situations outside one's home state are relatively rare and most other countries have lower cost health care, there is no reason not to provide coverage under those circumstances. Transfers to other states' policies would only be necessary when permanently relocating to another state.

The challenge is to prevent overconcentration or monopolization of the insurance market. With most of the administrative overhead removed, smaller insurers would be better able to compete. Since implementation would be in order of increasing population size, selection of qualifying insurers would also be in order of increasing capitalization. The number of licenses issued in each state should be limited to three to give consumers a choice, allow insurers to make a profit, and insure competition within each state. Once an insurer is selected for one state, it could not be selected again until all other qualified insurers had been selected (or refused selection) in other states, at which point bypassed insurers could once again be selected in states where they qualify. The selection process would be handled by the central computer with the results downloaded to branches. Households would then select their insurer of choice from the list of licensees, or any other plan from any other source that equals or exceeds the default plan. Once each year all parties would rebid either by itemized lists or percentage adjustments. New bidders would have an opportunity to enter the market if they meet the required criteria. Enrollees would then have an opportunity to switch plans if they so choose. The whole thing sounds much more complicated than it is. The entire process can be performed online and processed by the central computer.

The difference between CHAP and Tricare or Medicare is that CHAP does not dictate what it will pay for each service nor what premiums insurance companies can charge. Those charges are determined by providers and insurers. CHAP would be a non-profit government sponsored (not government run) enterprise whose function would be to provide administrative support services, monitor quality of care, and promote competition in health care. Its operating costs would be funded by the 6% up-charge on pass-through provider invoices.

Whether one chooses to accept it or not, most of us will get older and the vast majority will experience many more health issues at a time when, based on all available statistics, our health costs will escalate beyond the ability of many of us to pay, at which time the burden falls on everyone else, the taxpayers. By participating in universal health insurance coverage at a time we have minimal health issues, we are reducing the cost for all of us and, in essence, saving for the time that we will also have increased needs. It is therefore reasonable that we all be required to carry health insurance in the same way that we are all required to carry auto insurance.

We should also recognize that the reasons that so many are now uninsured is unemployment and wage erosion. Our failures to increase minimum wages in step with inflation, allowing unfettered immigration, and lack of competition in health care have put health insurance costs beyond the reach of many employers and individuals. Publicly funded health care is also beyond our reach because we have an inadequate tax base. Steps must be taken to correct these deficiencies. Implementing the Gross Revenues Tax system and allowing minimum wages to float up or down with the consumer price index would certainly help, but they would not immediately reduce unemployment. A move away from employer provided benefits would make businesses more competitive in a global economy, and it would allow work hour adjustments as a means of controlling unemployment. The resulting reduction of poverty from these moves should markedly improve the health of our population, reduce public welfare, refuel the economy, and begin to pay down our enormous debt. We would, in effect, be doing exactly what the insurance companies have been doing by buying back their own stock – taking back our country from its creditors.

There is one principle that cannot be repeated often enough: one's **obligations to society should be in proportion to the benefits one receives from it**. The notion that our success is strictly of our own making is nonsense, just as the notion that our failures are always of our own making. We succeed when our preparation and perseverance meets the opportunity provided by the environment in which we live. We sometimes fail in spite of preparation and perseverance because outside influences in our environment conspire against us through no fault of our own. There is no easy way of knowing whether one's wealth is due to one's merit, an accident of fate, or comes at the expense of others in some fashion. Conversely, there is no easy way of knowing whether one's poverty is due to one's ineptitude, an accident of fate, or comes due to the disproportionate advantage of the wealthy and powerful. What we do know is that we are all on this planet together, and that wealth is built on the backs of those who labor to provide the goods and services to earn the money that is then spent to enable those who create those goods and services. It is a symbiotic relationship, not a competition but a cooperation that benefits all concerned.

If **life, liberty, and the pursuit of happiness** are truly unalienable rights, then basic health care is also a right. It comes at a cost that is currently much too high in both dollars and human misery. If you read the chapter on Fair Tax carefully, and added up the potential savings in this chapter, then you should realize that there is a way that we can afford universal health care. If we implement a Gross Revenues Tax, a basic comprehensive health care policy for every legal resident would cost 4% of gross revenues. That is less than one-third of the 12.45% total combined federal, state, and local tax. The simplest method for paying the premium would be a direct deposit to the CHAP pool. The alternative is to have every household pay separately, but that would be far costlier to administer, and it would still leave too many without coverage at taxpayer expense. Is anyone calloused enough to refuse health care services to the uninsured? I am not.

Many of us might want a higher level of coverage. For example: I might prefer tooth implants over a bridge or dentures, or fancy metal eyeglass frames over inexpensive plastic ones, or the services of a nutritionist, massage therapist, extended physical therapy, or some other health related service. A few might choose to use a higher cost provider than those allowed by the default policy. Qualified insurers could certainly offer supplemental policies to cover such services, or we could choose to pay the difference out of pocket.

Those who benefit from the status quo will not easily give up their disproportionate advantage. They will try to label this proposal as 'socialism', which it clearly is not. It relies on a competitive free market between insurers and providers, does not dictate prices, and functions much like an insurance company which pools risk. For the first time, it gives all parties involved an incentive to control cost.

I have been in many countries of Europe, Asia, and the American continents. In many, the environment is inferior to ours, yet they have a lower incidence of cancer. Some people who have diets rich in fats may actually have fewer heart attacks than we do. To what can we attribute their longevity and apparent better health?

- They walk far more than we do, even in crowded Asian cities.

- Their family and social lives are less stressful.

- They get more time off from work.

- Their diets are much more varied than ours. Asian meals may contain several different vegetables, some of which are rich in protein, others are leafy green.

- Most of their fruits and vegetables are fresh. They are purchased and prepared daily. Their refrigerators are tiny.

- They eat less meat overall. Fish and fowl are seen more often than beef or pork.

- The meats are fresh, not frozen or canned.

- Meats are not colored, soaked in brine, or treated with preservatives.

- They rarely eat desserts. Fruit is the preferred dessert.

- They eat far fewer calories per meal and per day.

- Packaged foods are rarely seen. Those that are seen do not contain non-food products like colorants, preservatives, modifiers, or extenders.

- I have not seen pesticides used.

All you need do is look at longevity statistics and health care costs to realize that our killers are lack of exercise, excessive stress, bad eating habits, and the chemicals in our foods. The solution to many of our health issues is well within our capabilities. Many of the substances in our food are habit forming, sugar being but one example. Schools should be teaching our children the fundamentals of nutrition. Why aren't they? You probably guessed it: MONEY! Someone is benefitting from the status quo.

Of all the anti-social vested interests the worst is the vested interest in ill-health.

George Bernard Shaw (1856-1950), Irish writer.

No Child Left Behind

The United States has some of the best universities in the world. Citizens of foreign countries strive to have their children educated here. Nonetheless, we are losing our technological edge. Why is that? A fitting analogy may be a computer – the quality of the output cannot be better than the input. The problem is not at the university level; it is at the elementary level. You have undoubtedly heard some of the reasons: unqualified teachers, large class sizes, insufficient classroom hours, social promotion, tenure, unrecognized learning disabilities, underfunding, powerful teachers' unions, inadequate testing, etc. These may be contributing factors, but I don't believe most of them are causative. Most proposals to improve education address one or two of the symptoms, but fail to deal with many core issues. I am not an expert in the field of education, but I believe you will find my observations and suggestions to be correct, practical, and effective.

My education began in a United Nations refugee camp in Germany after World War II. By the end of first grade, every Polish child in my class could read everything it was given. I am not implying that each child necessarily understood everything it read, but it could read and pronounce the words correctly. There was no social promotion and no teachers' union, but all the other factors cited above were present. So why does it take children here four or more years to learn to read reasonably well? I believe I can explain it, starting with a few cultural issues.

My mother and I both grew up, although at different times, without access to recorded music, radio, television, movies, computers, computer games, and telephones. The world was much simpler before all those entertainment and communication devices, and smaller before automobiles became the primary mode of transportation. We often travel to work or school farther than my mother did in her entire young life. Consider how many streets and roads we must remember compared to our ancestors. All those things that have eased our lives and entertained us have also placed an inordinate demand on our memory capacity, and have reduced our attention spans. At the same time, there has been a tremendous explosion of knowledge in nearly every field, so there is much more that needs to be learned. The human brain is like an empty bucket that begins filling at birth. The fuller it gets, the less room there is for additional water. If we want to drink the water, we must not put dirty water in the bucket. We have limited memory storage and retrieval capability. All that sensory input we receive is like dirty water – it fills the bucket, but we cannot drink it.

Studies of child prodigies have shown that a child's level of achievement in a given discipline is often proportional to the level of parental commitment. There is a difference between a prodigy, who develops an exceptional skill in one field, and a genius, who has extraordinary intelligence and ability in a broad range of subjects. Child prodigies tend to learn by total immersion. That can become a full time job for a parent. The study habits formed this way often make it possible for such children to change interests and become high achievers in a new field. The key word is interests. Children rarely become proficient in subjects they find uninteresting or monotonous, or those that are so challenging that they can never experience some success.

Few parents today have the luxury of a stay-at-home spouse. My parents both had to work to survive. A single parent often has no choice but to work multiple jobs. The absence of parents due to divorce, multiple jobs, and irresponsible lifestyles, means that children must fend for themselves. Sometimes a family member can provide childcare, but most often it is entrusted to a childcare center or other non-family care giver who cannot give the individualized attention needed for the development of reasoning and memory. When the child outgrows the need for a childcare center, it is left without supervision of any sort for a significant part of its day – this is not a formula for success.

Even if a child has two parents, and one is a homemaker, it is difficult to provide structure and maintain control. Concepts of child rearing have changed. We are far more permissive than our grandparents were. Children jump from one activity to another, and have to be constantly entertained or kept busy. Sports, entertainment, and other extracurricular activities take precedence over learning. Getting the child to focus for any reasonable length of time becomes a constant challenge. I had occasion to substitute teach a fourth grade class last year. It was an eye-opening experience. Three of the students were completely out of control – jumping from one desk to another, fidgeting with their books, throwing things, and being generally disruptive. One recent study states that about ten percent of elementary school students have been diagnosed with attention deficit/hyperactivity disorder (ADHD), and two-thirds of them are being medicated. It seems to help, but who is it helping -- the teacher, the parent, or the child? And, what effect is it having on their academic performance?

My experience with our grandchildren and those of friends and relatives suggests that hyperactivity is not a congenital condition but one that develops as a byproduct of parental failure to provide structure and discipline. Their desire to be buddies with their children prevents them from exercising their parental authority. What the child wants at the moment becomes more important than what is actually good for the child. The child becomes the center of its own universe. The notion that someone else's opinions, wants, or needs should take precedence over their own never occurs to them. Since it never encounters resistance in its first few years, it does not develop the ability to cope with opposition, adversity, being ignored, meeting schedules, or needing to organize its activities or spaces. When they do encounter these situations, they are frustrated and bewildered. The result can be depression, rebellion, anti-social behavior, or even suicide.

An example of this "center of the universe" phenomenon is burned indelibly into my mind. We attended a birthday party for a five year old girl. She was an only child, as was her four year old cousin. After more than an hour of opening an obscene number of gifts, a final gift was given – a toy horse. Her little cousin also received the same toy horse in a different color. Birthday girl wanted the other girl's horse. More than a dozen adult relatives watched a ten-minute screaming, crying, wrestling match while the parents stood by helpless. I was embarrassed for the parents. The girls were knee deep in toys, but none could please them. My mind drifted back to how much I cherished the one and only toy I ever received, a toy wind-up tank. I was eight years old.

Children are rarely disciplined. In my second grade classroom, there was a tray of hard dried peas on the floor next to the teacher's desk. I no longer remember what I did to deserve the punishment of kneeling on it for five minutes, but I know I never did it again. My parents backed the teacher. Today, that teacher would be sued or fired. I don't approve of cruel punishments, even when they work, but discipline is essential to learning. We must find better ways to maintain discipline in our schools and homes. The best way to develop discipline is not through cruel punishment but through structure. Although an occasional swat on the behind or the hand may be called for.

Shortly after my first retirement, I babysat our two granddaughters when my wife was unavailable. They were two and three years old. The girls began banging their hands on the glass in the French doors between our family room and dining room. The small panes were not tempered glass, so they could break and cause serious injury. First, I explained that they could get hurt. Then, when they resumed banging, I first said "no, no", then a stern "No!". When they went to strike the glass with their toys, I slapped each one's hand just hard enough to sting, and for them to know I was serious. They burst into tears and wrapped their arms around me. They instinctively went to the person who loved them for sympathy and comfort, even though the same person had disciplined them. Love and discipline must go hand in hand to be effective. It is difficult to create structure if the child does not accept the parent's authority.

These days, bedtimes and study times are rarely enforced. Meals are often taken on the fly, or in front of the television. All of this makes it difficult for a family to communicate. That, in turn, leads to alienation. Children invariably do their homework in front of the television or listening to music. The parents allow it because it is easier to give in than fight. From earliest times, our children had a fixed bedtime that was increased by fifteen minutes each year until they graduated high school, at which time it was 10:00 pm preceding school days, and 11:00 pm on weekends. There were no allowances. They each had a list of chores for which they were paid. If the chores were done improperly, they would have to redo them. School assignments were always done before supper, with the television and radio turned off. Meals were always eaten together at the kitchen table after a blessing. We went to church every Sunday, where misbehavior would not be tolerated. Nothing illegal, immoral, or improper was allowed in our home. It was not easy to provide that structure, especially since many of their peers live in different circumstances, but the results were well worth it. They have accomplished much.

Many of the societal factors may be irreversible. We cannot go back to simpler times. What we can do is provide structure and discipline in the home and in the school, reduce the level of mind-numbing monotony, and develop less distracting and memory intensive ways of learning. Home study and homework can be a real problem for the 31.4% of high school students who also work. They were for me in my junior and senior years. I worked till 10:00 PM and took a bus home, often arriving after 11:00 pm. The choice was between homework and study or sleep. You can guess which won out. Sports and other extracurricular activities also squeeze the time available for schoolwork. Even when sufficient time is available, there are just too many distractions in the home.

It would make far more sense to revise our class schedules to permit study and homework in class without cell phones, iPods, and gaming devices. A class might consist of a 20 minute study/refresher period followed by 20 minutes of teaching and discussion, then 20 minutes for homework. Study, discussion, and homework would all be done while the teacher is available to answer any questions, memories are fresh, and there are no distractions. That would also give teachers sufficient time in class to grade papers and do lesson plans. The most demanding subjects should be taught early in the day when minds are fresh. Allowing a 30-minute lunch period and two 15-minute recesses would minimize students' need to leave class for restroom breaks, and give children and teachers a needed break. That makes for a nine hour school day with eight classes, but it comes with two additional benefits: reduced daycare costs and less unsupervised after-school time for children.

When we were an agrarian society and there was no air conditioning, taking three months off during the summer made sense.

Children could help on the farm during extended daylight hours and avoid stifling hot classrooms. Today, we have air conditioning, family farms are fewer, and modern farms and farm machinery are well illuminated. With both parents working, the child is either unsupervised for long periods of time or the parents are stuck with three consecutive months of daycare expense. Lack of supervision often provides an opportunity for kids to get into trouble. Some of what was learned before the summer break must be relearned. A better plan, in my opinion, is to spread the time off over the year, perhaps four eleven-week quarters with one week off each in the spring and fall, two during the winter holidays, and a four week vacation period in the summer. This allows children to participate in fun activities in each season of the year, adds four weeks of education, and lessens the risk of burnout.

Adding time alone will not improve the quality of education. Most discussions of the subject eventually get around to firing bad teachers. There is a near consensus that it is very difficult to get rid of bad teachers because of teachers unions, and that getting rid of them would improve education. There are a number of problems with this premise. How can we tell who the bad teachers are? Were they always bad, or were they somehow made bad by the system? Does money somehow figure in the equation?

You may have heard of Michelle Rhee, the chancellor of Washington, D.C., public schools from 2007 to October 2010. The annual cost per student was more than $15,000, more than most others in the nation. The student test scores were abysmal. Only 8% of students were reading at grade level. Numerous news reports on PBS, Time, the Atlantic, and newspapers lauded her efforts to turn the situation around. She fired nearly 100 of the central office staff, two dozen principals, almost that many assistant principals, approximately 260 teachers, and nearly twice that many teaching aides. She closed more than twenty schools and reorganized more than two dozen others. Rhee renegotiated the contract with the teachers union that would give them the option to give up seniority pay for a chance at much higher merit pay. There were some results. Graduation rate increased three percent. Reading and math scores came up a bit, and writing skills improved. If replacing teachers alone was the solution, the D.C. schools should have shown more significant results, even in that short time frame.

A PBS Newshour report on December 14, 2010, featured the Peer Assistance and Review (PAR) program started in 1981 by the Toledo, Ohio, public schools with the cooperation of the teachers union. It allowed experienced teachers to evaluate new teachers, who were then matched with a mentor to help them succeed. Eight percent of the new teachers were fired during their first year. PAR was also used to evaluate and mentor tenured teachers, although only fifteen tenured teachers were fired. One would think that this weeding process would result in a cadre of effective teachers. While there may have been some improvement, student scores continued to be among the lowest in the area.

Two of our children attended parochial schools. When we moved to an upscale community with a public school reputed to be one of the best in the country, we decided to enroll our children there. Within two months, our children were terribly bored. They were studying material they had learned in the parochial school eighteen months earlier. We had no choice but to put them back in the more distant parochial school. Parents of the public school children felt their children were getting an excellent education, and that the teachers were doing a good job. Their teachers were getting paid more than those in the parochial school. They had better facilities and larger budgets. What conclusions can we draw from that experience? I can think of several:

- We do not have effective ways of evaluating schools or teachers.

- Money alone does not guarantee good education.

- School choice is a good thing.

- More structured and disciplined environments are more conducive to learning.

In their book titled *Freakonomics,* Steven D. Levitt and Stephen J. Dubner write about the Chicago Public Schools' adoption of a testing program similar to that mandated by No Child Left Behind. Schools and teachers could be penalized for poor performance. Original test sheets were retained. When they were analyzed, a significant number of teachers were found to have cheated, actually changing poor students' answers to improve their scores. Subsequent retesting by school board authorities of students whose teachers were suspected of cheating showed that some students' performance was altered by nearly two grade levels. A July 5, 2011, article cites an investigation in Atlanta, Georgia, that found cheating on tests at 44 schools involving 178 teachers and principals, half of whom confessed. The administration of their highly acclaimed Superintendent was apparently involved in covering up the cheating. On August 1, 2011, MSNBC.com news reported that 89 schools in Pennsylvania were flagged as probably cheating on tests resulting in questionable gains on reading and math scores. Texas, an early adopter of a similar testing program has the second highest high school dropout rate in the country. Schools have found that pushing poor students out is every bit as effective at raising scores as educating them, and it is easier than getting rid of poor teachers. One news report pointed out that once alternative schooling has been recommended for a student, that student is removed from the rolls, thereby raising the schools performance numbers. Black and Hispanic students have by far the highest rate of high school dropouts – thirty to fifty percent. Not coincidentally, they also come from the poorest families.

It is difficult for a parent to know how good a school is or whether their child is performing satisfactorily. Report cards do not tell the whole story. The proliferation of privately operated charter, magnet, alternative, and church affiliated schools provides choices, but how are we to know that they are any better than the public schools? They should be subject to the same testing process with the same safeguards. Teachers should not be the ones to administer tests used to determine their own effectiveness. Teachers should be tested periodically to determine their knowledge of the subject(s) they teach. That testing should take place at a different facility and be administered by someone outside of their administration and district. Their students should be tested similarly. Any one test can be misleading, so testing should be done frequently, perhaps once per quarter, with each succeeding test somewhat more difficult. The exact test to be used should be a surprise to all parties concerned, being selected at random at the last moment. There should be enough different tests that teaching to a particular test or cheating would be less likely. Results should not be based on grade levels, which are a moving target, but on absolute percentage scores. Each question or problem should have a percentage of difficulty assigned. The test should be graded by the average difficulty ratings of the questions answered correctly times the percentage of all questions that were answered correctly. Ideally, both figures should be recorded because they would more readily identify developmental limitations.

Not everyone learns the same way. Earlier in my career, I hired a warehouse supervisor named Eddie. I used a non-verbal (picture-based) multiple choice intelligence test to screen applicants. My objective was to hire people who could easily understand instructions, solve problems quickly, and function autonomously. Eddie scored in the 99th percentile of intelligence. After a brief indoctrination period, he participated in daily operations meetings, and was given verbal assignments of increasing responsibility. Eddie could not follow the simplest of verbal instructions. His brain was wired differently. He could follow detailed written instructions of great complexity, but was completely lost in a fast-paced environment where verbal interaction was essential. It was with the greatest of sadness that we had to let this brilliant mind go. That experience spoke volumes to me about our teaching methods, which have changed little over the last century.

One of the best ways to learn is by doing, and seeing some principle demonstrated in practice. A student can learn much more about structural engineering from building a bridge model with Popsicle sticks than one ever could from verbal or written instructions alone. Science projects by competing student teams teach not only the science but also how to cooperate with others. Recreating the scientific experiments of earlier scientists helps a student to understand how we arrived at many of the current theories in physics, chemistry, and other disciplines. Of course, it takes a teacher with sufficient knowledge of the subject matter to properly guide and evaluate the work. After the second or third grade, teachers should specialize in the subjects they teach. Students should be able to jump grades on a subject by subject basis so they can continue to be challenged and advance most in the subjects in which they show the greatest interest and ability. That means classes should be set up to teach specific subjects with all the necessary equipment and supplies present. Moving from class to class would provide changes of scenery and reduce boredom.

Each student's education should be coordinated between the various classes. For example, if a student has interest in some period in history, reading that material would be far more rewarding than reading Shakespeare or Dickens. For another student, reading about some aspect of science or engineering would be more beneficial than the works of modern novelists. The same should apply to mathematics. The math taught to the student should be geared to the direction of the student's interest and ability. That makes it a lot tougher for the teachers, but it helps to develop expertise in areas that have occupational potential.

Educators have long labored under the notion that their students need to receive a well-rounded education. While some subjects are essential tools for learning, like English, math, geography, geometry, and some science, forcing other subjects upon students that they have no interest in may cause them to turn off to learning anything. Our daughter was studying to be a nurse. One of the subjects she was required to take was 'Music for the Listener'. It had absolutely nothing to do with her chosen profession, and stole time from what she really needed to study. It was merely a tool to increase revenue for the college. Most people develop their own tastes in music, art, and literature. It is certainly helpful for a student to learn how to do basic sketching for the purpose of communicating ideas graphically, but knowing what kind of style Van Gogh painted in or how he lost an ear is only useful to the student who chooses art or art education as a career. My wife studied piano for several years as a child. She was forced to memorize and practice long classical pieces she had no interest in. After each recital, she could never play that piece again. She gave up music entirely, lost interest in school, and never pursued another demanding course of study, but she did wonderfully master the role of wife and mother. I am very much in favor of a cafeteria system where a child can take short introductory courses early on to determine the child's aptitudes and interests. Developing those areas is most likely to benefit the child, the nation, and society in general.

Just last week Borders, the huge bookstore chain, announced that it is closing most of its stores and filing for bankruptcy protection. Rumors have been circulating that Barnes and Noble will soon follow suit. Much of the business is now being done online with Amazon.com taking the lion's share of the business. It is not just that books purchased online are cheaper. Amazon claims that there are nearly a million books available for its Kindle electronic book reader. It can wirelessly download and store more than a thousand books. The $139 device is smaller than one book, and it has many of the capabilities of a laptop computer. There are also Kindle applications available for cellular smart phones and Apple's iPad. Universities are issuing laptop computers to their students. Many of the students are also carrying Kindles. We have the capability to put much of the knowledge known to man in the hands of every child for a fraction of the cost of textbooks, and present it in color with video, audio, and text, much like reading a newspaper on your web browser. The ability to drill down into ever greater detailed explanations would enable even slower students to grasp complex concepts. I know that I can teach a child basic math concepts with a few pennies because it allows them to visualize what a mere verbal explanation or blackboard scribbles cannot. Developing multimedia learning applications could spawn a whole new industry. It might also diminish the power of the text book publishing industry which has done little to advance learning.

The high cost of higher education may be partly responsible for the astounding high-school dropout rate. It is certainly beyond the reach of most families. In 2000, 64% of college graduates financed their education with loans averaging $16,928, or nearly half of the $37,729 median annual salary of graduates with bachelor's degrees. Since then, college tuitions and student loan interest rates have soared without a commensurate increase in salaries of college graduates. The average college debt now exceeds $24,000. The uncertainty of later employment, staggering cost, and fear of indebtedness may scare off many high school students from pursuing higher education. The export of quality jobs makes repayment of student loans problematic. Student loans are not relieved under bankruptcy.

Another factor that may affect the quality of our education is the overemphasis on sports. Parents may push their children into sports in hopes of them earning college scholarships on the basis of athletic ability, overlooking the fact that only a tiny fraction of college students ever goes on to make a living in sports. This would not pose a problem if it did not relegate academics to a lower priority. What does it say about our priorities when a high school coach is paid much more than the school principal?

Firing people and closing underperforming schools is easy. The same students and teachers then go to other schools, and drag down their performance. Teachers should be tested for knowledge of the subjects they teach and their teaching skills, only be allowed to teach subjects in which they can meet certain minimal standards, and be required to either teach a lower grade for which the teacher can meet the standard or take remedial classes if there is a likelihood of meeting a standard. It is difficult, in terms of time and finances, for a teacher with a family to work and take classes. We should be willing to pay the teacher's salary for a few weeks while taking the classes. Failure to meet the standards after taking the classes would justify termination. There is no guarantee that replacement teachers will perform any better. Smart college graduates can earn far more in other professions than in teaching. If we want qualified teachers we must pay them what they are worth. How do we determine what they are worth?

Some have argued that teachers should be paid based on merit. This assumes that once a teacher has achieved proficiency they will remain proficient. That is not necessarily the case. I have had a number of outstanding employees who received repeated merit salary increases, but could not sustain that high level of performance, and were ultimately priced out of the market. Performance evaluations tend to be subjective, and vary broadly from manager to manager. They are rarely free of bias. The amount of education a person has received is also not a certain indicator of performance. I believe teacher compensation should be based on the difficulty of the subject taught, the amount of education required to achieve and maintain mastery, and the performance of their students compared to others in the same demographic based on impartial testing.

Primary and secondary education is funded largely by community-based property taxes. You may have heard it said that 'money does not guarantee good education'. That may be true, but why are the best schools typically found in affluent communities? Inequitable distribution of education funding affects class size, teacher compensation, ability to attract qualified teachers, and availability of the best materials and programs. The College Board, a non-profit organization that administers Scholastic Achievement Tests, has published figures showing that students from the wealthiest homes score the highest, while those from the poorest homes score the lowest. Property taxes are an anachronism. I believe two-thirds of all primary and secondary education should be paid for from the general fund based on the gross revenues tax on individuals and corporations in the nation. The remaining one-third should be based on the gross revenues tax collected from the postal code(s) in each school district. That would still allow wealthier communities to spend more per pupil, but would level the playing field somewhat.

Parents of private or parochial school students pay twice for their children's education, once in their taxes, and then in tuition. In many cases, these schools provide a better education at lower cost. Would we not be better off to put some of our tax money to work there? I do not believe that the separation of church and state clause of our Constitution, which prohibits the establishment of a state religion, would be violated if all religious and secular schools were treated equally.

In listening to the wrangling over the sad state of our educational system, I am appalled at the lack of any creative solutions in the proposals. I am generally in favor of a longer school day and school year, and I believe incompetent teachers should be dismissed after remedial efforts have failed. However, if such a large number of teachers need to be fired, the problem is greater than the teachers. It is the management and the system. For example, the labor contracts negotiated with teachers' unions were negotiated by managements of school districts. The defined benefit retirement plans that were negotiated are nearly impossible to fund, and make education unaffordable when they are funded. The resulting pressure on education budgets forces teachers' salaries down to unacceptable levels considering the amount of education required.

If money alone could cure the problems, then Washington, D.C., should have some of the best schools in the country. If it did indeed spend more than $15,000 per student annually, where was the money going? It was not to teachers' salaries. Teachers in our community often buy school supplies for their classes out of their own pockets because their schools' budgets are so tight. Perhaps the situation in Falcon, Colorado, near Colorado Springs might shed some light on the issue. Falcon has a population of 18,000 people in about 6100 households, a median household income of $70,591, ten public schools, about 14,700 students, and its own school district. Many of the students come from the surrounding rural communities. Over the past several months they debated how to cope with budget cuts due to declining revenues from the state. Among the proposed cuts were eliminating student bus service and lunch programs on which nineteen percent of the students depend. In addition, the school board decided to terminate the contracts of their school district's administrative staff as part of an initiative to move decision making lower down the organization structure to principals. According to the *Colorado Springs Gazette, KRDO.com Target 13 investigative reporter Tad Landrock*, and several other sources, the staff reductions required buyouts of about $1.1 million. They included:

- Chief Financial Officer $260,220
- Director of Human Resources $233,246
- Chief Information Officer $264,004

The Superintendant was to have his title changed to CEO, which would have relegated his role more to educational issues than administrative. Perceiving this as a demotion, he decided to resign instead. His buyout will be $225,000. He had been hired eighteen months earlier at a salary of $180,000. His prospective successor wants to match or exceed that figure. This raises a number of questions. Why do we need all these school districts each with their own expensive administrations? What functions do they serve? What do they do to improve quality of education?

School districts allow wealthier communities to have better schools because the property tax revenues that support them do not cross district boundaries. They have greater buying power than individual schools, so presumably they should be able to get a better deal. Suppliers love centralized purchasing. Without adequate controls, corruption often creeps in, not just in school systems, but in private businesses and government agencies. In 1980 in Chicago, I negotiated for a city-owned industrial building for my employer. In the building were 1050 brand new police cars that might not get used for years. According to a *1997 Heartland Institute op-ed by Joseph L. Bast*, in 1995, the Chicago superintendant of schools was convicted of tax evasion. When Chicago's mayor, Richard M. Daley, assumed control of the schools, his management team found warehouses full of rotting food, more than 4,000 desks, almost 9,000 chairs, and nine pianos. The director of facilities was jailed for accepting bribes to funnel projects to favored contractors. Many others were fired for corruption or incompetence. It should surprise no one that the public schools spent twice as much per student annually than Chicago's highly acclaimed Catholic schools. The business world is no different. I have on more than one occasion fired managers for taking bribes. That is why the purchasing, accounting, and operations functions should never be under common management.

All of the preceding factors have some impact on our children's education. Technological change has increased how much we need to know, while filling our minds with trivia and reducing our capacity for essential knowledge and reasoning ability. Every time I see a spelling bee, I am chagrined at seeing children memorizing words that they will never use. Have you noticed that most of the winners in recent years are Asian? Why is that? I believe it is because of close extended family relationships, more structured and disciplined home environments, and the importance placed on quality education as a key to future success.

Foreigners are generally more adept at learning languages than Americans. Most Americans cannot pronounce foreign words correctly. For example, the Revolutionary War hero, Kosciuszko, always comes out as either something unrecognizable or 'cozzie-ass-ko'. There is no effective way for me to give you the correct pronunciation in writing because there is no set way to transliterate that word into English. The closest I can come is 'cause-chew-sh-ko'. The soft 'sh' should actually be pronounced as 'sz', the sound of frozen chicken in a deep fryer. English is an agglomeration of many languages, each with its own spelling and pronunciation. Without knowing the etymology, or word origin, it is difficult to pronounce the word correctly, except by hearing and memorizing the correct pronunciation, a very memory intensive process.

That brings us back to the classroom in the refugee camp in Germany where every one of my classmates could read everything at the end of first grade. Why is it that these children could do what ours cannot? The answer is simple: they were learning Polish, a much more phonetic language. Most European languages are more phonetic than English. Trying to teach English phonetically is a study in frustration.

Children are born with logical minds. They learn quite easily what makes logical sense. If something follows simple straightforward rules, which are applied consistently in similar cases, then it can be learned easily, and it can be remembered easily. Unfortunately, the evolution of language has little to do with logic. Most languages are the product of the mixing of cultures, each with numerous loan words from other languages, and their own spellings and pronunciations. This creates the necessity for memorizing the spelling, pronunciation, and usage of each word, a tragic waste of learning effort.

Children begin to learn reading by sounding out the letters. As long as we deal with the very simplest cases like 'cat' and 'dog', 'mom' and 'dad', etc., they do well. Then, as we progress to multi-syllable words, the process comes to a grinding halt. Words that sound alike have different spellings and meanings. Letters and letter combinations are pronounced differently in different words. Some letters are silent. Several different letters can sound the same depending on the word they are used in. All the time we spend learning spelling and pronunciation stands in the way of extracting the knowledge in the educational materials we are trying to learn how to read.

Here's a little demonstration of how the mind works. This is not a trick. Have several people try it. Count aloud the number of F's in the following sentence, and write down the total. Count them only once.

FINISHED FILES ARE THE RE
SULT OF YEARS OF SCIENTIF
IC STUDY COMBINED WITH
THE EXPERIENCE OF YEARS

Now read the footnote at the bottom of the page. [1]

The English language is grammatically simpler than many others, but it is more difficult to gain proficiency in it because it is so memory intensive. The following examples should make the point:

- Words with nearly identical spelling sound different: bomb, comb and tomb; bough, cough, rough;

- Words that sound the same are spelled differently: air and err; bear and bare; beer and bier; bury and berry; deer and dear; do, dew and due; doe and dough; done and dun; dual and duel; draft and draught; hew, hue, and whew; hoar and whore; meat, meet and mete; per and purr; root and route, or rout and route; to, too, and two, etc., etc.

- Words that sound exactly alike have different meanings: matter and madder; bear and bare. Bear can be an animal, or it can mean 'to carry' or 'to tolerate'. Bare can be an adjective or verb meaning either 'exposed' or 'to expose'.

- Double letters are used when they are not sounded separately: abbot, arrow, illicit, pinnacle.

---

[1] Most people will count three F's even though there are six. The F's in 'OF' are perceived as V's, which is how they sound. The mind, which is phonetic, must translate them.

- Letter combinations are used to make sounds for which we already have single letters: photo, phrase, physics, laugh, cough. We already have the letter 'f' which sounds just like the combinations 'ph' and 'gh', why do we need the combinations? The same is true for the letter combination 'ck': clock, kick, pluck, rock. Since the 'c' and 'k' ending these words sound alike, what is the purpose of having them both? Another example is character and charisma. When we have the letter 'k' available, why do we need to use the 'ch' as a 'k' sound?

- Some letter combinations can have two different pronunciations: character and charter; charity and charisma.

- Two different letters can be pronounced the same: size, wise; waiter, wader. Why should an 's' sound like a 'z', or a 't' like a 'd'?

- Some letters cannot be individually sounded: quick, quake; extra and xylophone. Since the letter 'q' sounds like the combination 'kw', and the letter 'x' sounds like 'ks', 'kz' or 'gz', why do we need these letters? Would they not be better used for sounds not represented by our existing alphabet?

- Two different letters often are pronounced the same: celestial, selection; cell, sell. Why do we need a 'c' to sound like an 's' that we already have available?

- These and very many other words contain letters which are not sounded: cologne, foam, pier, pique, etc. Why do we need silent letters? What purpose do they serve?

- In some words, two different letters have the same sound: mystic. Why should the 'y' and 'i' sound alike?

- In other words, the same letter has two or more different sounds: reenter, reexamine

- The various forms used to communicate plurality merely add confusion to the English language: cat, cats; cannon, cannon; octopus, octopi; mouse, mice; goose, geese; is, am, are. . A common standard would simplify matters and accelerate learning. Why should the verb need to be plural when the noun already conveys plurality?

- We have many ways of expressing groupings in the animal world: flock of sheep, gaggle of geese, herd of buffalo, pack of wolves, pride of lions, pod of whales, etc. Why do we need all these ways of expressing what is essentially a group, family, clan, tribe, or herd?

Look through the dictionary. You will find many cases like these. One should not have to memorize the spelling and pronunciation of every word in order to be able to read it. Nor should one be dependent upon seeing a complete sentence to determine the context and meanings of the words in it. This factor is a major obstacle to developing people (and computers) that understand human speech and writing.

I don't underestimate the difficulty of making changes to the spelling, pronunciation, and grammar of our language, and I don't expect people will flock to the idea. A symposium would have to be held on revising the language, followed by a public education program. Changes in language have happened through a sort of evolutionary process in the past. One's language has always been a means of defining one's ethnic identity, something we cherish. As the process of globalization continues, the inconsistencies in grammar and pronunciation will be perceived as stumbling blocks to the free flow of information. If we could all agree on a logical standard format, the benefits would be tremendous. Our televisions or computers could automatically translate foreign news broadcasts, entertainment programs, and texts. A small handheld universal translator could allow us to communicate with others anywhere in the world in their own language. Learning a foreign language would become very much easier. At first, it seems awkward, but, never having to worry about spelling or pronunciation, because each letter and each letter combination can only be pronounced one way, and being able to read words as soon as the alphabet is learned has great appeal. It does not guarantee comprehension of what is read, but the fact that reading occurs earlier allows comprehension to develop earlier also.

National programs of this sort are not without precedent. In 1928, Mustafa Kemal Ataturk, first president of Turkey, began the conversion of Turkey's alphabet from the Arabic to a modified Latin one similar to those used by many European countries. The task was completed in four years. The result was a phonetic alphabet better able to express Turkish words. The change I am proposing is far simpler than the one he undertook, since it is merely a matter of establishing rules for pronunciation of individual letters and letter combinations. We have computers that can automatically translate everything ever written into the new form. That would spawn an entirely new industry.

Let's not confuse intelligence with memory. Many people with relatively poor memories have outstanding reasoning ability. On the other hand, there are people with phenomenal memories but limited reasoning ability. We need to unburden the process of learning language so that our children can concentrate on developing math, science, literary, mechanical, artistic, and creative skills. Simplify our language and every child will be able to read before school age, with the possible exception of the severely handicapped. A purely phonetic language is incredibly easy to learn so the effort goes into learning the meanings and usage of words and extracting knowledge rather than laboring over the tools of knowledge. The changes needed are intuitive enough that you and I will be able to read materials written in the new form, and learn to write in the new form in very short order, if we so choose. The youngsters who learn the new form will be able to begin the pursuit of useful knowledge far sooner.

The earlier we give our children the tools of learning, the sooner we can discover their aptitudes and interests, and develop them. Pursuing a course of study that brings rewards and recognition should reduce the frustration and boredom so many children experience. It may not solve all the problems of our educational system, but it will almost certainly improve our chances of meeting the technological challenges we will face in the future.

It has been estimated that 92% of college graduates are working outside their field of study. There are a number of reasons that may be deduced from this. We view high school as preparation for college, and college as preparation for the working world. Most high school students have no idea of what career they are best suited for, which occupations are most in demand, which pay a decent wage, what their future financial needs will be, how to manage their finances, and which occupation they might actually enjoy. This is a major failing of our secondary education system. Part of the explanation may be that the failures of the primary education system force high schools to teach what should have been learned in elementary school. That, in turn, forces colleges to spend two years teaching what should have been learned in high school.

Earlier, we mentioned a cafeteria system to determine elementary school students' areas of interest and aptitude. A similar system is needed in high school to help students decide on a career. During the first two years, one class could be devoted to exploring career choices. In the last two years, during part of their four breaks from school, students could do one-week internships, with or without pay, in industries in which they have some interest. That would require schools to partner with businesses and institutions. The ability to experience varied work environments should make the career decision much easier for students. More people ultimately working in the field they studied would raise the competency of employees. That assumes that they have an opportunity to go on to college. About one-fourth of high school students fail to graduate, and one third of those that do graduate do not go on to college. That means that nearly half of our high school students will become part of a permanent underclass.

Have you wondered why we have a shortage of college graduates in engineering, sciences, mathematics, medicine, and other demanding disciplines? We have exported the technical jobs to other countries, and driven down wages here by bringing in lower-paid foreign technical workers. The brain drain from those countries deprives them of their best and brightest, and deprives our best and brightest of good opportunities. The better schools are out of reach for most students. Too many college graduates have difficulty finding jobs in their own field, or jobs in their own field that pay enough to repay their student loans. Why undertake a difficult course of study if it does not improve your prospects? As an example, our nursing shortage is being addressed by importing lower-paid foreign nurses. Our nursing schools do not graduate enough nurses to meet demand. They cannot get enough qualified teachers because the pay is often less than they can earn as nurses.

Just as specialization based on student interest and ability, and commensurate specialization in teaching would improve education, it might have a similar effect if universities were more highly specialized around disciplines. The cost of a university education might be considerably lower if they were organized around occupational domains like medical, law, physics, chemistry, information technology, engineering, music, etc. In some of these technical fields, the rate of change is so great that much of what is learned becomes obsolete before a degree is earned. Specialization would make it easier for universities to stay more current in their chosen fields. The rate of change, facilities and equipment requirements, and cost for subjects like political science, history, sociology, theology, communications, marketing, and others, could be much lower. With rare exceptions, the proliferation of for-profit, online or on-campus, unaccredited, lower cost colleges does little to advance knowledge in technical fields or employability of their students.

We are at an important crossroad. Our future prosperity depends on high quality jobs. They, in turn, depend on innovation, and innovation depends on education. Consider the number of industries that have been spawned by technological innovations in the past century. Education enables research and development of new products and technologies that will provide high paying jobs of tomorrow. In the short term, we need to focus our energies on rebuilding our infrastructure. The jobs thus created will pay for our schooling while we wait for that education to bear fruit. Even with those interim jobs, the earnings will be inadequate to pay for a sufficient number of advanced degrees. How can we make up the difference? There is enough waste, fraud, and abuse in our system that we could easily provide an associate degree to every student with the ability and desire to pursue higher learning. Implementing the gross revenues tax system would enable us to do even more and pay down the national debt. Only one thing stands in our way: political ideology. We think it fitting that taxpayers provide an education to many military personnel, yet the very notion of doing it for our other best and brightest immediately raises red flags. Therein lies the dilemma: our choice is between political ideology and regaining our technological advantage in the world. You get to choose.

Winning the War on Drugs

Few of us are old enough to remember the **Prohibition** era in the
United States, but may be familiar with it from history books, movies,
or television programs. From 1920 to 1933, the Eighteenth
Amendment to the Constitution banned the sale, manufacture, and
transportation of alcohol throughout the country. It started with a noble
cause — to reduce alcoholism and its associated evils. Instead, it
created an enormous black market for alcohol, which criminal gangs
quickly organized to produce and supply. Bloody turf wars erupted.
The opportunity for quick money corrupted many law enforcement
officials and judges. The Great Depression drew many normally law-
abiding citizens into crime as well. Perhaps you remember the
television program 'Elliot Ness' that lauded the exploits of the
incorruptible lawman who fearlessly fought to enforce the law. So,
what did Prohibition accomplish? It created powerful crime syndicates
that are still with us, got a lot of dedicated law enforcement
professionals killed, corrupted many others, pushed many desperate
people into crime, filled our jails, and actually increased alcohol
consumption. What part of that history can we not understand?

Here we are, nearly eighty years later, doing exactly the same
thing. The violence under prohibition was far worse than we
experienced from legalized alcohol consumption. Last year, at least
15,000 people across our southern border were killed by drug gangs. I
suspect that many of the murders committed here are in some way
connected to drug use or trafficking. Random drive-by shootings as
part of gang initiations have become frequent events in our cities.
Drive-by shooters in stolen cars are rarely apprehended. Consider the
number of dedicated law enforcement professionals who have given
their lives in an attempt to reduce traffic in alcohol then and drugs now.
Why? To prevent drug induced violence, both willful and accidental?
Look around you. It hasn't worked! The prohibition of anything for
which there is popular demand creates a lucrative market for it, which,
due to its illegality, brings in criminals as suppliers, and makes
criminals of users. It has been estimated that 70% of our prison

inmates are there for drug use, drug trafficking, or indirectly related crimes.

One of my friends is a former drug enforcement agent with the Illinois State Police. He is very much concerned with the carnage on the highways that might result from decriminalization of drugs. He speaks of the difficulty of overcoming addicts high on PCP. I can only point out that at least 20,000 people a year die on the highways as a result of drugs and/or alcohol. Driving under the influence is and should remain illegal. My friend's experience with drugged up felons was gained while the use of controlled substances was and is illegal. Bringing drug addicts out of the shadows might give us the opportunity to intervene and help them.

Prohibitions against alcohol, gambling and prostitution have not worked. Similarly, prohibitions against drug use have not worked. Consider all the prominent sports and entertainment figures who, in spite of enormous incomes, are known abusers. Every attempt to legislate morality has failed miserably. People can be educated to the dangers of drug use, but there is no effective way to prevent them from engaging in it. They want government to protect them from external hazards, but don't want it to meddle in their private lives. A major attitude change is needed, one that allows people sovereignty over their own persons and denies the opportunity of profit to the criminal. Criminals are in it for the money. Remove the money, and the criminals go away. That is what has happened with legalized gambling – corporations have taken the place of the Mafia. That is also what happened with prostitution where it has been legalized. Sexually transmitted diseases, assaults on prostitutes, and drug use by prostitutes have declined. Don't misunderstand me. I neither engage in nor condone any of these activities, legal or otherwise, but I do want to bring some order to them. The lives and money we are wasting on attempting to enforce these laws would be better spent on educating our young people about the dangers of drugs, alcohol, gambling, prostitution, and other vices. We send very mixed messages to our young people when we sit in front of the television with our beer, wine, or cocktails while telling our kids that it is an adult activity. Anytime we prohibit something or label it an 'adult' activity, young people will be attracted to it because they want to be considered adult. Those who want to engage in risky behavior are less likely to engage in a behavior when the risk has been removed.

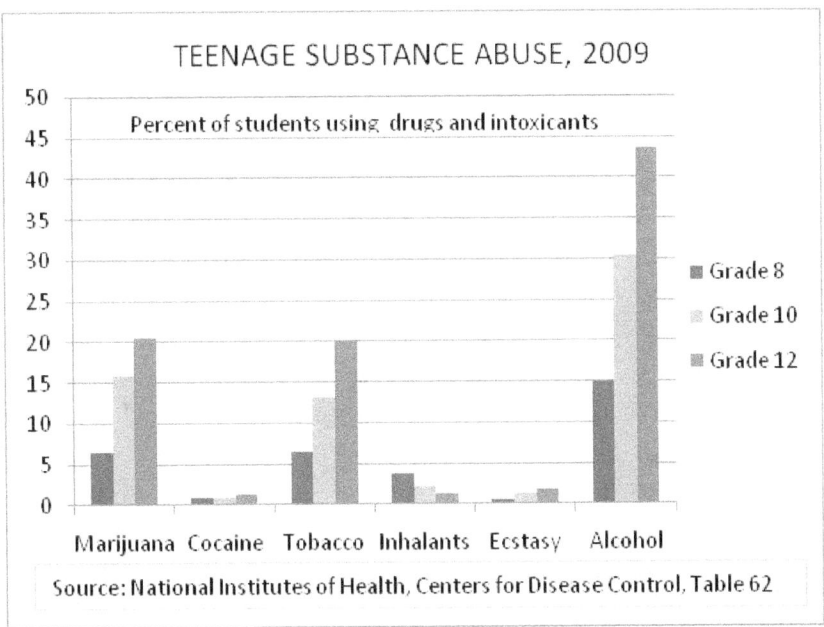

TEENAGE SUBSTANCE ABUSE, 2009

Percent of students using drugs and intoxicants

Source: National Institutes of Health, Centers for Disease Control, Table 62

Compare the laws regarding alcohol, drugs and cigarettes. We have subsidized tobacco growers, but want to burn the farms of coca growers. We put warnings on cigarettes, but allow alcoholic beverages to be advertised incessantly in every media with no warnings at all. Cigarettes kill about 480,000 people a year and alcohol kills about 80,000. We allow poppy growers to continue supplying the heroin trade in Afghanistan because stopping them would shut down the Afghan economy. We rail against drug traffickers crossing our borders, but jail border patrol agents who shoot them. None of this makes any sense. After all the lives, years, and dollars lost combating drugs, what have we gained? Many states, including Colorado, are legalizing medical marijuana. In a depressed economy, states will do whatever it takes to increase tax revenues. In our county alone there were 550 applications for licenses to grow and distribute it. Do the math. That is one application for every 1,100 residents. How many of the 1,100 people do you estimate will need medical marijuana? You guessed it! They will be selling it to you and your kids. The following table regrettably omits one of the most used substances: legal prescription drugs broadly available over the Internet and from your medicine cabinet.

Up until the past decade, there were drug addicts who were receiving Social Security Disability payments, even though they were not otherwise disabled. One of my nieces, who lives in rural Minnesota, came to visit us, and brought a friend who openly admitted receiving SSD payments. He merely smiled when I asked about it. He had no visible means of support but looked healthy. I strongly suspect he was a small-time drug trafficker. One has to wonder how such a program came into being.

Over the last few years, our government has waged a war on the use of steroids in sports. Marion Jones, the Olympic track and field star, was stripped of the five medals she received at the 2000 Summer Olympics for lying about her use of performance enhancing drugs. Shortly thereafter Barry Bonds, the Major League Baseball player, was indicted for obstruction of justice and perjury in an investigation into a designer drug ring. Roger Clemens, the outstanding pitcher for the New York Yankees, was listed in the Mitchell Report as a user of steroids and Human Growth Hormone (HGH), and continues to vehemently deny it. Lance Armstrong, the Tour de France bicycling champion, has also been accused and denies doping. If we look at the bodies of professional wrestlers and other athletes, there can be little doubt in our minds that human bodies do not naturally look that way. It is all about the money. Sports team owners and promoters, and the athletes themselves, stand to benefit financially from enhanced performance. While Congress is busy holding hearings on this issue, health, education, the economy, war, and myriad other issues are ignored. HGH is broadly advertised and available, and is being touted as the next fountain of youth.

Drug traffickers pay no taxes at all. Anytime we legalize something, we decriminalize it. We get to know who the users and providers are, the providers can pay taxes, and we can exercise some control over their activities. For example, letting doctors prescribe and the drug companies supply the drugs should have a number of benefits. Both would pay taxes. The potency and quality of the drugs would be controlled. Competition would drive the prices down, not only for these but for medically necessary prescription drugs as well. There would be no room for criminals to profit. Coca farmers and others supplying the raw materials will eke out a living. Lower drug prices might move coca and poppy farmers into growing food. Prison populations will gradually decrease. A prohibition on advertising drugs to consumers in any form and strong advertising campaigns against them might diminish their allure. Drug abuse is as pervasive for prescription drugs as it is for illegal drugs. I don't know how one can stop the advertising and distribution of them over the Internet. I get two or three spam emails for them every day. Pharmaceutical companies have managed to create drugs and vaccines for hundreds of conditions. I am reasonably certain that they could develop drugs to overcome addictive tendencies in our brains (much as they have for smoking), non-addicting substitutes for recreational drugs, or compounds to counteract the worst effects of using illegal drugs.

I have avoided using many of the statistics being quoted on this subject because the available data is fragmentary and contradictory. Sweden has the strictest anti-drug laws in the world. Netherlands has the loosest and least enforced, especially for recreational use of marijuana. An estimated 25,000 tourists cross the border from neighboring countries to smoke marijuana at Dutch cannabis cafes each week. The European Monitoring Center for Drugs and Drug Addiction (EMCDDA) publishes statistics on drug use by country (*http://www.emcdda.europa.eu/stats10/gps/tables*). The Netherlands shows a lower percentage of adults using drugs than a number of other European countries, and much lower than the United States and England. There is little evidence to suggest that restrictive laws have a measurable impact on overall drug use. Sweden has a lower rate of marijuana use, but no significant difference in the use of hard drugs. Both Sweden and Netherlands have very effective drug treatment programs paid for by the government. Netherlands has among the lowest rates of drug related deaths. Sweden is unique in that it also has among the lowest rates for cigarette smoking, alcohol consumption, and prescription drug use, but there appears to be no causal relationship with its restrictive drug laws. If it makes so little difference, why do we bear the expense and grief of criminalizing drug use?

I have not arrived at this conclusion lightly. My father was a wonderful hard-working and decent man when sober, but he was an alcoholic who became abusive to my mother and his stepchildren when he got drunk. Thankfully, he was able to quit drinking after our son was born, and spent the last two decades of his life sober. He loved his family enough not to risk losing it. My brother also became an alcoholic and nearly lost his family because of it, but he also turned his life around. One of my friends drank himself to death, and two acquaintances died as a result of drug overdoses. I quit smoking forty years ago, have not had a drink of hard liquor in nearly forty years, do not drink beer, and rarely have more than one glass of wine in a month. Having personally seen the damage being out of control can do to a family, I avoid any substance that can become addictive or deprive me of reason. Although I must confess that as a young man I once worked 102 hours per week for six months. A friend sold me a packet of Dexedrine to help me stay awake. That was my one and only personal experience with drugs.

The illegality of drugs might deter a few people from using them. I discern that from my wife's experience with seat belts in cars. Long before they were mandated by law, I installed and used seat belts in my cars. My wife could not be persuaded to do the same. After the mandatory seat belt law was passed, she immediately buckled up and still does. Most people are not so lawabiding.

According to the Bureau of Justice Statistics, there were 1.52 million prisoners in U.S. jails in 2008. In federal prisons, 50.7% were there because of directly drug related offenses. The median sentence was 55 months. Another 35.0% were there for public order offenses including immigration, weapons, etc. How many of those 'public order violations' were related to drugs is unknown. It is interesting to note that the median sentence for violent felonies was 63 months. I suspect that state and local jails have an even higher percentage of drug incarcerations. It costs more than $22,000 per year to keep a person in prison. The annual cost for all drug violators must therefore easily exceed $17 billion plus the cost of adjudicating and enforcing the laws here and aiding other nations in their war on drugs. The total almost certainly exceeds $40 billion. That money would be far better spent on drug regulation, prevention, and treatment.

ANNUAL NUMBER OF INCARCERATIONS
BY U.S. DISRICT COURTS 1980 — 2008

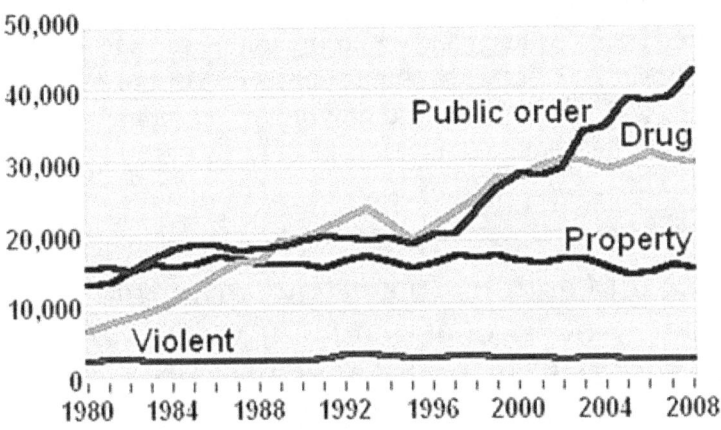

Source: Bureau of Justice Statistics

The crime rate in Netherlands is significantly lower than the United States. A Netherlands newspaper reports that the country has 14,000 prison cells but only 12,000 inmates (*http://vorige.nrc.nl/international/article2246821.ece/Netherlands_to_ close_prisons_for_lack_of_criminals*), so they are closing eight prisons. Since soft drugs and prostitution are both legal and regulated, criminal involvement in these activities is minimal, sexually transmitted diseases are rare, and violence is less.

Decriminalizing drug use does not mean that drug producers, distributors, or stores should be allowed to advertise or otherwise promote drugs. It also does not mean that anyone that endangers others or causes injury or property damage should not pay the consequences. Anyone that is reasonably suspected of driving under the influence (DUI), or causing an accident or violent encounter, should be required by law to submit to a drug test. If they are found to be under the influence beyond a reasonable level, a jail sentence and rehab program should be imposed. Upon a second conviction of DUI, the offender's vehicles and weapons should be impounded. Lax enforcement of DUI laws contributes to many hit and run accidents including fatal ones. Victims and their families are often left without recourse because offenders are uninsured.

If the criminalization of drug use does not make us safer, and it clearly does not, why do we continue legislating against them? If an activity is not injurious to others, it should not be criminalized. When we enlist government in policing and enforcing our moral standards, we get the exact opposite of what we set out to achieve. Most of us want a moral and decent society, but that is the province of religious institutions and families, not government.

"Tobacco and opium have broad backs, and will cheerfully carry the load of armies, if you choose to make them pay high for such joy as they give and such harm as they do."

Ralph Waldo Emerson (1803-1882), American poet.

Gun Control

Few subjects can raise emotions to a fever pitch as quickly as this one. It seems there is little middle ground. Opponents on this issue tend to go to opposite emotional extremes. Facts and statistics do little to persuade them. We need to recognize that most of us want the same thing, freedom from fear and violence. Only our preconceptions of how best to achieve our mutual goals differ. I'd like to share a few personal experiences that may illustrate the complexity of this subject.

I had seen too much violence as a small child in Nazi concentration camps. After nearly four years in refugee camps in Germany, we arrived in Perry County, Arkansas, then the poorest in the United States. I was enrolled in a small Catholic school, eight grades in a one-room log cabin. It was located five miles (a long walk) from home in a little village of about 60 people. A saintly old nun was the only teacher. The other kids near my age taught me to speak English, ride a bike, and play baseball. Poverty forced us to hunt rabbits and squirrels for food. All the kids were great shots. We even held BB-gun battles on logging trains parked on a rural siding. The objective was to hit an opponent's shoe. No one ever got hurt. There was no violence there. It was as if the church and school were on holy ground. Grinding poverty was our only enemy. Then, we moved to Chicago.

On my first day of school in Chicago, as I approached the school, I saw two bigger boys beating up a smaller boy. I put myself between them and said, "Stop! God will punish you." They laughed and began to push me around. That was to continue for about three years. I was two of the things they seemed to hate worst: a D.P. (displaced person, i.e. refugee) and a hillbilly – you know, those people that spoke funny and came to take their parents' jobs. The very notion of hurting someone, even in self-defense, was foreign to me.

I was about thirteen, and still relatively new in Chicago, when a neighborhood youth gang leader held a crude contraption to my head. It was called a zip gun. Kids my age were carrying them. They were manufacturing them in their basements using a hand drill, hacksaw, screwdriver, and pliers. Depending on the level of sophistication desired, it would take anywhere from one to perhaps five hours to construct a functioning firearm. At close range, it could kill as easily as a commercially manufactured one. I was petrified. Fortunately, he was just trying to scare me.

Twenty years later, I went to work for a manufacturing company located four blocks from a notoriously dangerous housing project in Chicago. People were being shot almost daily from the rooftops. I was hired to turn the business around, and that's what I was going to do. Two gangs, one Latino and one Black, were terrorizing the workforce. The previous manager lasted a few months and quit, a broken man. I couldn't quit. My wife and I had three children, one of whom was born with congenital defects and required frequent hospitalizations and medical attention. He was uninsurable, so we bore the cost out of pocket for six years, and were hopelessly in debt as a result. As an employee, I could get health insurance coverage for my family, the primary reason for leaving the management consulting business.

One of the worst offenders was a leader of one of the gangs. I caught him in the act of trying to knife my Production Manager. After I terminated him, another employee warned me that the manager and I were put on the gang's hit list. We were both to be killed. I thought they were idle threats, but over the next several days one employee was shot at behind the building, another was beaten and dumped in the front entrance, a carload of thugs tried to force me off the freeway, and then several hoodlums, apparently armed, were waiting on a railroad bridge above the freeway. I managed to evade both.

The police could not provide protection. I explained my concern for my family's well being. They suggested I vary my route home every day, check my car carefully, and avoid walking past doorways, around blind corners, and into alleys. If anyone suspicious approached, I was to run in the direction of the largest group of people and, if followed, I was to stay there and call the police. I frequently left after dark, our parking lot was in the alley, and the industrial area was deserted after normal work hours.

The uniformed police officers turned the case over to the gang crimes unit for further investigation. A few days later, I met with the gang crimes detectives. They confirmed that the threat was serious. The young man I had fired had a rap sheet that included twenty-seven juvenile arrests for violent crime. At the time of his termination, he was being tried for his first adult arrest, a broad daylight shotgun shoot-out with the police. Being a member of the inner council of his gang meant that he was a confirmed killer. The job was merely intended to display his best behavior during the trial.

I asked the officers "What can I do?" "Leave town", I was told. I explained why I couldn't do that, and asked for alternatives. "Do you want the official or the unofficial version?" The official version turned out to be the 'routes, alleys, doorways, corners, and crowds' speech. "What are the chances such measures will be enough?" "Not good", they replied. "If they want to get you, sooner or later they will."

The unofficial version went like this: "Buy a good gun, learn how to use it well, keep it with you at all times, and do all the other things we told you. Even then there are no guarantees." When I asked about applying for a permit to carry one, they replied "Don't waste your time. They're not issuing non-professional permits." I then asked, "Are you saying my only choice is to be a criminal or a victim?" They replied, "We don't make the laws. We just enforce them."

For days I struggled with their advice. Then, as I was driving with my wife and children in the car, returning from a visit with my parents, a terrible bang sent our hearts into our throats. There was no sensation of collision or a tire blowout. As I looked around, I saw a man clambering up an embankment. We sped away. Upon arriving home, I inspected the car. On the right front vent window, there was a smear of lead where a bullet had ricocheted off the glass, and dug a groove in the door. We had been shot at. Had the shot come from a shallower angle, it would certainly have struck my wife in the chest. I shuddered at the thought of some mindless punk taking my wife's life, and robbing our children of their mother. I learned that day that protecting my family is my responsibility. The police cannot guard everyone who feels threatened, and they cannot be everywhere. A period of intensive self defense training followed.

I became my Production Managers bodyguard, taking him to work, to lunch, and back home for the next several months. The stress of those days had a severe impact on him. He developed serious heart disease, had a pacemaker installed, left my employ, went through a divorce, and was never quite the same. Our adversary was ultimately found guilty in the shootout trial, and was sent to prison. After several additional incidents, things quieted down. Then I heard a rumor that he had been killed in prison.

The government not only failed to protect us, it tried to prevent us from protecting ourselves. The laws did nothing to prevent the criminals from being armed. Criminals, by their very nature, have a disregard for the law. Please don't tell me I must be a voluntary victim, or that I may not have the means to protect my family. That protection is my right and my obligation

Man has practiced violence upon his fellow man since the beginning of time. Before there were guns people killed each other with spears, swords, knives, bows, clubs, and even poisons. Richard Speck, the drug-addicted mass murderer of eight student nurses, said he had a gun but used a knife to commit the murders because the gun would have been too noisy. People have a misplaced fear of firearms. The young man that tried to kill my Production Manager was going to do so with a knife. He was an intravenous drug user. A mentally ill person or drug abuser who wants to do me harm can do so by any number of means. Laws that deprive the decent citizen of means of protection do nothing to reduce violent crime. In fact, wherever citizens have been allowed to carry concealed firearms, violent crime has decreased. Most weapons of the past required a degree of physical prowess. Guns, on the other hand, can even be used by the aged and infirm. They are an equalizer.

On January 8, 2011, Congresswoman Gabrielle Giffords of Arizona was conducting a meeting with constituents outside a grocery store in Tucson when an assailant opened fire with a 9mm pistol killing six people and wounding 13 others. Among those killed was a nine year old girl, a federal judge, and one of Giffords' staffers. Two more staffers were wounded. Giffords was shot in the head, the bullet passing through her brain. She survived, but is undergoing intensive rehab. Giffords was reelected over a Tea Party candidate the previous November. Her support of the health care reform bill angered some extreme elements. Her Tucson office was vandalized, and someone showed up at another gathering with a weapon. The shooter in this case, Jared Lee Loughner, 22, walked up to the gathering holding a pistol with a 31 round magazine and began firing. Loughner had a history of aberrant behavior that frightened those around him. He should have undergone psychiatric treatment, but there was no mechanism for getting him to do so involuntarily. He should never have been allowed to own a gun or an extended magazine.

There have been several cases of mass killings by mentally disturbed persons in recent years. One walked into a fast food restaurant and opened up with a semiautomatic rifle, sometimes mistakenly called an assault rifle, and killed several innocent people. Another walked into a subway car with a high capacity pistol and did the same. More recently, there have been mass shootings at several schools. In each case, no police were present. Consider how many lives might have been saved in the above scenarios if one or more properly trained and armed citizens were present, which was the case at New Life Church in Colorado Springs. A female guard in plain clothes brought down the gunman, who had enough arms and ammunition to kill many more than the two young church members. Most of the offenders in these cases had a history of mental problems, drug abuse, or alcoholism. Why were they allowed to purchase firearms?

Naturally, anything that has the potential for inflicting injury can be misused. Accidents can and do happen. Drive-by shootings and gang shoot-outs in increasingly congested urban areas often result in an innocent person being shot who is not the intended target. Mentally ill people can and do cause harm. The news media report most sensational events and sensationalize the events they report. Only rarely do they report deaths caused by less sensational non-natural causes.

"Man never legislates, but destinies and accidents, happening in all sorts of ways, legislate in all sorts of ways."

Plato, ancient Greek philosopher.

CAUSES OF DEATH BY MECHANISM AND INTENT, 2007

Mechanism of Death	Total of All		Unintentional		Suicide		Homicide		Undetermined		Legal Intervention	
	Number	Rate per 100,000	Number	Rate per 100,000	Number	Rate per 100,000	Number	Rate per 100,000	Number	Rate per 100,000	Number	Rate per 100,000
Total of All	182,479	60.5	123,706	41.0	34,598	11.5	18,361	6.1	5,381	1.8	433	0.1
All Transport	46,250	15.3	46,067	15.3	131	0.0	30	0.0	22	0.0	*	*
Poisoning	40,059	13.3	29,846	9.9	6,358	2.1	85	0.0	3,770	1.2	*	*
Firearm	31,224	10.4	613	0.2	17,352	5.8	12,632	4.2	276	0.1	351	0.1
Fall	23,443	7.8	22,631	7.5	731	0.2	15	*	66	0.0	*	*
Suffocation	14,930	4.9	5,997	2.0	8,161	2.7	637	0.2	135	0.0	*	*
Drowning	4,086	1.4	3,443	1.1	358	0.1	49	0.0	236	0.1	*	*
Fire, Hot things	3,774	1.3	3,375	1.1	157	0.1	141	0.0	101	0.0	*	*
Cut or Pierce	2,734	0.9	111	0.0	619	0.2	1,981	0.7	23	0.0	*	*
Natural/environmental	1,449	0.5	*	*	*	*	*	*	*	*	*	*
Struck by or Against	1,009	0.3	832	0.3	1	0.0	*	*	*	*	*	*
Machinery	659	0.2	*	*	*	*	*	*	*	*	*	*
All Other	12,862	4.2	10791	3.6	730	0.3	2791	1.0	752	0.4	82	0.0

Source: Centers for Disease Control, National Center for Health Statistics, Table 18

* Numbers are either insignificant or not available.

The above table shows some government statistics for 2007 (*http://www.cdc.gov/nchs/data/nvsr/nvsr58/nvsr58_19.pdf*). The numbers are in descending order of cause. You will notice that accidental firearm deaths, at 613, are among the rarest causes of accidental death. There are approximately 250 million motor vehicles in the United States, and a nearly identical number of firearms owned by civilians. We are 75 times more likely to die in transport accidents than accidental shootings. A more serious problem is higher up the chart, the 34,598 suicides and 29,846 deaths due to drugs or poison. Substance abuse is also suspected in as many as 20,000 deaths by vehicles. This suggests that mental illness and substance abuse may be the largest contributing factors to violence, suicide, and accidents.

In 2006, 14990 homicides were reported. Of those, 1781 or 11.9% were of family members, and 4554 or 30.4% were of friends or acquaintances. Alcohol or drugs may be involved in about 65% of those cases. In the case of homicides committed during felonies, about 35% of perpetrators report being under the influence of drugs and/or alcohol. Overall violent crime has declined over the last forty years. There were several periods when violent crimes spiked up. It is difficult to state conclusively what the causes are, but the spikes appear to coincide with periods of intense stress, and declines appear to be most pronounced during periods of prosperity.

Criminals do not obey gun laws. Why should the law-abiding citizen be at a disadvantage to the criminal? A few police groups have supported such laws in the mistaken hope that it will make the streets safer for police. Many of the politicians and lawmakers who have promoted restrictive laws have their own bodyguards or have carry permits. Most people have not had that option. I sympathize with the motive underlying the laws, a safer society. However, it hasn't worked! Wouldn't the police and populace be safer with a well-trained citizenry working as partners to prevent and deter crime?

Most police officers are honest, but, as history has shown us, there are plenty of the other kinds. Recently, a Chicago police officer was arrested by federal authorities for being a notorious supplier of drugs and firearms to gangs. He had gotten away with it for years. Within the same week, four police officers in New York fired 41 shots at an unarmed immigrant. They hit him 19 times and killed him. There appear to be no mitigating circumstances. A retired police officer has been accused of masterminding a notorious jewelry theft ring. Another has been implicated in a murder for hire. Can we trust a society in which only the police and criminals have weapons?

The law recognizes the right of citizens to defend themselves. In most cases, a defender who shoots an assailant in self-defense is not charged with a crime. If self-defense is a legitimate right, why is it illegal in many jurisdictions to carry a firearm for self-defense? I personally feel safer knowing that someone will be able to come to my defense if I am ever attacked.

Safeguards should be provided to prevent authorities from arbitrarily denying the right to purchase or carry a firearm to those who do not pose a threat to society. The various laws that have been passed restricting the size of weapons, forbidding concealed carry, and mandating that they be transported cased and empty, also play into criminals' hands by disabling citizens from defending themselves. The confusion over local gun ordinances should be resolved by a national standard.

I have been a member of the National Rifle Association (NRA) for about forty years because I value the right to protect my family and myself, to hunt, and to engage in shooting sports, and the NRA has been a champion of those rights. In all of those activities, I never found it necessary or practical to use a thirty round pistol magazine, even when facing the probability of multiple assailants. They made the pistols and spare magazines I carried too bulky to conceal and too heavy to carry comfortably. Those extra rounds do not make up for lack of skill. They are primarily offensive devices. I am not an advocate of private citizens possessing fully automatic weapons (those capable of firing multiple rounds with a single pull of the trigger), grenades, bombs, rockets, cannon, tanks, etc. Most of these cannot easily be employed selectively against one or two attackers. They are military weapons designed to fight wars, and are not truly personal defense weapons. I'm also not sure it is a good idea to proliferate .50 caliber rifles capable of taking out targets more than a mile away. They are an invitation to assassination. Provision can always be made for museums, collectors of military hardware, and long range shooting competitors.

The takedown of a Mexican drug cartel recently yielded an enormous cache of money, drugs, and hundreds of weapons. Many of the weapons were AK47s first imported into the United States, while many others were M16 variants of U.S. manufacture. About 70% of the weapons used by Mexican drug cartels originate in the U.S. Most of them were sold by U.S. dealers to straw purchasers (intermediaries) in violation of U.S. laws. Surely, the dealers should have known that individuals purchasing dozens of rifles at one time were not purchasing them for their personal use. According to a March 3, 2011, Los Angeles Times news report, U.S. authorities allowed weapons to pass to suspected gun smugglers so they could be traced to leaderships of Mexican drug cartels over the objections of some federal agents. Many of the firearms were used in various crimes, including the murder of a Border Patrol agent. The Obama administration is proposing a law that would require the reporting of multiple weapon purchases of semi-automatic versions of battlefield rifles by dealers in southern border states. The measure is vehemently opposed by the NRA. The House of Representatives has voted to defund the multiple purchase reporting effort. I believe they are both wrong. The right to keep and bear arms does not give us the right to arm private armies. There are a number of ironies in all this.

Over the last several years, I have sold several of my guns. In each case, I received and verified the purchaser's identity and address, as well as his dealers name, address, and Federal Firearms License number. It is illegal to ship a firearm directly to a purchaser. Neither FedEx, UPS, nor the Postal Service would ship a pistol, so I was unable to complete several transactions. UPS would only ship a rifle or shotgun back to the manufacturer. The rules and regulations only make it more difficult for law abiding people to buy and sell a firearm. Criminals simply ignore the laws.

One can go to a gun show and purchase a weapon legally. One-third of states regulate gun show sales to varying degrees, usually a background check; the remainder do not. There is no way of knowing whether the purchased gun was stolen or used in the commission of a crime, or whether the buyer is a felon, mentally deranged, or legally blind. In order to drive a car or motorcycle, one must pass a written and driving test. In most states, one must have taken a hunter safety course in order to obtain a hunting license. One need not actually own a gun to take a hunter education class or to hunt. It is shocking to me that there is no such requirement for buying or using a gun.

In chapter 5 on immigration reform, I wrote about the need for an interactive multi-purpose positive national identification card. The same card could access databases with medical, criminal, immigration status and other essential data. Scanning the card in a gun shop or gun show would immediately display a photo of the card owner, other identifying information, and any restrictions on firearm ownership or use. It would make much sense to have firearms education in the schools covering topics such as conflict resolution, anger management, legal issues, firearms safety, and firearms use. Different levels of training and certification could be indicated on the national identification card. Just like a drivers license, it could be suspended or revoked for criminal misuse, drug or alcohol abuse, carrying a weapon while under their influence, mental illness or incompetence, or poor vision. Persons receiving certification need not necessarily own a firearm. Those that choose to own firearms will be properly trained in their safe and effective use and storage, and the legal issues involved. Most importantly, they will learn when and how not to use them.

During my early troubles with the gangs, I provided basic firearms training to our children when they were still in elementary school. They clearly understood the power of firearms, their associated hazards, and how to handle them safely. The mystery was gone. They never developed the desire to play with even toy guns. They enjoyed our occasional target shooting sessions, but, by their teens, their interests turned elsewhere. However, if the need were to arise to protect their families, they would know how.

While firearm registration may have some limited benefit for solving crimes, I don't believe it is either workable or wise. A registered weapon in the hands of a lunatic is every bit as dangerous as an unregistered one. The danger is not the firearm, but the violent abuser. Registration laws are unenforceable. Black market firearms will never be registered. Criminals most certainly will not register their guns. Tyrants love gun registration. When the Nazis overran Poland, they went directly to the police stations, got the registration records, and disposed of the firearms and their owners. Corrupt and tyrannical governments have killed far more people than criminals have. Don't assume it can't happen here. The United States would not exist today as a free entity if its citizens had not been armed.

If we want a safer society, we must work to eliminate poverty, provide adequate mental health care, reduce militarism, minimize the desensitization to violence caused by entertainment programs and violent computer games, and change the way we raise our children so they learn respect for authority from their parents and schools..

There will always be those who willfully or negligently injure others, the mentally ill or impaired, those who use weapons as an aid to their criminal pursuits, and those to whom weapons are more important than the people they are intended to protect. No amount of education, laws, or weaponry will eliminate the lunatic fringe. We must provide moral teaching and good example, turn from competitiveness to cooperativeness, and resolve the social issues that breed violence. In the meanwhile, let's protect our own.

"Laws that forbid the carrying of arms ... disarm only those who are neither inclined nor determined to commit crimes ... Such laws make things worse for the assaulted and better for the assailants; they serve rather to encourage than to prevent homicides, for an unarmed man may be attacked with greater confidence than an armed man."

Thomas Jefferson quoting from *On Crimes and Punishment* by criminologist Cesare Beccaria, 1764.

Correctional Institutions

Ask anyone what the purpose of prisons is, and you will likely get one of two responses: to punish criminals (repaying a debt to society) or to rehabilitate them. Neither premise works. According to the Bureau of Justice Statistics, 77.1% of criminals released from jail are rearrested within three years, 57.5% are reconvicted, and 47.9% wind up back in jail or prison. Apparently, they have not been rehabilitated, nor punished severely enough to be deterred from further criminal activity. That should lead one to conclude that some of the principles underlying our penal system may be wrong.

RECIDIVISM RATE OF RELEASED OFFENDERS

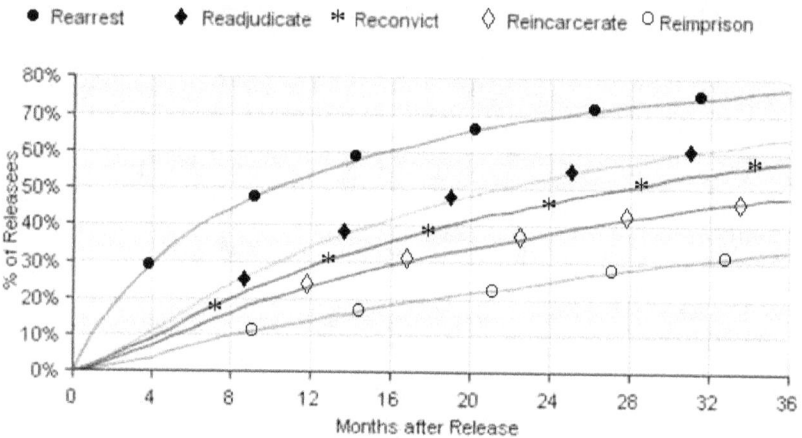

Source: Bureau of Justice Statistics, study of 15 states 1994-1997
(Most recent data available)

Through most of recorded history, systems of justice revolved around punishment. It was intended as a deterrent, but I suspect that desire for revenge played a part. It did nothing to help the victims of crime, and merely angered the perpetrator against society. To counter this anger, reformers introduced the concept of rehabilitation, the premise that treating criminals well will somehow motivate them to abandon their evil ways. Providing exercise yards, workshops, televisions, conjugal visits, and other amenities has done absolutely nothing to stem the criminal tide. The freedoms accorded prisoners have turned prisons into universities for crime, and increased the cost of operating them.

A television report on Richard Speck, now-deceased mass murderer of eight student nurses, showed a video made by Speck and two other inmates. In the video, Speck was interviewed by his homosexual lover, described the murders in some detail, denied any remorse, snorted cocaine from an ample supply, was said to have engaged in sex acts on video (although that portion was edited out), and displayed a large hoard of cash which, presumably, he had earned by selling liquor he had brewed in jail. How is it possible that all these activities can take place in jail? The guards and prison administrations must either be intimidated, involved, or oblivious to what is happening on their watch. The prisons appear to be run by gangs, the same gangs that wreak havoc on our streets. Their influence extends beyond the prison walls. The inmate who might have a tendency to go straight cannot avoid being dragged into drugs, sex, theft, and violence.

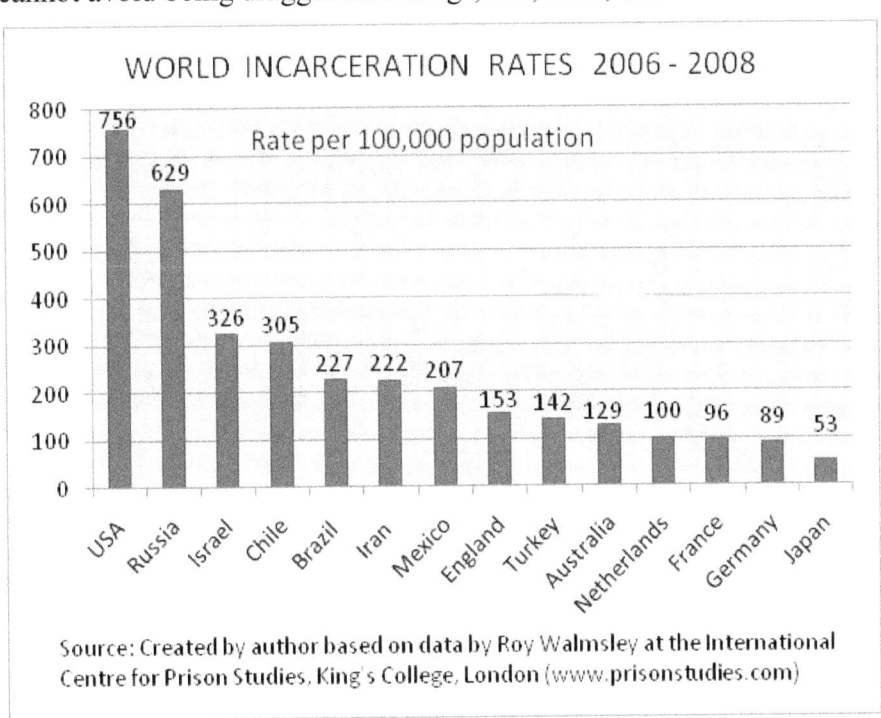

Source: Created by author based on data by Roy Walmsley at the International Centre for Prison Studies, King's College, London (www.prisonstudies.com)

In the United States, there were 2,297,400 inmates in state and federal prisons and local jails in 2009. We have the highest incarceration rate of any nation on earth. Only Russia comes anywhere close. The New York Times reported on February 12, 2009, that two Pennsylvania judges pleaded guilty to wire fraud and income tax fraud for taking more than $2.6 million in kickbacks from a for-profit juvenile detention facility for sentencing youths to juvenile detention for minor offenses. One student built a spoof MySpace page mocking the assistant principal at her high school. She was sentenced to three months in the detention facility. She was a good student who had never been in trouble, and the page stated clearly that it was a joke,.

Prisons are being privatized in an attempt to reduce costs. There are now more than 260 private prisons in the US. Most of them are operated by three companies (Corrections Corporation of America, GEO Group, and Community Education Centers), and most of them are located in the South and West. It is noteworthy that the incarceration rate in several southern states is much higher than elsewhere in the country.

REGIONAL INCARCERATION RATES, 2009					
South		**Midwest**		**Northeast**	
Louisiana	881	Michigan	457	Delaware	447
Mississippi	702	Indiana	447	Pennsylvania	406
Oklahoma	657	Ohio	446	Connecticut	382
Alabama	650	South Dakota	420	New York	298
Texas	648	Wisconsin	369	New Jersey	291
Florida	559	Illinois	349	Vermont	277
Georgia	526	Iowa	292	Massachusetts	213
Arkansas	522	Nebraska	243	Rhode Island	211
South Carolina	512	North Dakota	228	New Hampshire	206
Missouri	509	Minnesota	189	Maine	150
Average	**617**	**Average**	**344**	**Average**	**288**
Source: Created by author based on data presented by the Henry J. Kaiser Family Foundation at http://statehealthfacts.org/comparemaptable.jsp?ind=760&cat=1					

There is no way of knowing whether the concentration of private prisons is somehow responsible for the high incarceration rate. Race alone does not appear to be a driving factor. About the only generalization that can be made is that incomes are generally lowest in southern states and highest in the northeast.

A New York Times article by Richard A. Oppel Jr., dated May 18, 2011, states that data from Arizona shows that the annual cost in private prisons is as much as $1,600 per year higher than in state run prisons, even though private prisons avoid getting the sickest and costliest inmates. Other states have found the savings, if any, to be minimal. Outsourcing the management of prisons to for-profit companies, which may hire low-wage guards with little or no training or background checks, is a very bad idea. It guarantees continued gang dominance, abuse of prisoners by other prisoners and guards, frequent escapes, and riots. Such prisons do not provide an environment capable of rehabilitating prisoners. If we really want to reduce cost, we should release the drug addicts and put them into mandatory drug rehabilitation programs. Even that will not help if we do not find better ways to reintegrate them into society.

Capital punishment has been with us since the beginning of recorded history, but there is not one shred of evidence to suggest that it deters crime. According to a survey conducted by the Death Penalty Information Center, 88% of criminologists say that executions do not lower the homicide rate, and only 5% say that they do (*http://www.deathpenaltyinfo.org*). The state of Texas executed more criminals since 1976 than any other state – 466 of the 1243 total for the United States. Still, the murder rate, 5.4 per 100,000 people in 2009, was higher than any of the 15 states plus District of Columbia that did not allow the death penalty at that time. The state of Illinois, whose murder rate was 6.0 per 100,000, has since stopped executing prisoners after several death row inmates were exonerated by DNA evidence.

Texas has two-thirds the population of California, yet it has a virtually identical number of prisoners under state jurisdiction (171,249 in 2009), the second highest in the nation after California. The logical conclusion is that capital punishment is not an effective deterrent to violent crime. Texas is the only state that does not give juries the choice between execution and life in prison. That may explain why 24 of the 52 executions in the US were in Texas.

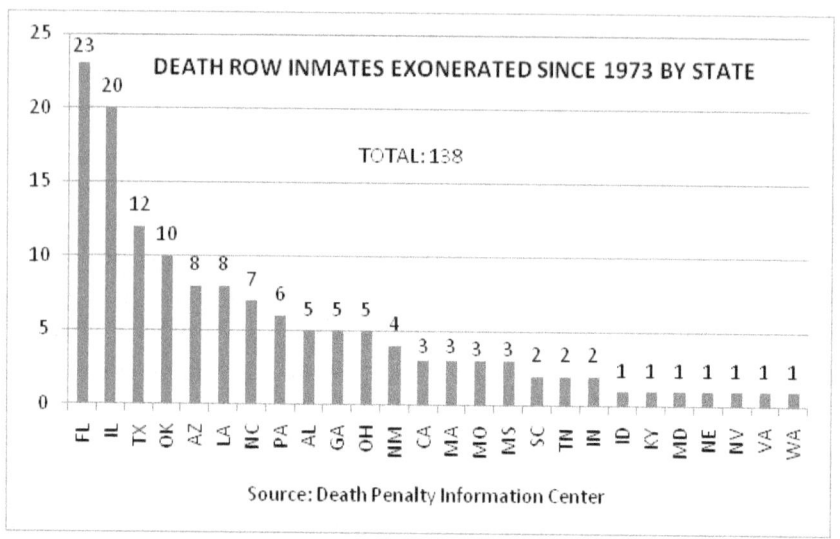

It has been estimated that it costs upwards of $2.5 million to execute a criminal, including the cost of mandatory appeals. A prisoner may remain on death row for years before finally being executed. Keeping that prisoner in prison costs less than $27,000 per year – approximately $1.3 million for the average life sentence – far less than the cost of executing him. Only lawyers benefit from capital punishment. If it is not an effective deterrent, and it is costlier than life in prison, we must question its effectiveness and morality, especially since DNA testing has demonstrated that many convicts are indeed innocent of the crimes for which they are imprisoned.

All too often we hear that a murderer has been imprisoned, served two to four years, was released, and then committed murder again. Parole hearings, presumably aimed at determining if convicts have been sufficiently rehabilitated to be released, go on interminably. Victims and their relatives are forced to relive the horrors of the crimes repeatedly. Why? Remember the old radio program introduction, "Who knows what evil lurks in the minds of men? Only the Shadow knows!" Well, the Shadow is a fictional character. He does not sit on parole boards. I believe they should be eliminated. Ideally, mandatory fixed sentences should be imposed for each type of crime. Judges are subject to intimidation and corruption, like anyone else, and should be relieved of that burden. Repeat offenders should automatically receive a sentence double the previous one for each subsequent offense of the same kind. Generally, sentences for first time offenders could be much shorter.

Ex-convicts with a sincere desire to go straight upon release find themselves facing nearly insurmountable obstacles. Employers are reluctant to hire them. Those who come from dysfunctional or economically deprived families will find little help. Many suffer from diminished mental capacity, as well as emotional and psychological problems. Prospective employers and families alike shy away from them. One can find them among clients of homeless shelters. Even when they come from relatively normal backgrounds and are healthy, reintegration into society is extremely difficult. Complicate that with a substance abuse habit, and return to crime becomes the overwhelming probability. A program of education and career training during incarceration, mental health care, a guaranteed job and housing, and denial of access to harmful drugs would dramatically reduce the likelihood of reoffending.

Systems tend to change slowly even when based on faulty assumptions. Those in control have a vested interest in keeping things as they are. It is much easier to make relatively minor adjustments than to effect fundamental changes. The first change that must be made is in our attitude. Our motives must go from punishment or rehabilitation to the **protection of society.** Rehabilitation is a wonderful objective, but the only person that can bring it about or know that it has happened is the convict. I learned a lot about punishment from my rebellious son. Sometimes paddling his butt was necessary, but having to do it often only served to alienate him. It took a while for me to realize he was just like me, then a few more years to rebuild the relationship. We cannot force people to change; it has to come from within. We need to develop a new kind of prison that increases the probability of rehabilitation, costs less to operate, and prevents inmates and guards from abusing or corrupting each other. Bear with me as I describe such a prison for you, and the benefits it should provide.

The way to protect society from criminals is to isolate them from society – every kind of society: family, friends, the public, professional, and criminal society. Inmates should have private cells that they never leave. The cells should give no opportunity for visual, voice, or personal contact with other inmates or guards. A simplified built-in computer terminal would provide for family and friends to visit from remote locations, a means of communicating with prison administrations regarding any special needs, and as an educational terminal. It should allow access to the news once or twice a day, and perhaps exercise programs, but not television programs or music that contain violent or otherwise objectionable material. Restricting the amount of time spent with sources of entertainment would almost certainly move the inmate to take advantage of educational programs, if only to avoid boredom. Making the programs such as correspondence courses interactive would permit testing and awarding of credits toward a college degree.

All the inmate's needs, including food, laundry, toiletries, should be supplied and removed through a blind opening in the wall, preferably by an automated system. Every effort should be made to provide a safe and pleasant environment, possibly including a small desk with writing materials, some exercise equipment, a chair, water cooler, toilet and shower. Nothing should be allowed into the cell from anyone outside the prison. That should prevent any kind of contraband from reaching any prisoner. All deliveries should be to cell numbers, not to prisoners by name. Maintaining the prisoner's anonymity is a way to insure the prisoner's safety and everyone's security.

There may be times when it is necessary to enter the prisoner's cell to perform repairs, provide medical care, or some other valid reason. A dispatcher at a remote location should control all such access. Ideally, each cell should have a vestibule with an inner and outer door, only one of which can be open at one time. Closed circuit TV cameras in the cell, vestibule, and corridor should permanently document all access, but only while guards and service providers are accessing the cell or are inside. Their identities must be verified electronically at time of entry, in addition to being recorded on video and audio. Having access controllers selected at random at the beginning of each shift and maintaining prisoner anonymity should minimize the possibility of collusion to bypass security protocols. As you have probably figured out by now, such a prison could be operated with a much smaller staff, and would probably not require large walled compounds, workshops, guard towers, etc.

An inmate's stay would begin with indoctrination on how to use the equipment, what the educational choices are, what the rules and regulations are, what the consequences are for violating them, and the process for getting reintegrated into society. Near the end of the sentence, inmates would be required to return their cells to the condition in which they received them. Then, they would be allowed to work for a few weeks to service other inmates' needs in the kitchen, laundry, warehouse, or in janitorial services. Their performance and behavior during that period would determine whether they get released or returned to confinement. When released, they would be provided with housing and work until they become self-sufficient. If we don't want people to be forced back into crime, we must provide alternatives.

There will always be a few who choose to damage their cell, terminal, or other equipment. I believe very few will damage their only access to the outside world. Having all water sources controlled electronically and prevented from overflowing by sensors would leave little else that could cause severe or costly damage. The inmate should have to live with damage caused intentionally, and be required to repair it as a condition of release. All of this serves to communicate that actions have consequences, and may instill a sense of responsibility.

If I were ever incarcerated, whether justly or unjustly, that is the kind of prison I would prefer to be in. Prison inmates are people, and should be treated as such. If we want them to be rehabilitated, then we must provide a safe environment that is free of criminal influence, sex, drugs, alcohol, or even cigarettes. Inmates should receive proper nutrition and all their essential personal needs. If they choose to participate in religious services, they should be allowed to do so by terminal, providing no other inmate can be seen or heard. Most importantly, there must be no opportunity for criminal activity of any kind.

So much crime and violence stems from substance abuse that breaking those habits must become a top priority. Success in that area will dramatically lower prison populations, and the costs of prisons. Much sexual predation is related to substance abuse, as is much violence and property crime. This method of incarceration provides no opportunity for riots or abuse by guards or other inmates. Deprived of human contact and lacking other forms of diversion, the inmate may be more likely to pursue self-education. It is also possible that it may cause the inmate to long for, and possibly to develop a greater respect for other human beings. I believe very strongly that it would dramatically reduce the recidivism rate.

There may be people who think this cruel and unusual punishment. It's not punishment at all. The inmate's physical needs are met. He is not abused in any way. Some psychologists could speculate that social deprivation might cause the inmate psychological harm. I would ask them, "As compared to what – getting gang raped, forced into drugs or criminal activity, intimidated, injured or killed?" A criminal who has committed the acts that put him in jail is already psychologically harmed. I reject the notion that someone can be guilty of a crime against society yet be considered sane. Truly sane people do not murder, rape, rob, cheat, or otherwise abuse their fellow man. Charles Manson is still sitting in prison. Few of us would go so far as to consider him sane.

In a previous chapter, I told the story of my encounter with a violent juvenile offender and his gang. Why was he allowed to commit twenty-seven violent crimes before the age of seventeen? The young criminal can be the most dangerous of all, and should be treated as such. Age is not a factor, the willful commission of violent crime is. I don't believe we want them placed in the present prison system, which is little more than a university for crime. Reform schools and juvenile detention centers do little to rehabilitate them. We must always keep the protection of society foremost in our minds.

How can we replace our current penal infrastructure with this kind of system? Slowly. Build one isolation unit in each major metropolitan area, and use it for violent and career criminals, then expand it to include other crimes. Leave the existing prisons for white-collar criminals who pose no physical danger to society. Even there, modifications can be made to have existing prisons approximate the conditions in the new facilities. I had occasion to visit the Metropolitan Correction Center, a high-rise federal jail in downtown Chicago, which has individual cells, provides a safe environment for inmates, and good supervision. It did not have the kinds of problems that the jail in which Richard Speck was housed. I deduce from this that jail design can play a major role in minimizing criminal activity in prisons.

There should be little doubt that an environment free of sex, violence, drugs, and alcohol could reduce prison populations dramatically, and reduce the cost of operating our prisons sufficiently to offset the cost of new construction. The high technology equipment required is far less costly today than it was just a few years ago, and it is essentially a one-time expense. A high-rise prison requires far less land, is easier to secure, requires less staff, has lower utility costs, and can be located anywhere. I believe that sentences could be shortened in such an environment. Consider that, using 2009 cost and population figures already cited, cutting prison populations by half would reduce incarceration costs by approximately $31 billion (1,148,700 X $27,000) plus the reduction in operating cost.

An acquaintance of ours had a long term substance abuse problem. She held a responsible position as a public employee. Her family was aware of the problem, but they could not afford to pay for drug treatment, and there was no way to get her into such a program involuntarily. She embezzled more than $100,000 from her workplace to support her habit, and was ultimately arrested and convicted. The family mortgaged their home to pay her legal fees, and is in dire financial straits. After serving two years of her sentence, she was released. Released to what? After more than a year without a job, she found she could get a job by lying on her application. She was hired by two successive employers, and, in each case, was fired within weeks after the employers did background checks. She came out of prison clean and determined to change her life, but there was no way for her to do that. Although she cannot afford hard drugs, she is abusing alcohol again. She is married with children, but the future of her family is very much in question. I have seen many like her when I volunteered among the homeless. Her story is repeated thousands of times every year. It is a tragic waste of humanity.

Statistics suggest that there is a racial component to the incarceration and recidivism rates. Blacks are incarcerated at more than twice the rate of Hispanics, and more than five times that of whites or Asians. That might lead one to conclude that there is some inbred or ingrained tendency toward criminal behavior, but that would be incorrect. A careful examination of available data shows an enormous disparity in income, health, life expectancy, and family structure between whites and blacks. The data for Hispanics is unreliable because approximately 25% of their population consisted of illegal immigrants.

RACIAL CHARACTERISTICS OF INCARCERATED POPULATIONS, 2008								
	All Races		**White**		**Hispanic**		**Black**	
Population total (1)	301,483,000	100.0%	197,159,000	65.4%	47,485,000	15.8%	38,076,000	12.6%
Incarcerated (2)	2,305,919	0.76%	864,700	0.44%	432,300	0.91%	887,800	2.33%
Rate per 100,000	765		439		910		2,332	
Households (1)	117,181,000	100%	82,884,000	70.7%	13,425,000	11.5%	14,595,000	12.5%
Median Income (1)	$ 50,303		$ 55,530		$ 37,913		$ 34,218	
Per Capita Income (1)	$ 26,964		$ 31,313		$ 15,674		$ 18,406	
Persons per household	2.6		2.4		3.5		2.6	
Civilian workforce (3)	132,255,000		107,849,000		18,235,000		14,973,000	
Unemployed (1)	6,094,000	4.6%	4,475,000	4.1%	1,120,000	6.1%	1,187,000	7.9%
Workers per household	1.13		1.30		1.36		1.03	
Persons in poverty (1)	39,829,000	13%	17,024,000	8.6%	10,967,000	23%	9,379,000	24.7%
In fair/poor health (4)	9.5%		8.4%		12.8%		14.6%	
Uninsured (1)	46,340,000	15.4%	21,320,000	10.8%	14,558,000	30.7%	7,284,000	19.1%
Life expectancy (5)	77.9		78.4		?		73.6	
1. Census Bureau, Current Population Survey 2008				4. Centers for Disease Control, Table 57				
2. Bureau of Justice Statistics, federal, state, & local data				5. Centers for Disease Control, Table 103				
3. Bureau of Labor Styatistics, Table 592 (Total includes other races. Some White and Hispanic numbers cross-reported.)								

How do we explain the incarceration rates? We should realize that the median black family's income is insufficient to afford adequate legal representation. The family of the acquaintance referred to above mortgaged their house to pay for legal fees rather than risk having their daughter defended by a relatively inexperienced public defender. The median household income of the black family does not give them that option. The black offender is much more likely to take a plea that involves jail time. Since there is only one wage earner, their household income almost certainly comes from working two jobs. Inevitably, the children are without parental supervision. Unemployment often exceeds 50% among black youth. If jobs are unavailable, higher education is not affordable, nutrition is lacking, and the parents have no money to spare, why bother to chase the dream? Drugs, alcohol, and crime are the inevitable result. The stress level tears families apart. More than half are single-parent households. Even if some balance could be established, it might take one or two generations to turn the cultural tide. There is nothing in the color of a person's skin that limits a person's ability to do well.

Just this week, a friend asked me, with a hint of racism in his voice, to explain why when hurricane Katrina hit New Orleans there was massive looting, but after the earthquake and tsunami in Japan people who had lost everything banded together to help each other. My response was that the Japanese have the third largest economy in the world with a much better social safety net, less poverty and unemployment, better education, and a culture of civic responsibility. Their stress level is lower, they are healthier, live longer, and have less crime. Look at any other developed country with a good social safety net, and you will find the crime rate is much lower than ours, and they spend less for prisons and their safety net than we do.

A 2011 Gallup poll surveyed the level of happiness in various countries. In the top ten were Denmark, Canada, and Sweden. The United States did not make the top ten. A year earlier, Forbes published similar results with the US fourteenth on the list. In Denmark, 82% of people considered themselves as 'thriving' compared to 57% in the US. The crime rate in these countries is also very low. A famous Bible passage (*Matthew 7:16*) says *"By their fruits you will know them."* Why is it that we consider ourselves so superior when we produce such bitter fruit? Perhaps it is time to reexamine our ideology.

"Distrust everyone in whom the impulse to punish is powerful!"

Friedrich Nietzsche *(1844-1900) German-Swiss philosopher and writer.*

Just War.

Wars have been fought since the beginning of time for primarily two reasons. Offensive wars were most often waged for the expansion of empire or territory, either (1) to increase the rulers' wealth and fame, or (2) to promote their political or religious ideology. Conversely, defensive wars are fought to (1) retain one's wealth and (2) to retain one's government or religion. All wars are therefore fought over wealth, ideology, or both. For much of our history, rulers waged offensive wars openly without having to justify them. The Roman and Greeks made no excuses for their wars of conquest. Their soldiers followed willingly because they received a share of the spoils, the wealth of conquered peoples. Under the feudal system, military service was obligatory. The serf went where he was told and did as he was told without question, receiving little more than a ration of food for his service. Over the centuries religious leaders, notably Augustine of Hippo and Thomas Aquinas, tried to provide moral guidelines for the appropriate use of force. Their findings are codified in the Catechism of the Catholic Church as the Just War Doctrine:

- *The damage inflicted by the aggressor on the nation or community of nations must be lasting, grave, and certain;*
- *All other means of putting an end to it must have been shown to be impractical or ineffective;*
- *There must be serious prospects of success;*
- *The use of arms must not produce evils and disorders graver than the evil to be eliminated. The power of modern means of destruction weighs very heavily in evaluating this condition.*

As the feudal system broke down, giving people greater independence, it became expedient for rulers to justify going to war in order to gain popular support. A favored tactic was to make all wars defensive. Hitler justified the invasion of Poland by the takeover of a German radio station by Polish troops, but the troops were actually bilingual German troops dressed in Polish uniforms. Patriotic fervor swept the nations, and the war was on. Demonization of Jews and most

East Europeans as 'subhuman' removed them from any moral consideration. Slave labor and extermination became major industries. Heads of the German military-industrial complex were thrilled. It seemed every German had something to gain. Much of Poland was depopulated. Germans replaced Polish farmers and business owners. Initially, German military seemed unstoppable, and casualties were light. How could any reasonable German not support the war?

We now know that our full-scale entry into the Vietnam War was based on an incident in the Gulf of Tonkin that never actually happened. The Gulf of Tonkin Resolution gave President Lyndon B. Johnson authority to wage all out war against North Vietnam without ever securing a formal Declaration of War from Congress. We put more than 550,000 troops into Vietnam. We killed about 1.5 million North Vietnamese, and lost 58,000 American lives. About ten percent of my high school graduating class did not come back alive. We bombed on a massive scale, defoliated the dense jungle with toxic chemicals to uncover supply routes, and fought bravely against communist supported North Vietnamese, who were not originally communists themselves. They merely wanted their country back from the French. Some of my friends still decry our pullout. They speculate that we might have been victorious if only we had stayed the course. It was our support of the French that drew the North Vietnamese into communist China and Russia's sphere of influence. In retrospect, what did we have to gain? Who had anything to gain from the conflict? You have probably guessed the answer. If we wanted our ideology to prevail, we should have promoted Vietnamese independence from France, built roads, schools, hospitals, and factories, and given them to the Vietnamese. Then they would have experienced the benefits of our ideology. The cost, by every measure, would have been a tiny fraction of what we spent to rain destruction on that country.

Over the past ten years, we have been fighting wars in Afghanistan and Iraq. It is important to understand the historical context of our involvement there. In 1953, the United States Central Intelligence Agency (CIA), at the request of British Intelligence (MI6), mounted a campaign to oust the democratically elected Prime Minister of Iran, Mohammed Mosaddeq. Mosaddeq had tried repeatedly to negotiate a deal with the Anglo-Iranian Oil Company (AIOC, later renamed British Petroleum, or BP) to get a bigger share of the company's profit for his country. When his efforts failed, he nationalized Iran's oil industry. Britain accused him to the United States of turning toward communism. The accusation was false. Nevertheless, the CIA overthrew him and placed the titular monarch of Iran, Shah Mohammed Reza Pahlavi, in complete control of the country in violation of Iran's constitution. The pro-Western secularist Shah became our biggest customer for military hardware. Over the next quarter century, the Shah served to restrain Soviet ambitions in the Persian Gulf. His huge security apparatus maintained tight control of Iranian society. Opposing the Shah was an anti-American fundamentalist Shiite cleric named Ayatollah Khomeini. After being arrested twice, Khomeini was exiled from Iran for fifteen years, spending most of that time in Najaf, Iraq.

In early 1979, the Shah, suffering from cancer, left Iraq as the people revolted. Khomeini returned to Iran and began the process of rewriting the constitution to make Iran an Islamic state governed by Sharia (Islamic law), with Khomeini at its head. In October, the Shah was admitted into the United States for cancer treatment. This angered the Iranians, who wanted the Shah returned to Iran for trial. Islamist students took over the American embassy in Tehran, and held 52 of its employees hostage for nearly fifteen months in what became known as the Iran hostage crisis. The US imposed an arms embargo on Iran. President Jimmy Carter ordered a rescue attempt, but it failed. Years later, former hostages identified Mahmoud Ahmedinejad, the current president of Iran, as one of their captors.

Iran's neighbor to the east, Afghanistan, was in a state of revolt against its widely unpopular Soviet-supported government. Groups of Islamic fighters, mujahedeen, had been attempting to bring down the Marxist government for several years. The government, which had close relations with the Soviets for decades, asked them to intervene. The Soviet Union put more than 100,000 troops into Afghanistan. Muslims from many countries, including the United States, flocked to Afghanistan to participate in the **jihad**, which means **struggle** in Arabic. The Soviets were still a superpower and ruthless in the prosecution of the war, nevertheless, they were unable to defeat the insurrection. The United States helped the mujahedeen by supplying Stinger anti-aircraft missiles. I recommend Steve Coll's book *Ghost Wars* for a more detailed treatment of our efforts there. Saudi Arabia, Britain, and other nations also supplied money and weapons. In recent years, we were offering $80,000 TO $150,000 per missile to recover all unused Stingers. Hundreds may still remain in circulation. The Soviets fought for ten years losing 15,000 troops and killing countless Afghan and allied Islamic fighters. By early 1989, they pulled out. A key figure in the fight against the Soviets was Usama bin Laden, a name all too familiar to us now. As soon as the Soviets were gone, we withdrew our support, leaving the country with a power vacuum that the Taliban and Al Qaeda were happy to fill.

In September of 1980, after years of border disputes, Iraq, under Sadaam Hussein, invaded Iran partly out of concern that the Iranian revolution would spread to the Shia majority in Iraq, and partly out of desire to be the dominant power in the Persian Gulf. The incoming Reagan Administration negotiated a deal with the Iranians for the release of hostages, agreeing to sell missiles to Iran in violation of the arms embargo by using Israel as an intermediary. The money was then used to aid the Contras, anti-communist rebels in Nicaragua. Oliver North and other Reagan Administration officials were convicted of felonies in the matter, but were subsequently pardoned by President H. W. Bush. The US and other nations supplied weapons to both Iran and Iraq, including chemical weapons. A stalemate led to a ceasefire agreement in 1988.

We have repeatedly acted to support our short term business interests even when it undermined our standing in the world in the longer term. This was clearly the case in Iran, Iraq, Afghanistan, and many other countries. Chile is another example. In 1973, President Nixon authorized a coup against the democratically elected president of Chile, Salvador Allende. The CIA had tried unsuccessfully to prevent his election in 1970. In 1971, Allende nationalized US copper firms, banks, and other interests, and began to expand social programs. If he had been left alone, he might not have been reelected because of the failure of his economic policies. Instead, the US government and several large US corporations spent millions of dollars to replace him with General Augusto Pinochet. Pinochet's government reportedly killed at least 3,000 Chileans and tortured about 29,000 during his seventeen years in office. He was subsequently indicted for human rights violations, embezzlement, tax evasion, and many other crimes. He died before he could be prosecuted.

The 1990 Gulf War started when Sadaam Hussein invaded Kuwait. His dispute with Kuwait stemmed from their use of modern horizontal drilling techniques to extract oil from nearby Iraqi oil fields. Sadaam's response was to conquer Kuwait. The risk that he might raise the stakes and attempt to move into Saudi Arabia, thereby threatening one of our major sources of oil, motivated us to form a coalition of thirty-four nations, including Islamic countries, to oust Sadaam's forces from Kuwait. Bin Laden offered the services of Al Qaeda fighters to drive out the Iraqis, but the Saudis, fearing his ambitions, refused his offer. Coalition forces drove Iraqi forces far back into Iraq, but stopped short of a complete takeover. After the war, American troops continued to be stationed in the region. The coalition imposed a no fly zone over much of Iraq. Weapons inspectors were sent in to find and destroy any weapons of mass destruction (WMD) that could be found. Large quantities, including chemical weapons, were found and destroyed. There were no nuclear weapons.

From the time of Mohammed, a portion of Saudi Arabia called the 'Sacred Triangle' (bounded by the cities of Mecca, Medina, and Yamama), was considered off limits to non-Muslims. Even today, a special highway bypass takes non-Muslims around Mecca. That is the cover photo on this book. It was taken by my friend Dennis Chaltry who was a contractor in Saudi Arabia. Many of the more conservative Muslims consider all of Saudi Arabia holy ground. The presence of foreign troops there is considered an affront to Islam. Bin Laden used it as justification for Al Qaeda's attacks on the United States and its allies, and his attempts to overthrow the Saudi monarchy. Had Al Qaeda succeeded in overthrowing the Saudi royalty, it would certainly have threatened our access to Saudi oil. Gerald Posner, in his book *Secrets of the Kingdom*, speculates that, in order to forestall such a possibility, the Saudis have rigged their wells with self-destruct devices that would shut down its productive capacity for a long time.

In 1993, Al Qaeda bombed the World Trade Center in New York. In 1996, Bin Laden issued a fatwa (religious ruling) against the United States, in essence declaring war. He followed that up with one in 1998 declaring war on American civilians. At about the same time, Al Qaeda bombed U.S. embassies in Nairobi, Kenya, and Dar es Salaam, Tanzania, killing more than 200 people and injuring several thousand. In 2000, they bombed the USS Cole, an American warship, killing seventeen sailors. The most severe blow came on September 11, 2001, when four airliners were hijacked. Two were crashed into the World Trade Center towers in New York, one into the Pentagon, and one was crashed into a field in Pennsylvania when passengers tried to overcome the hijackers. About 3000 people died in these coordinated attacks.

Bin Laden's headquarters and terrorist training camps were in Afghanistan in the mountains bordering Pakistan. The radical Islamic Taliban were in control of the government. They had been Bin Laden's allies in their struggle with the Soviets, and were happy to provide him a safe haven. After the 9/11 attacks, the US demanded the Taliban turn over Bin Laden and other Al Qaeda leaders. When they refused, the CIA, with a few hundred operatives and Special Forces working with several anti-Taliban groups, mounted an effort to bring down the Taliban regime and Al Qaeda. The CIA's operations are described by the key CIA field commander in Afghanistan, Gary Berntsen, in his book *Jawbreaker*. Berntsen tells that, in December of 2001, Bin Laden and his fighters were pushed back into the mountains at Tora Bora. Berntsen requested 600 to 800 additional Special Forces troops from CENTCOM to be positioned behind the Al Qaeda fighters to prevent their escape into Pakistan. Incredulously, his request was denied. General Tommy Franks, CENTCOM commander at the time, tried feebly to explain away the failure in his testimony before the Senate Armed Services Committee in July 2002. Many sources have since stated that preparations were already being made for the invasion of Iraq.

The reasons given for the invasion of Iraq were their support of terrorism, possession of WMD (weapons of mass destruction —

chemical, biological, and nuclear), and to free the Iraqi people from the dictator Sadaam Hussein. Iraq had no connection with Al Qaeda or the events of 9/11. Iraq's WMD had been destroyed after the 1990 Gulf War operation Desert Storm. David Kay, our chief weapons inspector in Iraq, cautioned the Bush Administration that our weapons inspectors found no evidence of any recent WMD activity. A massive disinformation campaign was launched to persuade Congress and the public that they did exist. Who can forget the warnings about a 'mushroom cloud'?

Most of the information regarding Iraq's WMD came from a single source, the Iraqi expatriate we called Curveball who was living in Germany. Tyler Drumheller, our CIA Station Chief in Europe, advised the administration that the German intelligence services warned us that Curveball's information regarding Iraq's WMD program was unreliable. He was an alcoholic and had provided information that proved to be false on other occasions. Drumheller describes these events in his book *On the Brink.*

Documents, which were apparently forged, were found in Italy indicating Sadaam had tried to acquire large quantities of yellowcake uranium from Niger in Africa. The CIA sent former Ambassador Joe Wilson to Niger to determine whether Sadaam had acquired uranium there. He had not. His findings are described in his book *The Politics of Truth.* The Bush administration ignored all the warnings, and included statements about Iraq's pursuit of nuclear weapons in the President's State of the Union Address in January 2003. When Wilson challenged the statement, the administration leaked the name of Wilson's wife, Valerie Plame, a covert CIA agent working on non-proliferation of WMD. They ruined her career and endangered her and every asset she worked with. Scooter Libby was convicted of lying to investigators in the matter, but President Bush commuted the sentence. It is clear others were involved in leaking her identity and had lied, but the chain of evidence was too convoluted for further prosecution. In case you are tempted to think that these are politically motivated statements, let me point out that most of the sources referenced above are Republicans, and the Vietnam War was waged by presidents who were Democrats.

It is quite likely that the threat to our oil supply was a factor in the strategic decision to invade Iraq. A friendly government there would have assured us of a reliable source. Our motives are brought further into question in a report by Rajeev Chandrasekaran, *Imperial Life in the Emerald City,* as quoted by Nobel Prize winning economist Joseph E. Stiglitz and Linda J. Bilmes in their book *Three Trillion Dollar War*. The report claims that our administration intended to privatize Iraqi industries including oil. When that proved impractical, we removed our troops from Saudi Arabia to minimize further radicalization of its populace. It also helped Improve cooperation between Saudi security forces and our CIA.

Our presence in Iraq became a magnet drawing Islamic extremists from around the world just as the Soviet presence did in Afghanistan. Apparently, we learned nothing from the experiences of the Soviets in Afghanistan, the Nazis in World War II, or ours in Vietnam. After ten years fighting in Iraq and eight years in Afghanistan, more than 5000 of our troops have died, and more than 20,000 came home missing body parts or otherwise injured. An estimated 100,000 Iraqi civilians lost their lives, plus at least 12,000 combatants. The cost to date of these wars is about $1 trillion, and the impact on our economy has become obvious. Our troops have done everything that has been asked of them, and have done it well. General Petraeus did a masterful job. They are not the problem. They did not choose this war. Our leaders, who had not experienced war themselves, and understood neither the nature of this type of war nor Islamic religion and culture, made the choice for them. Of course, we must take some of the blame. We allowed ourselves to be convinced we were defending the United States. Would you like to reread the first few paragraphs of this chapter – you know, the part about false premises, patriotic fervor, and military-industrial complex?

There are two ways wars can be fought. Conventional wars are fought by armies that are usually dressed in uniforms so one can know who the enemies and who the friends are. That can help to minimize the destruction of people and other assets that might be useful to the victors. You may recall that one of the first moves in operation Iraqi Freedom was to secure the oil fields. Asymmetrical wars are fought by an army facing enemies that cannot be easily identified. You may have heard of Vietnamese children with grenades strapped to their bodies, Iraqi women wearing suicide vests, or nameless and faceless booby traps and improvised explosive devices in both conflicts.

Traditional military tactics do not work in asymmetrical wars. To win a war militarily, you must know who the enemy is, and the enemy must care about either his own life or the lives of others. When the enemy looks just like your friend, everyone becomes your enemy. As ruthless as the Nazis were in World War II, they were unable to eradicate the resistance. When someone killed a German soldier during their occupation of Poland, one hundred civilians were executed in retaliation. When organized resistance arose, as in the Warsaw uprising, the entire city was leveled. Nevertheless, the resistance continued. Unrelenting sabotage prevented nearly forty percent of the supply trains crossing Poland from reaching German troops fighting in Russia. As an aside to the Soviet experience, we know that the Soviet Union came apart shortly after their pullout from Afghanistan. Some have attributed their collapse to Ronald Reagan stepping up our military spending to a level they tried to compete with but could not. Others credit John Paul II, the Polish Pope for uniting people against Soviet authoritarian rule. While both are true, hardly anyone points to the horrible drain on their resources posed by the ten-year war in Afghanistan.

On the surface, it would seem that the only purpose for overthrowing the Taliban in Afghanistan was to get rid of Usama bin Laden. If so, why then did we abandon the effort to capture him when we had the opportunity to do so early in the battle at Tora Bora? Why did the Defense Department refuse the CIA's request for a few hundred troops to cut off Bin Laden's escape? Once Hamid Karzai had been installed as provisional president of Afghanistan, it seemed the Taliban and al Qaeda were put on the back burner. Karzai was the ideal candidate. He was fluent in English. It was rumored he had been involved with a US oil company to promote building an oil pipeline from the Caspian Sea region to the Gulf. It was unlikely the Taliban would have supported such a project. The Taliban had killed Karzai's father, and he was unlikely to espouse their extremist beliefs. Since then, according to the New York Times, huge deposits of lithium, estimated to be worth about $1 trillion, and other minerals have been found in Afghanistan. Lithium is used extensively in advanced battery technology used in electronics, power tools, as well as hybrid and electric vehicles. We may never know whether any of this had anything to do with the decisions that were made.

Nine years after ousting the Taliban, on May 2nd, 2011, a Navy Seal team stealthily crossed the border into Pakistan in special helicopters. Good intelligence work led to the discovery that Bin Laden was hiding in a large compound in Abbottabad, Pakistan. They killed Bin Laden and several others, only one of which was armed, and collected a massive amount of intelligence. Within hours, he was buried at sea according to Islamic custom. He was living with his family, a virtual prisoner in his compound, and plotting future attacks. Muslims around the world protested his killing. What effect his death will have on terrorism worldwide remains to be seen.

Over the past several months, many predominantly Muslim countries are in popular revolt against their dictators. The Tunisians overthrew their long time President Zine El Abidine Ben Ali. The Egyptians deposed Hosni Mubarak. Both of them left without significant violence. Libyan, Syrian, Yemeni, and Bahraini regimes are brutally suppressing the revolts within their borders. There is much we do not know about the players in each of these revolts and what direction each of them will take. Under Hosni Mubarak, Egypt, which has a large Coptic Christian population, was relatively stable. Recently, fighting broke out between Christians and Muslims, and a large church was burned because of an unsubstantiated rumor that Christians had abducted a woman who had converted to Islam. Hopefully, this was an isolated incident. Only in Libya have the US and NATO, mostly Britain and France, intervened militarily, presumably to drive Muammar Qaddafi from power after his forces brutally attacked civilians in rebel held areas. Given the uncertainties in a post-Qaddafi Libya, why intervene there? Could Libya's huge oil reserves have been a motivating factor?

We have promoted, supported, or tolerated various dictators over the years, often for good reasons. There is no doubt that ruthless dictators have sometimes managed to provide a sense of stability by keeping sectarian and ethnic differences in check. In the former Yugoslavia, when it was allied with the Soviet Union, that was certainly the case under Tito. When Tito died and the Soviet Union collapsed, the various ethnic groups tried to assert their independence or dominance. Bosnia-Herzegovina and Kosovo, which are largely Muslim, tried to gain their independence from mostly Orthodox Serbia. Intervention by the US and NATO returned the region to relative stability after an estimated 100,000 people had been killed. Until World War I, much of the Muslim world was part of the Ottoman Empire ruled by the Sultan of Turkey. Turkey was allied with Germany during WWI. After the war, the Allies redrew national borders in the Middle East based on their spheres of influence without regard to the ethnicity and religion of the people there. Only a powerful tyrant could keep the various groups under control. That was the role Sadaam Hussein played in Iraq. Iraq is made up of about 60% Shia, 20% Sunni, 15% Kurd, with the remainder in other Islamic sects and a few Christians. While the Iraq war is largely over for us, sectarian violence continues almost daily. As this paragraph was being written, 27 Iraqi police recruits were killed and about 70 wounded in a series of bombings.

We have a fundamental misunderstanding of Islamic history, social structures, scriptures, and culture. The concepts of nationhood and democratic government are foreign to theocratic and tribal societies. The patriarchs of the clan, tribal sheikhs, and local clerics have far more influence than any outsider. In the absence of a strong central figure, often a brutal dictator like Sadaam Hussein, these societies break up into ethnic and tribal units. Such decentralization makes it extremely difficult for democracies to develop, especially in an atmosphere of theocratic fundamentalism, but it is not impossible.

Turkey is among the countries in the Islamic world which chose the path of democracy. Their example is worth understanding. Turkey had a mutually beneficial relationship with Germany for more than four centuries. The Turks sought German technology and trade. Turkey was an ally of Germany in World War I. After World War I, Kemal Pasha Ataturk, a general in the Turkish army, came to power. He moved Turkey toward the European sphere of influence. Among his most astonishing achievements was replacing the Arabic alphabet with the European, which was better suited to the Turkish language, and reeducating the population in just four years. After the defeat of Germany in World War II, Turkey became an ally of the US through the cold war. The Iraq war has turned Turkish popular sentiment against the US. Turkey has been seeking admission to the European Union. The key to winning hearts and minds lies in mutually beneficial relationships. It is not easy for outsiders to establish such relationships in the Islamic world. To understand why, we must understand how Islam evolved.

In a sense, many Muslims are very much like fundamentalist Christians. They believe every word in the Quran is literally the word of God. The Quran was compiled into book form more than two decades after the death of Mohammed, not unlike the Gospels in the New Testament. The chapters are arranged in order of length, not chronologically as they were given. This would not have been a problem except that Mohammed allowed God to change his mind on a number of issues, without explaining why an all-knowing and all-seeing God would need to do so. Consequently, there are contradictory passages that allow one to pick and choose which commands to follow: love and respect or dominance. The situation is even worse with the *Haddith*. These words and deeds of Mohammed were collected over several decades, and numbered in the hundreds of thousands. Islamic scholars winnowed them down to two authoritative collections of a few thousand. Some of Mohammed's deeds in the last decade of his life, if they were correctly passed down, were less than admirable.

As a young man, Mohammed led trading caravans from Mecca throughout the Middle East for a wealthy widow who later became his wife. In the process, he encountered Christians, Jews, and Sabaeans. He called them 'people of the book' because of their monotheistic beliefs and written scriptures. Mohammed was illiterate, but learned much of the Torah (first five books of the Old Testament) from Jews and the Gospels from Christians. Mecca was a commercial and religious center for the surrounding Arab tribes. Meccans worshipped about 350 different tribal deities. Mohammed was dismayed with the polytheism and materialism of the Meccans. He experienced visions of the angel Gabriel who recited God's words to him. He began to preach the new religion, and gained a following. Islam means 'submission' (to God). Muslim means 'one devoted' (to God). Most Muslims are decent, law abiding, hard working, peaceful people, but the decentralized nature of religious authority makes it possible for radical clerics and others to misuse the Quran to advance their own agendas.

In 2005, a Danish newspaper printed a series of cartoons that caricatured the prophet Mohammed. Violent protests sprang up around the world, in which more than 100 people were killed. The cartoons may have been offensive, but they did not justify killing anyone. The Quran dictates that any response to an offense must be in proportion to the harm done – words for words, an eye for an eye, etc. Many Muslims have elevated Mohammed to the status of a god. That is as blasphemous as lampooning a prophet or saint. Most religions have evolved beyond killing each other over their beliefs.

How do we win the hearts and minds of Muslims around the world? Violence will not do it. Our experience in Vietnam and the Russian experience in Afghanistan has shown that it does not work. We must open an inter-faith dialog. There is much good in the Quran to enable us to use it to bring about a change in attitude. Moderate Muslims can shame the radicals, and they can frustrate their recruiting efforts. The following are several references from the Quran that are relevant to the discussion. The numbers in parentheses refer to chapter and verse in the Quran.

Throughout the Quran, God is called the all-knowing, all-seeing, the true, and many other names that comport with the understanding of Christians and Jews. That tells us that God cannot make mistakes, cannot deceive, and need never change His mind. Any contradictions or reversals in the Quran must be human error, not God's. He does not make mistakes.

- God's word is perfect. He does not give different messages to different people (6.115).

- God states plainly that He has given the Torah and the Gospels to mankind (5.46-47; 57.26-27; 2.136). The only conclusion possible is those Scriptures should be obeyed where the Torah, the Gospels, and the Quran agree.

- God does not differentiate between Muslims, Christians, and Jews. All are to be held in high regard (2.62; 2.136; 3.55; 5.82-83).

- In the Quran, as in the Gospels and the Torah, God tells us that we cannot compel others to believe as we do, and that any discussion of religion must be done with kindness (2.256; 109.1-6; 10.40-41; 16.125-126).

- Mohammed's mission was to warn unbelievers of God's judgment and possible punishment (42.48; 3.20).

- It is clear that the One who will determine who is and who is not a believer is God (Allah) Himself (7.87; 22.56-57).

- Almighty God does not need our help to punish unbelievers. The Quran states unequivocally that God will hand out the punishment. It also states that those that try to divide Christians, Jews, and Muslims, are the ones to be punished (4.150-151).

- We are certainly allowed to defend ourselves. God instructs Muslims that it is their duty to defend monasteries, churches, synagogues, mosques, and their communities (22.39-40).

- Fighting should never be prolonged once an enemy expresses a desire for peace 98.61).

- God has a special love for those who forgive others (3.133-134; 2.109; 5.45; 42.40-41).

What about those who claim to be Muslims, but who causes the deaths of other Muslims, Jews, and Christians, as has happened in Iraq, Afghanistan, Sudan, and other places around the world? They are murderers, not true Muslims (5.32; 4.92)

The concept of Jihad as a war against others does not fit with the words of the Quran, even though some may interpret various verses that way. Jihad is a struggle against our own evil impulses, not a war against people of other beliefs. We certainly have a right to justice, and a right to defend ourselves, but there is no heavenly reward for those who die while committing acts of terror. In all scriptures may be found seeming contradictions. It is for us to decide whether we choose to follow the better path or the worse, keeping in mind that God can only dictate the better path.

There is no such thing as holy war, and there are no winners in war — only losers. Some lose less than others, but all lose. Those who promote violence in the name of religion are simply striving for political power. Politics is not religion, and religion is not politics. If we wish to change the world for the better, we must do so by our example — living in peace, love of God, and love of humanity. Let us focus on the riches we share in common rather than the things that divide us.

"I hate war as only a soldier who has lived it can, only as one who has seen its brutality, its futility, its stupidity."

- - - - - - -

"The problem in defense is how far you can go without destroying from within what you are trying to defend from without."

- - - - - - -

"Every gun that is made, every warship launched, every rocket fired, signifies in the final sense a theft from those who hunger and are not fed, those who are cold and are not clothed."

Dwight D. Eisenhower (1890-1969), 34th President of the United States, Supreme Allied Commander Europe in World War II.

Separation of Church and State

We continually play with our language to make our words more pleasing or innocuous. "Lady' once meant woman of noble birth or refined manners; now, it is applied to any woman. A television news reporter recently referred to a murderer as 'that gentleman'. 'Personnel Department' is now 'Human Resources'. 'Used' is now 'pre-owned'. 'Gay' once meant carefree and joyful. Now it means 'homosexual'. 'Right to work' now may mean 'right for employers to fire indiscriminately'. 'Politics' was once related to 'polite' or 'civilized'; now, it is anything but. The same is true with 'freedom of religion'. It originally meant we should be free to practice whatever religion we choose. The state could not dictate the religion we were to believe or practice, and no religious institution could dictate government policy or laws. Its intent was to maintain a separation of church and state.

From earliest times, governments have tried to dictate what its subjects should believe. When Socrates taught that there was one God, The Greeks tried him for atheism, and sentenced him to drink poison. Religion and the state were intertwined. Heresy was akin to treason. The Romans were tolerant of other religions up to a point. Once per year, everyone was required to offer sacrifices to the Roman gods and the Emperor. Jews and Christians refused to do so. For a while Jews were exempted. Christians were brutally persecuted for nearly three centuries. Until the last three centuries, forcible conversion was a common practice. The Muslim religion was spread mostly by the sword. The Inquisitions were as much a political tool as religious oppression. Zwingli, leader of the Reformed Churches died in a war to forcibly convert Catholics. Martin Luther approved the burning of Anabaptists as blasphemers, the deportation of Jews to Palestine, or the burning of their synagogues. Calvinists killed Anabaptists in Switzerland. Catholics and Protestants were alternately persecuted and killed in England. Witch trials were a blot on the American continent and Europe. We should not judge past actions by today's standards.

In the eighteenth century, absolute monarchies began to be replaced by more democratic forms of government. Revolutions in the

United States and France aimed to give individual citizens a voice. But, it was not quite that easy to separate church from state. The churches' role in preserving public morality was replaced by civil and criminal laws. Prohibitions were imposed on drinking, drugs, prostitution, gambling, polygamy, homosexual activity, and indecency. They had little or no effect. Sects or cults proliferated under the banner of 'freedom of religion'. Instead of governments and churches imposing their religious will on the populace, people could impose their religious or irreligious will on governments and churches—forbidding prayer in schools, religious observance in public places, etc.

A man in California sued to have the phrase 'one nation under God' removed from the Pledge of Allegiance. He tried to use the Constitution to accomplish what the Constitution forbids — forcing his belief on everyone else. No one compels him or his child to utter that phrase. Why should he be able to compel others not to? They could simply say 'under me' if they chose to. If there is no harm, there is no foul. As an aside, the Pledge of Allegiance could be changed to make more sense. For example, am I really pledging allegiance to a symbol or to a nation? If I do not believe in a supreme being, am I not my own god? How about this version?

"I pledge, by all that I hold sacred, my allegiance to the United States of America, home of liberty and justice for all its people, and pledge to honor its flag."

In another case, a judge resigned his position rather than remove a statue bearing the Ten Commandments from a courthouse. No one was compelled to read the Ten Commandments. No one was compelled to believe that God exists, or anything else for that matter. No symbol of any particular religion was displayed. The government was not forcing us to believe anything. It was not setting up a state religion. The problem is that the proliferation of denominations, sects, and cults makes it extremely difficult to maintain fairness to all of them. In a pluralistic society, there could be dozens or even hundreds of groups wanting their symbols to be displayed, or services to be performed on public property. There is no practical way to accommodate them, so it is probably best to disallow all of them on public property. However, people should be free to display whatever religious symbols they wish on their own property. Whatever one calls a tree with decorations on it, it is a tree with decorations, not an official symbol of a religion. Our nation's capitol contains works of art depicting religious observance by various historical figures. Such historical representations of important figures in our history, even if they contain some religious symbols, are not the same thing as promoting their religion.

When the Russians, under Stalin, invaded eastern Poland in 1939, they imposed their atheistic belief on the populace. Churches were converted into warehouses and stables. Teaching of religion was prohibited. My mother was imprisoned for defying their orders. The Nazis who invaded Poland killed more than 9,000 Polish Catholic priests, six million Jews, and many millions of Poles and Russians. Both Hitler and Stalin attempted to replace religion with irreligion. Are not the people behind the Pledge of Allegiance case and similar efforts actually trying to do the same thing?

The reverse is also true. We want government to impose our doctrinal and moral standards on everyone, even when we ourselves fail to live up to them. For example, we want government to define what constitutes marriage, beginning of life, limits of decency, how we should teach the origins of man, and countless other issues. Government is made up of people like us. They don't know. All they can do is set minimum standards. It is up to churches and schools to set the bar higher, but, because they too are made up of people like us, they have had limited impact on our behavior. This is particularly true in the public school system where discipline and teaching of moral behavior has been abandoned. Apparently, it is also not happening at home. Before we ask why, let's consider what may actually be going on in our kids' lives.

"I am tolerant of all creeds. Yet if any sect suffered itself to be used for political objects I would meet it by political opposition. In my view church and state should be separate, not only in form, but fact. Religion and politics should not be mingled."

Millard Fillmore (1809-1865) *13th U.S. President*

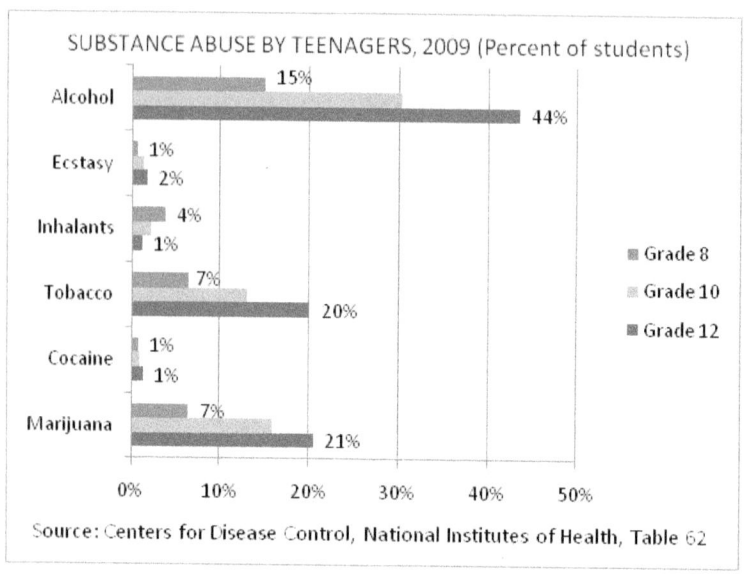

SUBSTANCE ABUSE BY TEENAGERS, 2009 (Percent of students)

Source: Centers for Disease Control, National Institutes of Health, Table 62

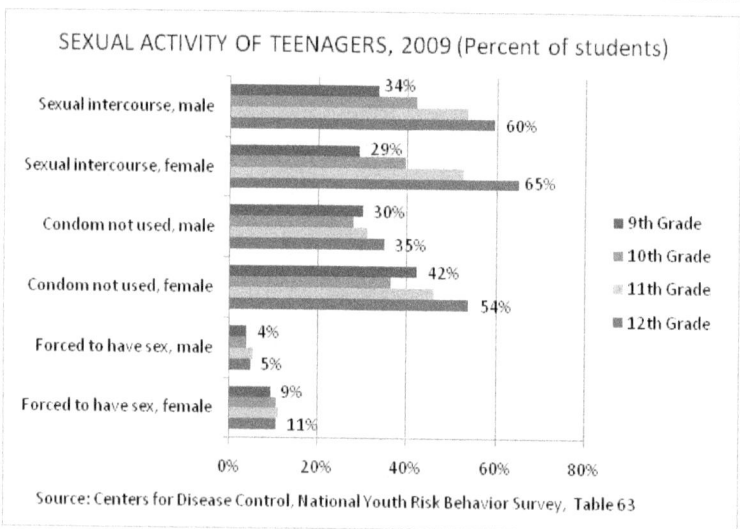

SEXUAL ACTIVITY OF TEENAGERS, 2009 (Percent of students)

Source: Centers for Disease Control, National Youth Risk Behavior Survey, Table 63

A study released recently stated that 25% of girls aged 14 to 18 had some form of sexually transmitted disease, with human papilloma virus (HPV) that causes cervical cancer being most prevalent.

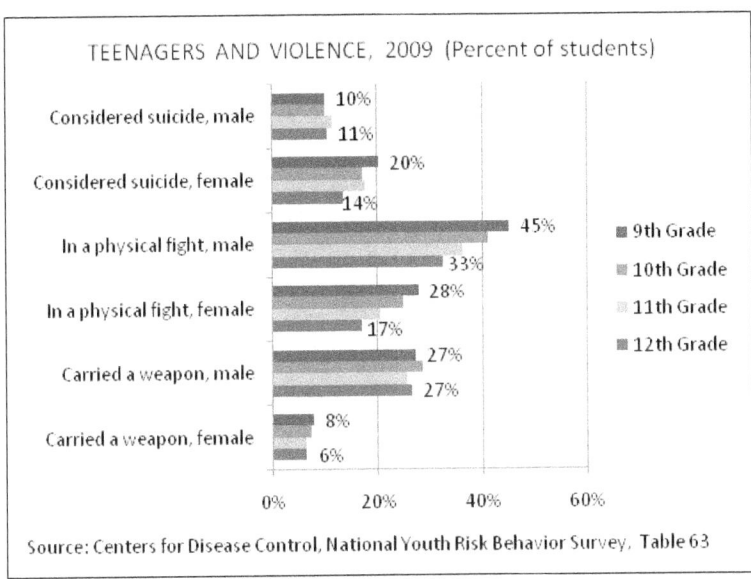

TEENAGERS AND VIOLENCE, 2009 (Percent of students)

Source: Centers for Disease Control, National Youth Risk Behavior Survey, Table 63

Most of us are either unaware of what our kids are doing, or we are in denial about it. It seems that everyone else's children behave that way, but not ours. However, the numbers are large enough that they cannot be confined to one or even two demographics. Even if we believe ours are engaging in risky behavior, we are at a loss to explain why. There appear to be two explanations. The first is lack of supervision. Kids have much free time, and, unlike in previous decades, parents have inadequate time because they are both working, often multiple jobs due to declining wages. Women are increasingly becoming primary wage earners.

MEN AND WOMEN IN THE LABOR FORCE				
	1950		2000	
Civilian labor force	62,208	100%	140,863	100%
Men	43,819	70.4%	75,247	53.4%
Women	18,389	**29.6%**	65,616	**46.6%**
Source: U.S. Bureau of Labor Statistics http://www.bls.gov/opub/mlr/2002/05/art2full.pdf				

The second factor is the disintegration of the traditional family. More than half of all couples live together (cohabit) before marriage. About half of first marriages end in divorce, as do two out of three second marriages and three out of four third marriages. Those who are engaged when they decide to cohabit are twice as likely to remain married as those who are not. Those who grow up with both birth parents present are twice as likely not to cohabit before marriage. There are too many studies on the subject to list individually. A 2010 report by the Centers for Disease Control *(http://www.cdc.gov/nchs/data/series/sr_23/sr23_028.pdf)* is a good starting point to verify the numbers. A search on the keywords 'divorce and cohabitation' will lead to many more. Some may be misleading. For example, some indicate that the divorce rate has been declining, but that is only because fewer people are getting married. Those who cohabit without plans to marry tend to break up more often, and their cohabitations are shorter. Several surveys find cohabiting more stressful than marriage. Married men are twice as likely to remain faithful as cohabiting men.

A Dallas Morning News article by Christine Wicker in 2000 quotes a study by Barna Research Group, headed by evangelical George Barna, which shows a much higher rate of divorce for born again non denominational Christians (34%), Baptists (29%), Mormons (24%), than Catholics and Lutherans (21%). Even more surprising, the rate of divorce for atheists and agnostics is also 21%. The divorce rates are highest in the South. The lowest are in the Northeast. One reason given is a higher concentration of Catholics in the Northeast. That is true, but there are other equally compelling explanations.

The tragedy in all this is that they are having children out of wedlock. No one cares as much about a child as its birth parents and grandparents. It is difficult for a child to bond with their cohabiting parent's serial partners or their parent's partners' parents. The inevitable result is alienation and depression, constant custody battles, and financial disruption. That and the difficulty of raising children while working may explain why so many are raised by their natural grandparents.

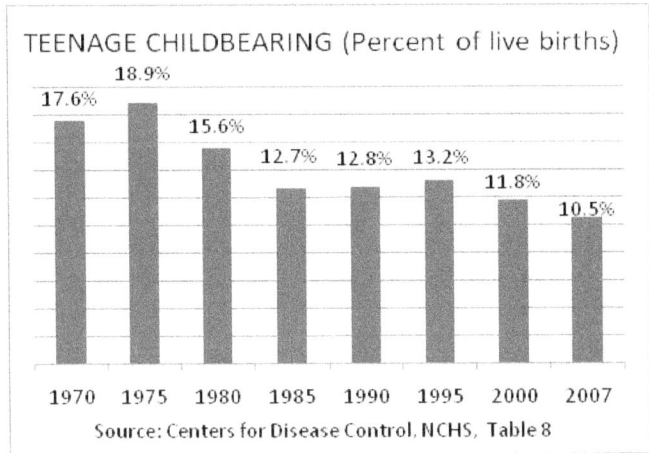

TEENAGE CHILDBEARING (Percent of live births)

Source: Centers for Disease Control, NCHS, Table 8

According to the Center for Disease Control, in 2008, 40.6% of children were born to unwed mothers *(National Vital Statistics Reports, Volume 59, Number 1, December 8, 2010)*. Once again, as in the case of divorces and criminal incarcerations, the statistics are worst in the South and among blacks. It is best in the more prosperous and better educated Northeast where women are having fewer children and having them later in life. Considering that 10.5% of the births are to teenagers; that means that 30% of births are to adult unwed mothers. Both are having frequent unprotected sex even though most claim to be using some form of birth control.

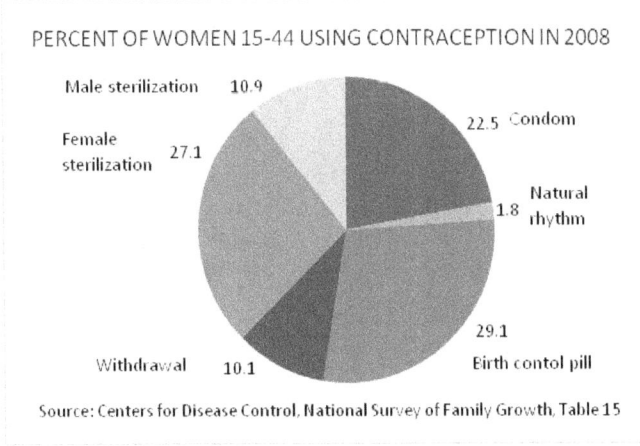

PERCENT OF WOMEN 15-44 USING CONTRACEPTION IN 2008

Source: Centers for Disease Control, National Survey of Family Growth, Table 15

All the teaching against premarital sex, contraception, abortion, homosexuality, sex abuse, and substance abuse by churches has done nothing to reduce any of these practices. That is why we ask government to enforce moral standards. Government is run by politicians. Have we forgotten the dozens of politicians' sex scandals in recent years? Parents are rarely aware of their children's sexual activity before it becomes obvious. Parents and teachers are then faced with choices: earlier sex education, teach abstinence, or give contraceptives to all children. Nothing has worked because the focus has been on sex rather than on love and social responsibility. What do our kids know about the pain of having a baby, the difficulty of raising it and providing for its support, budgeting time and money, the psychological damage caused by abortion, and the logistics of a teenager trying to be a parent? What do we teach them about how to select a proper mate for life, rather than letting it become a chance encounter? These should be taught to all children before puberty.

Throughout history, young women were generally married between the ages of twelve and fourteen. At seventeen they were considered old maids. Young men were somewhat older. Most kids were illiterate, and learned enough from their parents to get by in an agrarian society. Virginity before marriage was expected and sometimes even achievable. Industrialization, technological innovation, and the need for women to work outside the home and farm, made additional education, and therefore delay of marriage, necessary. Modern conveniences have increased young people's free time. Electronic media have filled that time with sexually suggestive and stimulating material. It has conditioned our children to believe that having sex is making love, and every child wants love. Sex is an adult activity, and most children want to be adult. How many times have we heard the expression that there are many kinds of love: romantic, sexual, familial, brotherly, platonic, friendship, etc? This may come as a shock to some, but there is only one kind of love, and sex is not love. Sex is a purely chemical and biological function instilled in living creatures for the purpose of procreation, thereby assuring the survival of the species. Because it is pleasurable, we have turned it into a recreational activity.

The confusion of love with sex is largely responsible for the horrible divorce rate, abortion, and unloved children. If sex were love, or even a form of love, there would be no rape, child molestation, masturbation, voyeurism, or other forms of sexual deviancy. The primordial urge is difficult to control, but it is not love. To prove the point, ask yourself the following:

- Does the typical rapist love his victim?
- Does a child molester love the child he molests?
- Does a man who has sex with a prostitute love her?
- Does a sex addict who pursues one sexual partner after another love them?

Why are we unable to restrain ourselves? We are all addicted — not just to narcotics and intoxicants, but to a drug produced by the pleasure center in our brains. Many animals have a biological clock that governs when they mate. Deer, for example, mate during a few weeks in autumn. It is called the 'rut', during which the pheromones females emit before ovulation drive males crazy. People are in a perpetual rut — a state of permanent craziness. That is what has made us the dominant species on earth. I am awed by the ubiquity of life, the variety of ways in which all living organisms reproduce and evolve. It is clear to me that there is some overarching intelligence far beyond ours that created the process and sets the rules by which it all operates. Man's brain has evolved beyond those of animals, yet it seems powerless against this animal instinct.

Many animal species have young that are born almost ready to walk and feed themselves. They need no clothing, shelter, transportation, or money. Human babies need all of these. That is why throughout history women's place was in the home. They did most of the work. Men provided protection and necessary resources. Babies grew to become helping hands. Then they supported their parents in their old age. The elders helped care for the children. It was a symbiotic relationship. The industrial revolution began to change that balance. Babies became increasingly expendable — a hindrance to both our occupations and leisure time activities, and a strain on parents facing economic hardship.

News reports over the last decade showed an increasing number of murders of children by sexual predators, embarrassed teenagers, party-minded adults, and murder-suicides by parents who snapped under stress, often due to economic hardship. Millions more are killed by abortions. We try to sanitize the term 'abortion' by referring to it as 'reproductive rights' or even 'reproductive health'. The lead-up to the legalization of abortion in 1973 was full of discussion of rape victims and mothers whose life would be at risk if they delivered their babies, and women who were being injured and killed in illegal abortions. There are no verifiable figures for rape caused pregnancies or those threatening the life of the mother. My guess is that they would not exceed five percent. If I am correct, then 95% of abortions fall into the category of inconvenient pregnancies.

Two-thirds of high school girls are having sexual intercourse, and more than half have had unprotected sex. They are not telling their parents about it, and they are not asking them for contraceptives. As the first draft of this chapter was being written, a sixteen year old girl who had concealed her pregnancy gave birth to what a child she claimed was stillborn. She placed the body in a plastic bag, and dumped it into a trash container. It is not altogether certain whether the child was alive at birth. The prosecutors were trying to decide whether to charge the girl with murder. Is the person on the inner side of the birth canal different from the person on the outside? Advances in technology allow us to see a fetus developing all the physical attributes of a baby within a few weeks of conception, and hear a heartbeat shortly thereafter. Is not the fact that the fetus has its own heartbeat suggest that this is a person? The argument that the fetus is not viable also makes no sense. A newborn baby is also not viable without support of a parent or surrogate. The truth is no one knows when a fetus becomes a person, or how person is defined. Courts can set a legal arbitrary standard, but that is all it can be – arbitrary. The very word '**fetus**' sounds like something foreign, when, in fact, it looks like a child, moves like a child, and is a **child**. What makes it acceptable to **kill** the child before birth but not after? What else can you call depriving a living organism of life? When someone speaks of having a household pet **put to sleep**, I am tempted to ask, "When will you wake it up?" The innocuous expressions cannot change the reality.

Of course, a woman has the right to decide what happens with **her body**. Does that automatically give her the right to do what she wants with the **child's body**? If it were her body, would the DNA not be completely identical? As you well know, the child's DNA is different. The woman is merely a conveyance for bringing it into the world, like a bus or train or airplane. Why do relatives sue for damages when someone gets killed or injured in a public conveyance? Their relative is not part of the conveyance. The conveyance is merely carrying the relative, and has the responsibility for delivering the relative safely to the destination. It makes no difference if the relative got on the bus by mistake, or is mentally or physically handicapped. The bus company is still responsible.

There is always a possibility that a child will be born with a physical or mental handicap. Genetic science now makes it possible to detect many such problems before birth. That may cause some parents to question whether to terminate the pregnancy. My wife and I have some experience in this matter. Our firstborn son, David, was born with multiple birth defects, and spent much of his early life in hospitals. He was uninsurable, so we paid his medical bills ourselves, and, as a consequence, were several years of income in debt. When he was four years old, we took him to a specialist in downtown Chicago. The specialist said, "Forget it. The kid is retarded. He won't live to the age of seven, but, if he does, he'll be a total vegetable". God knew better. David grew up, and led a relatively normal life for much of his thirty-two years, in spite of numerous health crises. In his teens, he ran and bicycled several miles per day and played tennis until his knees wore out. He became engaged to his high school classmate and had many friends. He held jobs as a groundskeeper and then as a bindery assistant in a printing company. He had zero math skills, but was quite intelligent in other ways, and had a wonderful sense of humor. Over the last twenty years of his life, David experienced total kidney failure, seizures and comas, heart disease, bone disease that reduced his height by eight inches, and finally thyroid cancer. He feared death, but trusted in God. He passed away at the age of thirty-two. Some would call him a "special needs" child. We prefer to think of him as a "special gift" to our family, and a "very special man". There were a lot of things David could not do. For example, David could never complain, could never hold a grudge, could never refuse a friend's request, could not stand to see someone sad, could not feel sorry for himself, could not give up when the going got tough, could not project machismo, could not refuse the most menial or unpleasant task at work, and could not care about or manage money. The most important thing he could not do was to leave our presence or end a telephone conversation with us without saying, "I love you!" Had we known in advance that fetus had defects, we might never have known such perfect love.

Abortion did not start with Roe vs. Wade. Estimates for illegal abortions and those obtained legally in other countries varied from 500,000 to 1,000,000 per year before abortion was legalized. The (not so) Supreme Court used the incredibly weak argument of 'right to privacy' in their decision. If privacy is truly a right, then we should not have to opt out of various businesses' privacy policies, have our private communications monitored, or even have businesses collect and sell our private information, all of which the Supreme Court has allowed. Even before Roe vs. Wade, I do not recall any cases of women being prosecuted for getting abortions. The fact that laws against abortion are unenforceable does not make abortion right.

The law makes no difference to my wife and me. We did not and would never have an abortion because logic and our religious beliefs tell us it is wrong. But, the politization of the issue has done nothing to minimize abortions. It is being used to capture the Evangelical and Catholic vote. For example, during a 2008 presidential campaign interview, John McCain was asked how he would handle the abortion issue. He answered that he would leave it up to the states, all the while insisting he was pro life. That would not prevent someone from crossing state lines to procure an abortion, and is not a pro life position. During Hillary Clinton's presidential campaign, former president Bill Clinton responded angrily to an anti-abortion heckler with, as best as I can remember "You want us to throw mothers and their doctors in prison." This too is strictly political pandering to abortion advocates.

My personal belief is that the Church is correct in its teaching, however difficult it may be for us to comply. It defines what constitutes **sin**. Government defines what constitutes **crime**. The two do not always coincide. When we conflate religion and government, we get the worst of both. If the debate were truly about saving the lives of the unborn, we would risk a constitutional crisis to repeal Roe vs. Wade. We would undoubtedly be forced to compromise by allowing abortion for rape, incest, and to save the life of the mother. We might even agree to provide contraceptives to minimize illegal abortions. We could never allow any abortion once the fetus has a heartbeat. We would make adoption easier and less costly. We would not reward irresponsibility by giving tax breaks and welfare payments to people who are incapable or unwilling to properly care for a child.

Abortion is not the only right to life issue. Just in the past month, I read of the death of Dr. Kevorkian, who had reportedly assisted more than a hundred terminally ill people to die and was convicted of second degree murder. He was no hero to me. Let me tell you who was. My father, who had survived Nazi concentration camps, died of lung cancer at seventy-two. During the last few months of his life, he was in terrible pain. The doctor gave him a narcotic cocktail, which did ease the pain somewhat. Dad used it sparingly because he wanted to be in control of his faculties so he could interact with his family. I sat at his bedside. He held my hand and said, "I love you son. I want to live." I mumbled, "You will, Dad – forever." I walked into an adjoining room to hide my tears. By the time I came back in, he was gone. There is no greater gift he could have given his family than to let us know how important we were to him. He would gladly have continued to bear the pain so we could remain together. Sometimes it takes a lot of love and courage to keep on living.

Our son David made his own decision not to be resuscitated and not to be put back on the ventilator. The doctors did ask us, in case he was unconscious, what would be our wish regarding resuscitation. Our response was, "What would we be bringing him back to?" His chances of survival were about zero. To bring him back for two or three more days of suffering, or to keep him on a ventilator for several days in a state of coma with no prospect for a life, seemed far more cruel than letting him go. Machines can keep a person nourished and breathing indefinitely, but that is not the same as living. Withholding such extreme life-prolonging measures when there is no hope for recovery is not the same as mercy killing.

Often, it is the children who cannot let go. In a room adjoining David's, in the Intensive Care Unit, was a man in his mid eighties. Many of his bodily systems had failed. There was no hope for recovery. The children insisted that every life prolonging measure be used to keep him alive. Whatever their reasons may have been – guilt feelings, religious convictions, or fear of loss – they were not thinking of him, but of themselves.

There are cases where the children are too anxious to turn off life support. The parent may have a chance to return to an assisted living condition, needing some support from family or other caregivers, but the children see it as an inconvenient burden. Memories are short. Didn't the parents put up with many years of even worse inconvenience and sacrifice in raising their children? Is there not a debt that needs to be repaid?

Abortion, euthanasia, and assisted suicides are contrary to the doctors' prime mission – saving lives. In Hitler's Germany, countless thousands of handicapped people were sent to 'special hospitals' where they were exterminated. Any prisoner who was too old or too weak to work was sent to the gas chambers. To the Master Race, they were all expendable. The notion that any human being is of no value because they are too old, too disabled, too poor, too sick, or too costly to maintain cannot be part of our ideology,

The right to life is a very complicated issue. It forces all of us (doctors, patients, and families) to examine our motives. There are many implications we may rarely think about. If we truly have a right to life, then we must have means of support and health care, capital punishment cannot be allowed, violent criminals must be removed from society, the mentally ill and handicapped must be cared for, the environment must be protected, and wars must be avoided.

Although my initial focus was on abortion resulting from teenage pregnancies, available statistics show that 20-29 year olds are having 57% of the abortions. Teenagers are having 16.8% and adults thirty years and older are having 26.1% of abortions. This suggests that something more than a mere unrestrained sex drive is involved.

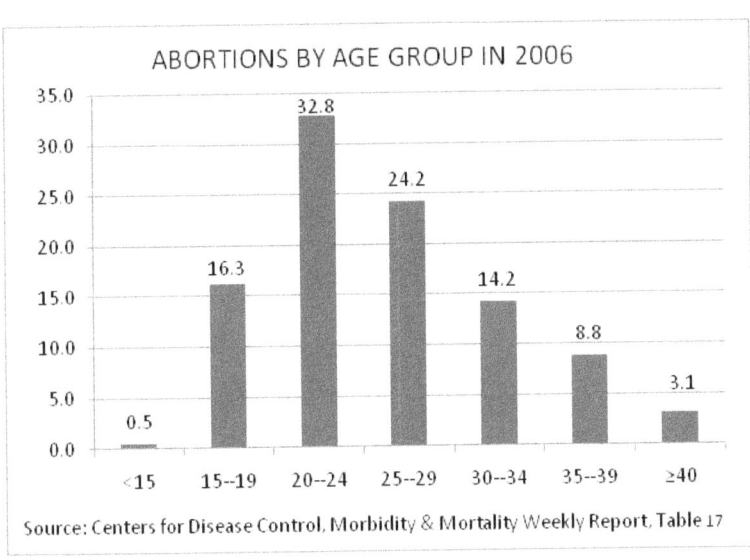

Source: Centers for Disease Control, Morbidity & Mortality Weekly Report, Table 17

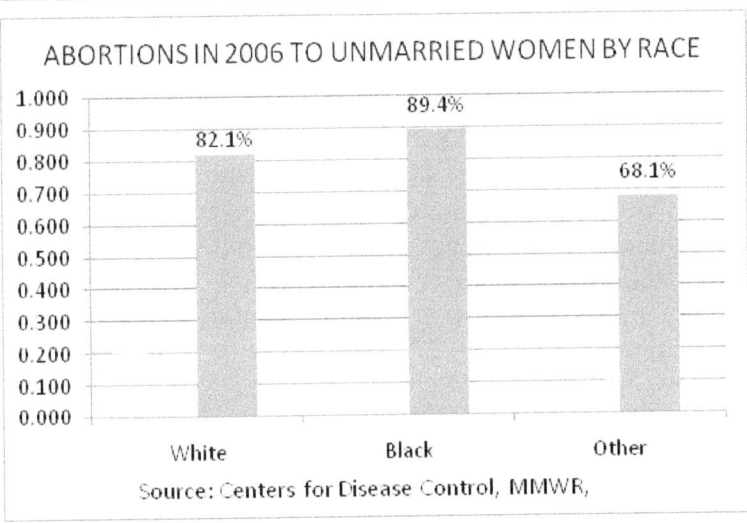

Source: Centers for Disease Control, MMWR,

Most of the abortions are performed on unmarried women. Black women are least likely to be married. Other race women are less likely to be unmarried than white or black women, possibly due to a significant portion of the Hispanics, the largest component of the 'other race' category, being Catholic. Black women are having far more abortions than white women or those of other races. This might lead one to conclude there some genetic factor is involved. I believe otherwise.

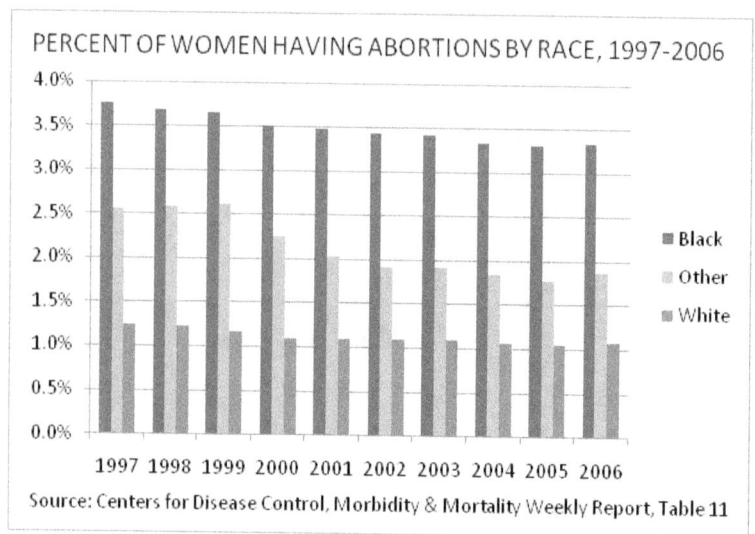

PERCENT OF WOMEN HAVING ABORTIONS BY RACE, 1997-2006

Source: Centers for Disease Control, Morbidity & Mortality Weekly Report, Table 11

In their otherwise excellent book titled *Freakonomics,* Steven D. Levitt and Stephen J. Dubner, conclude that crime rate in the United States has declined significantly because legalized abortion has removed many potential offenders, who are predominantly black. I believe they overlooked a number of factors. The number of abortions has been declining for more than two decades. Under their premise, the crime rate should have gone up, but it continues to decline. You may notice that the decline of abortions coincided with an economic recovery that began in the early 1990s and leveled off as the current economic crisis unfolded in 2005.

"Terrorism isn't insanity. It grows out of social conditions that are well known: poverty, social oppression, dictatorship, and a void of meaning in the lives of ordinary people."

Deepak Chopra (1946-   ), self help author

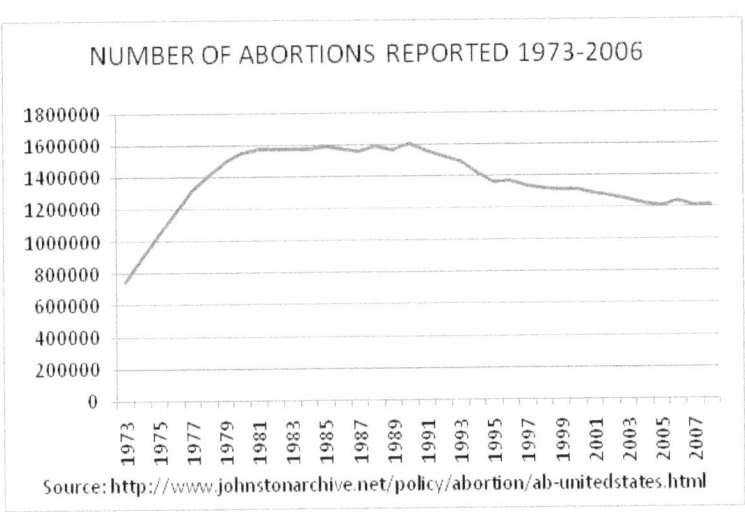

NUMBER OF ABORTIONS REPORTED 1973-2006

Source: http://www.johnstonarchive.net/policy/abortion/ab-unitedstates.html

The Civil Rights Act of 1964 and Voting Rights Act of 1965 reduced discrimination against blacks and women. As the Vietnam War heated up, unemployment dropped to 3.2%. More blacks were employed in private sector, military, and government occupations. Many pursued higher education. The rise of the black middle class began the decline in the crime rate. Development of DNA and other forensic technology, computer networks, and satellite communications made getting caught more likely. Police were also better trained. All of these factors suggest that the reduction in crime is not because of abortions, but because of economic factors. Blacks commit more crime and have more abortions than whites because, in spite of a growing middle class, the median income, unemployment and underemployment rate, access to proper nutrition and health care, and education levels are far worse than for any other demographic.

"Lack of money is the root of all evil."

George Bernard Shaw (1856-1950), famous Irish writer.

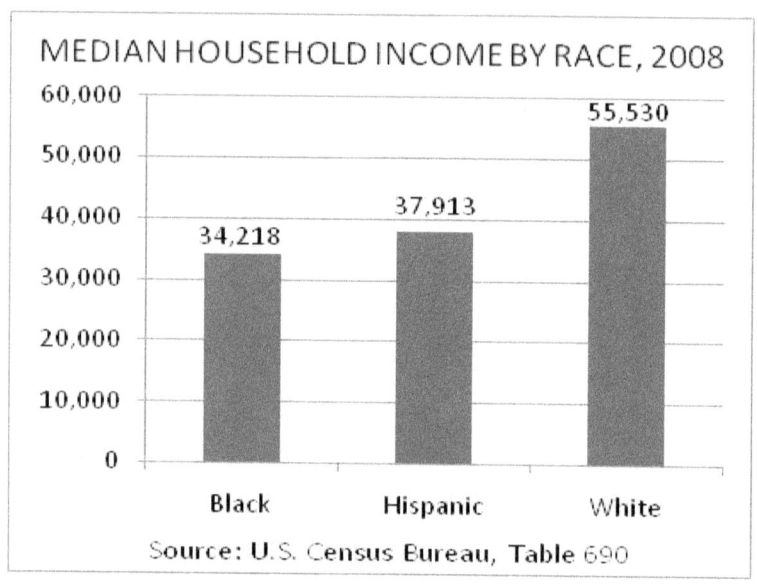

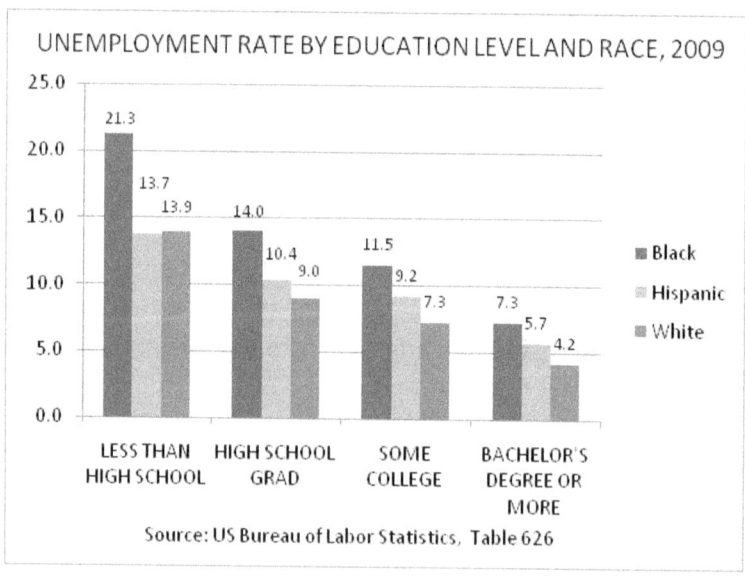

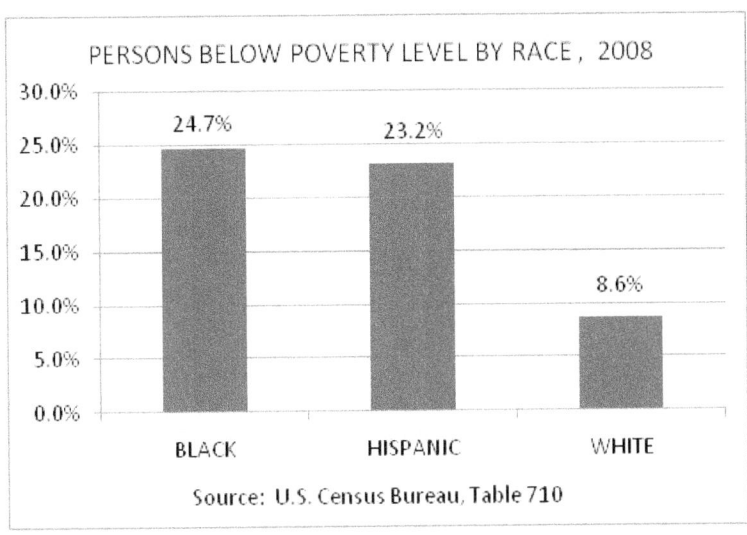

PERSONS BELOW POVERTY LEVEL BY RACE, 2008

Source: U.S. Census Bureau, Table 710

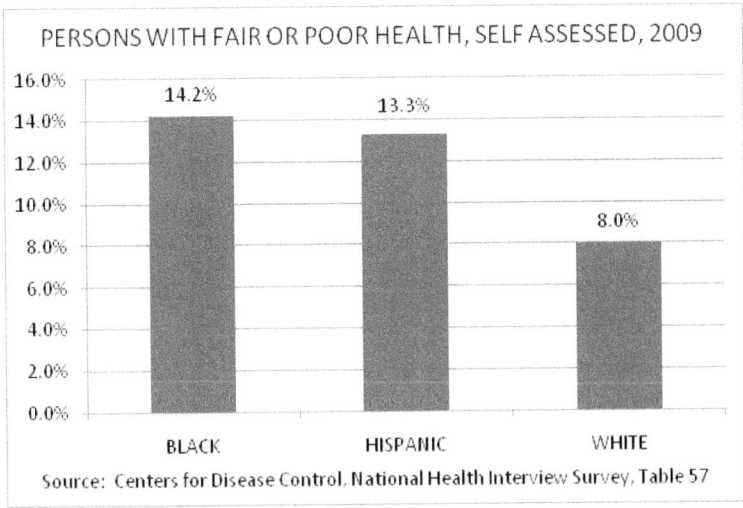

PERSONS WITH FAIR OR POOR HEALTH, SELF ASSESSED, 2009

Source: Centers for Disease Control, National Health Interview Survey, Table 57

You should have noticed a direct correlation between income, education, poverty, welfare, crime, substance abuse, abortion, and health from the above charts. Erosion of moral values certainly contributes to cohabitation, divorce, and abortion, but it does not tell the complete story. People are living together without getting married because most cannot afford to get married in the traditional way. The cost of college forces many to stretch their education out over many years, or abandon it altogether. The impermanence or unavailability of jobs forces many into group living arrangements. Having a baby may be their only way to get some financial support and health care. Many abortions are also for economic reasons. How else can we explain the fact that Hispanic women, many of whom are raised Catholic and are as white-skinned as women we classify as white, are having more abortions than white women? It is not about the color of the skin or ethnic origin.

Henry David Thoreau once said "Most men lead lives of quiet desperation and go to the grave with the song still in them." All too often I have heard someone say that there are no really poor people in America. They point to countries in Africa or South America where people are 'really poor.' The truth is that no one will let you build a mud hut, dig a well, cut firewood, plant a garden, or hunt for food year-round on land you do not own. We will not allow a witch doctor to practice medicine. We have built a society where the poor must pay for lodging, heat, electricity, water, food, health care, and transportation. It is a different type of poverty, but it is poverty nonetheless – a poverty of perpetual debt. The only relief seems to be in drink or drugs.

A growing attitude toward the plight of the poor is to disconnect social issues from our religious beliefs. This is exemplified by comments made by Glenn Beck on a recent television show. He suggested that the terms 'social justice' or 'economic justice' used by churches were merely code words for Nazism and communism. His words:

> *"I beg you look for the words social justice or economic justice on your church Web site," ... "If you find it, run as fast as you can. Social justice and economic justice, they are code words. ... Am I advising people to leave their church? Yes! If they're going to Jeremiah Wright's church, yes!*

> *"If you have a priest that is pushing social justice, go find another parish," ... "Go alert your bishop and tell them, 'Excuse me, are you down with this whole social justice thing?' If it's my church, I'm alerting the church authorities: 'Excuse me, what's this social justice thing?' And if they say, 'Yeah, we're all in on this social justice thing,' I am in the wrong place."*

Mr. Beck, I have lived under Soviet communism and Nazism. I found no social justice or economic justice in either ideology. They neither taught nor practiced it. However, I did find much reference to it in a book you should read – the Bible, especially Deuteronomy 15:4-6.

> *"And **there shall be no poor nor beggar among you**: that the Lord thy God may bless thee in the land which he will give thee in possession. Yet so if thou hear the voice of the Lord thy God, and keep all things that he hath ordained, and which I command thee this day, he will bless thee, as he hath promised. Thou shalt lend to many nations, and thou shalt borrow of no man. Thou shalt have dominion over very many nations, and no one shall have dominion over thee."* (Douay-Rheims Bible)

In the Bible, **God promises prosperity to our nation only if we care for our poor.** In the New Testament, Jesus repeatedly reinforces the message that a heavenly reward awaits those who provide care for their needy neighbors. Most of us do not have the resources to prevent a friend's home from being foreclosed or to care for them when they lose their jobs. Our churches and charitable organizations also lack the resources. Welfare as it is now done offers no path out of poverty. Government policies and business practices that deny people the opportunity for a job that pays a living wage are responsible for our personal and national economies.

Instead of dealing with our most critical issues, our politicians devote an inordinate amount of time to deciding whether gays should be allowed to serve openly in the military, or whether gays should be allowed to marry. Until I was seventeen years old, I had no idea there was such a thing as a homosexual. My first exposure came when a group of my friends and I drove to a Lake Michigan beach. Among the sand dunes in that state park was a group of about fifty young people wearing funny looking clothes. My friends told me they were 'queers', and warned me to stay away from them. I had no idea that had anything to do with sex. Some of their clothes and hairdos looked queer, but I thought it was just a gang thing. Later I learned that the police were doing 'queer patrols' in public park restrooms looking not for muggers but homosexual predators. I grew up in an environment where no one ever talked about sex, so I was understandably naive. Even after I learned what being homosexual meant, I could not understand it because I never experienced the least physical attraction for any male.

In the past there were, and in some places still are, laws against sodomy, adultery, and nudity. These are carry-overs from days when government dictated religion and religion dictated laws. We tend to have a twisted sense of morality. We want the rest of the world to abide by our rules, even though we often fail to do so ourselves. I will not bother to name the politicians and religious leaders who have railed against homosexuality to get our votes, but have engaged in the very practices they condemn. Please do not misunderstand me; I consider most homosexuality unnatural and practicing homosexuality a sin. Nothing will make me become a homosexual regardless of what the law says. Most of the laws against it are punitive in nature. They do not actually prevent people from becoming homosexual. So why do we bother to make them? We should concern ourselves with human rights, not gay rights. Gays should be treated like everyone else. We do not need yet another way to divide people.

An example of the hypocrisy is our treatment of openly gay people in the military. In many cases they have performed their duties heroically, and have not engaged in sexual activity while on duty. Why should they lose their career, pension, and other benefits? We allow men and women to serve side by side in the military. It is not uncommon for them to engage in heterosexual activity, even though many of them have wives and husbands at home. I also consider adultery a sin. A CNN news report showed that about 22% of women serving in Iraq experienced sexual harassment or rape during their deployment. Are their abusers being kicked out of the military? Why are they not treated the same as the homosexuals? The Constitution guarantees us equal treatment under the law, and the right to privacy. I don't want Big Brother invading my bedroom or yours. I get my moral teaching from my church, not my government.

Another example is the attempt to pass the Defense of Marriage Act to define marriage as the union of one man and one woman. Why do we need a law to tell us what we already know? Given our ridiculous divorce rate, should not the Act read, "the union of one man at a time to one woman at a time"? We honor marriage by bonding for life in mutual support and bringing new life into the world. It represents the complete union of two people. Is anyone clamoring for a law against divorce? In many cases, divorce is also a sin. The truth is that the Defense of Marriage Act has nothing to do with defending marriage, and everything to do with politics. It is yet another way to divide us. Some laws aimed at homosexuals have serious consequences for heterosexuals as well.

Consider this example. Two heterosexual divorced women, or perhaps single mothers, each with young children, decide to live together so one can care for the children while the other goes to work to support them. They form a household. Should the stay-at-home mom and her children be deprived of health insurance? If the working woman dies, should she not be able to bequeath her pension, home and other assets to the other mom? In the absence of closer family, should the stay-at-home mom not be allowed to raise the working woman's children? How about siblings living together? Should they not be able to form a household and share benefits? The law should be concerned with the household, not people's personal and private relationships. We should all be free to determine what constitutes our household, and it should have equal protection under the law.

People have gone to great lengths to explain homosexuality. Scientists have searched for a gene that may be responsible. It is like any relatively new science – people try to apply it to everything, until they find something to disprove it. Genetics may play a part, but it cannot explain much of what we see. I do not doubt that there are people who are born with a predisposition to homosexuality. I believe there are ways by which people choose homosexuality either consciously or subconsciously.

Most children's first sexual experiences are with close friends of the same sex. There is a barrier between the sexes that makes such experience more convenient. For most children masturbation is their first sexual experience. Boys will tend to voyeurism to stimulate themselves. If they do not move beyond that phase, they continue as peeping toms. Some of the hidden camera stuff on the Internet is indicative of that. I won't get any more graphic. You can figure out how this works for cross-dressing, various fetishes, and other deviant behaviors. I am not proposing this as yet another theory of everything, yet if you consider various forms of deviancy, you will see some underlying truth, perhaps even as it applies to some forms of homosexuality.

Heterosexual adults can also become homosexual or bisexual. A significant number of heterosexual prison inmates emerge as homosexuals. People who have been married for many years, have had good relationships with their spouses, and raised children, suddenly announce they are gay. A governor, with his wife beside him, announced he was resigning because he is gay. A senator was arrested for disorderly conduct for allegedly soliciting gay sex in a public men's room. You will notice that I have switched to the term 'gay' now. I define the term as 'carefree'. Some of these people are obviously free of any care for their spouses, preferring the satisfaction of their sexual appetites to the honor and dignity of family life. If they were born gay, they would have recognized it long before getting married and having children. Even if they did not know their sexual orientation and avoided premarital sex, they would certainly have figured it out after a year or two. But that explanation fails when a fifty or sixty year old person discovers it after twenty-five years of marriage. The answer lies elsewhere.

We miss the point when we focus on homosexuality rather than what has become an epidemic – sexual addiction. We are continually bombarded by sexually explicit material, much of which is easily available to any twelve year old on the Internet. A particularly disturbing element is the degradation of women. How do young people with raging hormones resist such an assault? Where do we set the limits? Should we institute censorship? It is probably too late. The Internet is available to everyone, and it is not easily controlled. Pornography leads to social paralysis – an inability to establish really meaningful loving relationships – and to dissatisfaction with one's spouse. We may associate sexual arousal with love, but it is not. That feeling does not and cannot last.

Perhaps the following analogy will explain how human sexuality works. Think of sex as eating ice cream. A person who gets a cup of vanilla ice cream once per month will savor the moment, and will continue to enjoy vanilla ice cream for a long time. Allow him to have it every week, or even more often, and he will begin to grow tired of it. He will begin to experiment with different ways of serving it. He will continue to want ice cream, but will want to try more exotic flavors. Fantasizing about the more exotic flavors makes plain vanilla less palatable. Once he has had the more exotic flavors, he can never fully enjoy plain vanilla again. He will move on to ever more bizarre combinations until the ice cream can hardly be recognized as such. In the process, he destroys his health and any chance of happiness. Ice cream has become his god, and yet, no ice cream can ever please him again. In sex, as in eating ice cream, novelty is exciting. It is nature's way of limiting inbreeding, thereby assuring a strong species. The genetic clock limits sexual activity in many animals. Man has learned to turn back the clock.

Sexual addiction can sneak up on us just like addiction to alcohol, drugs, or gambling. It takes a conscious effort to redirect our thoughts to decency, loyalty, honesty, integrity, modesty, kindness, compassion, and forgiveness. Without those, there is no romance and no true love. Most of us want our children and grandchildren to respect us for having put them and their mothers and fathers first before our animal instincts or our egos.

More of us are living longer than ever before in living memory. As we get older, we usually lose our occupations, are less able to enjoy our recreations, and many of our friends and relatives die off leaving us surrounded by strangers. Even if they are well meaning, it is not the same as family. How can I express to you the joy we feel when one of our grandchildren looks up at us and says, "Grandpa, I love you" or "Grandma, I love you." We treasure every opportunity to be with our children and grandchildren. What would holidays be without them? To love and be loved is the greatest gift there is. It is a tragedy to miss the opportunity to experience it.

Mainstream religions have been the source of moral teaching since the beginning of time. Some may try to deny it, but what institutions can they point to that teach moral principles? Certainly it is not the public schools. Even those who deny it are the beneficiaries of standards established by religious institutions. Look at the various news and entertainment media. Do any of them teach the evils of abortion, divorce, violence, crude behavior, or the virtues of marital fidelity, respect of others, caring for the needy, and a peaceful lifestyle? Those who choose to send their children to private schools where these subjects may be taught, are forced to pay twice for their children's education, once in the taxes to support the public schools, then out of pocket for all private school costs.

I once read about some fundamentalist missionaries arriving in Siam, now Thailand, in the mid-nineteenth century. The king asked them, "Why have you come?" They replied, "To bring God to your people." The king then asked, "Tell me, where was God before you came?" Apparently, the king knew a little something about God. Another story told of a famous American evangelist, Billy Graham if I remember correctly, who was preaching in Asia. He visited a Buddhist monastery. He sat down with a monk, but had difficulty finding words to express himself, so he took out his Bible and began reading about Jesus Christ from the Gospels. After a while, he noticed that the monk was crying. Thinking he had offended the monk, the missionary asked, "What's the matter?" The monk replied, "I have known him all my life." The missionary was overcome by the monk's tears of joy. Jawaharlal Nehru, a former Prime Minister of India, was asked his opinion of which religion was most beneficial for mankind. His response was something like this: "I believe it is Christianity. If I had ever met a real Christian, I might have become one." How sad!

If we care about the welfare of our nation, we should encourage the practice of religion, not discourage it. Nothing gives anyone the right to dishonor another person's sacred symbols. We must build bridges of mutual respect to people of other faiths. Mohammed said, "There is no compulsion in religion." If we want others to accept our particular persuasion, let it be done charitably, through sound teaching and good example. That's the way Jesus Christ did it. In the end, God is the only judge.

Race for Space

Over the past decades, we have spent fortunes trying to get off this planet. To some it may seem like a horrible waste of our resources. Billions of dollars went into going to the moon, sending satellites to other planets, and building a space station in which people can live for short periods of time. What for? Any habitable planet is many light years from here. No technology exists that will enable us to reach it anytime within the next few centuries. Why would we want to get there? Because we may not have a choice. The rate at which we are gobbling up our natural resources and destroying our environment makes it an imperative. The population of the world has tripled since I was born, and it will continue to grow although at a somewhat slower pace. More than 7 billion people now share space on this rock. All of them require air to breathe, water, food, shelter, and fuel for heat, cooking, and transportation.

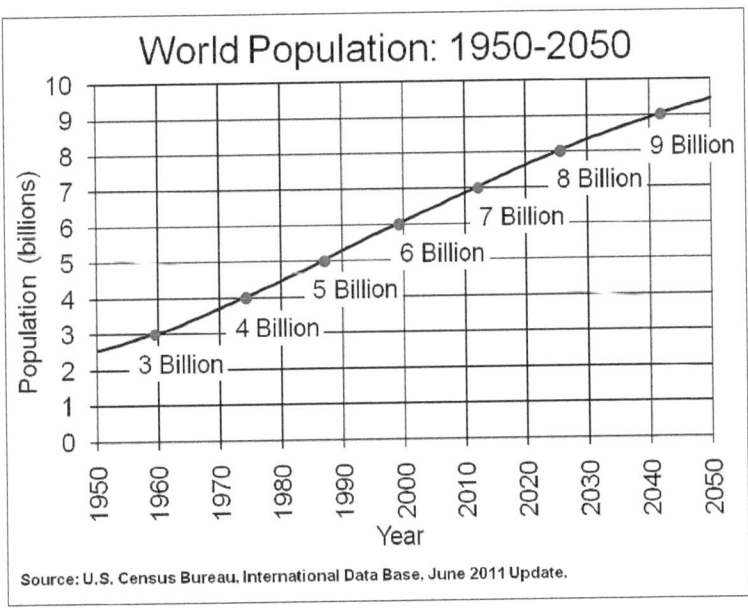

Source: U.S. Census Bureau, International Data Base, June 2011 Update.

We behave as if these resources are unlimited. No thought is given to what our children and their progeny will need to survive here. According to the CIA World Factbook, 70.9% of the world's surface is water, 29.1% is land. Only 10.57% of the land, or 3.1% of the earth's surface, is arable (usable for growing food), and much of that requires irrigation. Very few plants can thrive in salt water, and fresh water resources are diminishing worldwide. Desalination is much too costly to use for irrigation. Much of the land beneath us was under a sea at one time or another. Modern drilling techniques for oil and gas, aimed at increasing output, force water under very high pressure into the wells to fracture oil and gas bearing rocks to release their valuable contents. The water we pump in dissolves the salt deposits that have been buried for millions of years. Salinated water is released into rivers, creeks, and irrigation wells contaminating the soil and destroying the vegetation that feeds us and our livestock. Several television news reports showed flammable well water coming out of faucets in areas where these techniques were being employed. A spark would cause the effluent to burn. Non-stop advertizing by the industry claims hydraulic fracturing is the answer to our nation's energy independence, although most reliable estimates place our oil reserves at a maximum of 3% of the world's reserves. Pursuing our short term interests may very well bring on the famines predicted in the Bible (Revelation 6:56).

A tsunami in Japan earlier this year killed thousands of people and caused three of four reactors at the Fukushima Daiichi nuclear plant to melt down releasing radioactive matter into the air and water and causing the government to evacuate all residents within thirteen miles of the plant. The area remains in crisis for an undetermined amount of time. According to BBC News, Germany has shut down eight of its nuclear power plants, and will permanently shut down all others by 2022. In contrast, according to an Associated Press (AP) investigation, nuclear power plants in the United States, which were built to a useful life limit of 40 years, are being relicensed for an additional 20 years, often without proper safety reviews or much public attention. So far, 66 of 104 reactors have received license renewals, and no applications for renewals have been rejected. Regulators and the industry contend that there is no technical limit on the useful life of nuclear power plants. Some in the industry are planning for additional license extensions to 80 or even 100 years. AP states that "Records show that paperwork of the U.S. Nuclear Regulatory Commission sometimes matches word-for-word the language used in a plant operator's application." Nuclear power plants have been touted as being the cleanest, safest, and lowest cost source of electricity. You probably could not tell that to the folks at Fukushima, Chernobyl or Three Mile Island. Nuclear power plants cost billions to build. They do not normally produce air pollution. When nuclear fuel rods are spent, they remain radioactive. We have no absolutely safe way on earth to store them. They may remain radioactive for thousands of years. The desire of terrorist organizations to acquire nuclear materials speaks against their proliferation. As nuclear plants age, accidents become more likely. Exposure to radioactivity can be deadly rather quickly. In the two World Wars, we sank many German submarines. The batteries contained mercury, which is very toxic to humans. Now, we are routinely cautioned to avoid consuming more than small quantities of ocean fish because of their mercury content, even though fish in the diet reduce the risk of heart disease. When will we ever learn? We tell our kids not to play with fire, yet we do so all the time.

Hundreds of millions of vehicles, airplanes, ships, power plants, and heat sources are powered by fossil fuels. All of them are spewing heat and tons of pollutants into the atmosphere, which are said to cause global warming and climate change. There is no doubt that global ice caps are melting. We have satellite photographs showing miles of them disappearing. Flooding has become a worldwide problem, as has the incidence of severe weather. These have always been with us, but never as widespread and severe in recorded history. Scientists at the National Oceanographic and Atmospheric Administration (NOAA) have tracked the amount of carbon dioxide (CO_2) released into the atmosphere for decades. A majority of scientists agree that the rise in CO_2 correlates closely with the increase in global temperatures. Yet, the oil, gas, and electrical power generating industries have somehow managed to stifle their voices, claiming that these are merely natural weather cycles. Even if that were true, should we not be trying to avert these global catastrophes? Once again, money and politics trump common sense.

Plants consume CO_2, use the carbon for their growth, and release the oxygen that we breathe. Forests are the most efficient purifiers. At the same time as our emission of greenhouse gasses increases, forests are being cut down to make room for agriculture. Japan alone has a sustainable forestry program. We should remember that the Sahara, largest desert on earth, was once a lush tropical paradise. I highly recommend Jared Diamond's book, **Collapse**: *How Societies Choose to Fail or Survive*, in which he discusses current and past examples of short-sightedness that led to collapse of various societies. Bible prophecies predict global warming (Isaiah 30:26 and Revelation 16:8).

Every time gasoline tops $3.00 per gallon, politicians begin to speak of our addiction to oil. We are not addicted to oil; we just have not been given an alternative. I think it is more likely that our politicians are addicted to oil money. Otherwise our public transportation systems would not have been so neglected, and our vehicles would be fueled by something other than gasoline and diesel fuel. We need truly renewable energy sources. Unfortunately, research into alternative energy is controlled by the industry that is most threatened by it.

While we were in Brazil, all the cars were fueled with ethanol. A big deal has been made here of E85, or 85% ethanol and 15% gasoline. There is a lot about ethanol they do not tell you. To begin with, ethanol has approximately 60% of the energy content of gasoline. If your car gets 20 miles per gallon with gasoline containing the usual 12% ethanol, it will probably get about 14 mpg with E85' especially in larger and heavier vehicles. That means E85 should cost no more than $2.10 per gallon for you to break even. Ethanol is made from corn, the same corn that is used to feed livestock and dairy cows, and that provides about 40% of the calories we consume. The increased demand for corn due to ethanol production has already resulted in significant increases in food prices, in spite of the 51 cent per gallon subsidy to ethanol producers and farm subsidies to corn growers. There are far more cars here than in Brazil. There is no way to produce enough ethanol to meet our demand for motor fuel. Even if there was, a lot of fuel must be burned to produce ethanol, so the cost will always be unacceptably high. Research is underway to produce ethanol from wood. Our forests are already being destroyed.

Diesel fuel is much like kerosene, heating oil, and jet fuel. It is much less refined than gasoline, and should be much cheaper to produce. Why then is it priced 60 cents higher than gasoline? Diesel fuel also burns dirtier than gasoline, so its impact on the environment would be greater if more vehicles burned it. Bio-diesel, which has been promoted as fuel for vehicles, is vegetable oil, the stuff we use to deep-fry our foods. Some of it can come from discarded cooking oil, but no way is there enough of it to power a lot of vehicles. It does not provide a significant benefit to the environment because it is very similar to regular diesel fuel. Petroleum comes from rotted vegetation that has been buried in the earth for millions of years. Bio-diesel also comes from vegetation, but is captured before it is buried. If it were to be more widely used, food prices would increase even more.

The problem with petroleum-based fuels is that they will ultimately be depleted. Most of our plastics are petroleum based, as are many of the chemicals we use. Allowing that resource to be depleted would drive up the cost of most products. Aluminum is abundant, but it takes a tremendous amount of energy to produce. Glass is very abundant and requires less energy to produce, but we need to research ways of modifying its properties to make it more suitable for most consumer goods. In the end, other materials would have to be discovered. Plastics can be made from the cellulose in trees and various plants, but that would increase the rate at which we destroy our forests. Plant based fuels pose another problem – soil depletion. Farmers know that crops must be rotated to preserve the soils capacity to provide adequate quality and quantity of food. So much of our food comes from corn and soy beans that it becomes extremely difficult, if not impossible, to rotate those crops. Dedicating more land to ethanol production will, in the long run, threaten our food supply. Chemical fertilizers can boost yields, but have several downsides. The nitrogen in them is derived from natural gas, which is another resource that can be depleted. Nitrogen based fertilizers are mostly nitrogen, phosphorus, and potassium. Some may contain other so-called macronutrients and even a few micronutrients. No one really knows the effect of long-term use of chemical fertilizers. They drain into rivers and are carried into oceans. How they will affect marine life, which is already being depleted by overfishing, remains to be seen. No one knows for sure what effects the Gulf of Mexico oil spill, Exxon Valdez incident, and dozens of other spills into our oceans and waterways will have on our food chain. Pollution of oceans and waterways, and the destruction of marine life, is also predicted in the Bible (Revelation 16:3-7).

The holy grail of vehicular fuel is hydrogen. Hydrogen has higher energy content than gasoline, so fuel mileage would be significantly improved. Hydrogen fuel cells have been powering electrical systems on spacecraft for decades. There are two ways to get hydrogen. We can get it from natural gas in a process akin to what is used to extract nitrogen, or we can get it from water, the most abundant resource on earth. The beauty of hydrogen is that burning it produces only water. It is the most environmentally friendly fuel. It produces no carbon dioxide, so contributes very little to global warming. There are a few technical issues to be resolved, and the oil companies are pursuing solutions, but they are pursuing solutions they can control. You don't need oil wells to get gasoline when you can get water from the ocean. There are two ways to approach the problem. One company is developing hydrogen generators to be placed in gas stations. You would simply refill your tank much like refilling a propane cylinder for your barbecue grill, or you could just exchange cylinders. The other way is to build a small hydrogen generator right into your vehicle. Of course, then you would not need a gas station. Imagine that, no gas stations, no oil companies involved, no $4.00/gallon gas. Condensers could be used to recapture much of the water. The result would be as yet unimaginable fuel mileage. Why do you think your car is not already powered by hydrogen? Your car would cost a bit more, and would require periodic maintenance, but the total cost to you would be much less.

Vehicular fuel consumption is only part of the problem. Industrial, commercial, governmental, and home energy consumption is equally serious. Coal fired power plants supply most of the electrical needs of our country. Coal is plentiful and cheaper than other fuels, but it is the dirtiest to burn, mining it is dangerous, and it generates tremendous amounts of greenhouse gases that contribute to global warming. They can be cleaned up considerably by installing scrubbers to remove the pollutants. The industry has convinced our government that a 'cap and trade' system is a good idea. It allows companies who implement clean air technologies and reduce their emissions to sell so-called 'energy credits' to polluters. That allows them to continue operating such plants indefinitely. This market in energy credits creates a whole new level of middlemen, the brokers who make money handling the transactions. The cost of the credits and the brokers' commissions get passed on to you, the consumer. This is on top of the commissions paid to the brokers who deal in energy futures. The power companies don't care. They are a 'cost plus' business. Where else can you go for your electricity?

Power plants fueled by oil or natural gas are subject to the same price manipulation as gasoline. Oil and coal fired plants are dirty. Natural gas burns cleaner, but both are depletable resources better used for other purposes. That leaves us with two alternatives: natural power sources and conservation. Natural power sources include hydroelectric, geothermal, wind, and solar. They might be adequate to meet our demands for electricity if we eliminate much of the waste. The earth has a hot core of molten iron. Gravitational force and friction from slippage of the continental plates assures that it will remain molten for a long time. Steam from that heat can be used to power turbine generators without need for any fuel, and with no pollution whatsoever. Geothermal power plants are much less costly than nuclear ones. All that is needed is a water source. All the electrical power needs of the island nation of Iceland are supplied by geothermal power plants. There are many locations in the United States with access to geothermal energy, including Arkansas, Colorado, and Wyoming. Wind power is being used around the world for generating electricity and is gaining in the U.S. Aside from being a bit of an eyesore, and somewhat variable in output, they are environmentally friendly. The Netherlands and other countries are successfully using wind-powered generators to supply much of their needs. There is no reason for us not to do the same. Hydroelectric power is also a low cost way of generating electricity. It does not pollute the air, but it does have some environmental impact. Dams also prevent silt from traveling downstream. Silt is important for supporting marine life and building buffer zones in coastal areas to protect against storm surges.

Solar power alone at this time has the advantage of being usable at point of consumption, your home or business. New developments, such as photosensitive coatings that can be painted on, could reduce the cost of solar panels. Solar panels only produce electricity during daylight hours. If it is to be the only power source, a means of storing electricity is required. Batteries large enough to meet typical demand are expensive and may need to be replaced every few years. This suggests that they are best used as a supplement to other power sources.

My personal dream for energy independence is a combination of solar power and any other technology that would enable us to disconnect from utility companies. One possibility is small hydrogen generator to supply heating and cooking fuel, and fuel for a hydrogen fuel cell to supply electricity. Perhaps an intermediate step would be to use the hydrogen to power a small friction-free turbine to generate electricity. Such turbines, running on air bearings, have been developed. They could be inexpensive and have very long service lives. Even these solutions are probably crude compared to entirely new ways of generating electricity that have yet to be developed. In the meanwhile, I encourage everyone to conserve energy and to insist governments at all levels do the same. It will save you some money so you will be able to afford the new technology when it does arrive.

It is high time for our government to take back the lead in energy research. I believe that hydrogen is our best shot at energy independence in the short term. In the longer term, finding the keys to understanding and controlling gravity is our best hope for reducing fuel cost, saving our environment, and making long space voyages practical. The oil/gas/coal/energy companies have no interest in lowering our costs or saving our environment. They are cost-plus businesses concerned only with their own profits. If we truly want energy independence, the solution lies not only with independence from foreign countries but independence from oil/gas/coal/energy companies. They will not easily relinquish their favored positions. As long as the political process is so dependent on money, the lobbyists will use our money to get favored treatment for their clients. We can only achieve energy independence by taking back our government.

Freedom of Speech

Freedom of speech has been used as an excuse for peddling pornography, smearing opponents in political races, revealing the most intimate secrets of celebrities, inciting riots, lying about others, telemarketing, and verbal abuse. The time has come to clearly define the purpose of this precious right. It allows us to state our opinion on matters of politics, religion, economics, or any matter of interest to us. It does not, in any way, obligate others to listen to us, nor does it obviate the right to privacy. This freedom should allow us to express anything we want, but not necessarily any way we want. Too many lives have been ruined by lies and innuendo.

Civilization is founded on truth. We believe that when we put our money in a bank, it will be there when we need it, and that it will accrue interest at the rate promised. When we give a contractor a down payment to cover the cost of materials for a remodeling job, we can believe he will complete the job. When we hand our credit card to a store clerk, we expect that our credit card bill will only show the items and amounts we charged. When someone testifies in court, they are required to tell the truth. We have a right to the truth in most matters.

In the 2000 presidential campaign primaries, George Bush was facing John McCain in South Carolina. McCain was leading. Voters in the state received phone calls asking whether they knew that McCain had a black daughter. The implication was that he had fathered her with a black woman. The truth was that he and his wife had adopted a Bangladeshi girl. Their act of kindness became McCain's undoing. The Bush campaign took advantage of the racial prejudice there. McCain's loss drove down polls in other states. Constant media coverage did the rest. Politics trumps charity.

Two years earlier, in the impeachment process against President Clinton for lying about his affair with Monica Lewinsky, I received many derogatory messages about the President. Some implied that the President might have been somehow involved in the deaths of more than twenty of his friends who might have been involved in business dealings with him. Others implied that he was somehow involved in a drug cartel, or that he was helping the Chinese develop sophisticated weapons that might later endanger us. Who could believe any of these implications after Kenneth Starr spent more than fifty million dollars relentlessly investigating every aspect of the President's life, and all he came up with was a sex scandal? Politics trumps common sense.

In the 2004 election, John Kerry, a decorated veteran of the Vietnam War, who commanded a swiftboat on the rivers there, was accused of fabricating his exploits. One man he rescued and seven of his crew fully supported the official report that gave Kerry the medals. One crewmember did not. Kerry had turned against the war after serving in it. Somehow he was made to appear unpatriotic. He lost the election. Politics trumps truth.

I often receive pass-along emails. Many are from devout Christian friends. Generally they contain clean humor, poetry, or inspirational stories, until someone of an opposing political view enters a political race, commits some error, or is associated with someone else who does. Some claimed President Barack Obama was born in Kenya so was not qualified to be president. Others claimed he is a closet Muslim. The fact that the man has been attending a Christian church for more than two decades and professes his faith seems to make no difference. I had not been an Obama supporter before the general election, but I resent character assassination. I generally respond by directing the senders and recipients to the *snopes.com* website, and chide them for ignoring the teachings of their own faith. A few get upset with me. Politics trumps faith.

A few years ago, I was turning around a newly acquired company in a small town in Illinois. The previous owners had constructed a plant adjoining a residential neighborhood. The rezoning and construction was done so quickly that the neighbors had little or no opportunity to protest. Then, the company created an eyesore by storing hundreds of steel drums containing environmentally sensitive materials outside the building. I set out to rebuild the relationship with the community. First, we spent a lot of money to remove the unsightly waste materials. Then, we requested to be put on the village council's agenda so we could present our plans for expansion. Twenty-four neighbors showed up for our presentation. We laid out our plan for immediate expansion, then the various future options we might entertain if further expansion became necessary. The immediate expansion posed no difficulty for any of the neighbors if we could reduce the paint spray exhaust and reduce truck traffic on an adjoining residential street, both of which we agreed to take care of immediately. The long-range plan would have put the side of the expanded plant directly across the street from an elderly lady's home. We committed to buying the home, demolishing it, and replacing it with a berm covered with trees to isolate the residential areas. Only three neighbors presented issues, and all were resolved. A reporter from a newspaper serving the region was in the audience. Two days later, the headline read "Neighbors Fight Manufacturer's Expansion." The article failed to mention that only three of the neighbors raised issues, that all of the issues were resolved to the satisfaction of all parties, and that the neighbors complimented us on our openness. The story would probably have been more interesting if it had been accurately reported. The newspaper refused to correct the story. The next time they called for an interview, I refused their request because they could not be relied upon to report accurately.

The news media should report facts accurately, and not manufacture or sensationalize the news. They can certainly state their editorial opinions, or report the opinions of others, but facts should not intentionally be misstated, nor should others' statements be taken out of context. Tabloids have ruined people's lives by printing totally false stories about them. News media should be held to a higher standard. It is true that people can defend their reputations in the courts, but who can afford to do so? Freedom of speech should be the freedom to speak the truth or state an opinion without deriding others or inventing news.

There is a tendency in our society to value ourselves more highly than others. For example, we write the personal pronoun 'I' as a capital letter, but 'you' or anyone else is always lower case. We have lost the sense of 'us' being more important than 'I'. Winning has become the ultimate objective regardless of how the win is obtained. We taught our kids that how you win is more important than the win itself. When our younger son was twelve, he was enrolled in a Catholic school and played basketball. On several occasions, while playing against other

Catholic schools, parents cheered when an opposing team's player got knocked to the floor by an intentional foul. This attitude has carried forward into political races where outrageous mudslinging has become the tactic of choice. The media suck it up because sensationalism sells. Real information about candidates is difficult to get. Investigative reporting costs money and news budgets are getting slashed as the economy weakens. Is it any wonder that voter satisfaction with politicians is so low?

When we hire an executive in business, he or she must submit a resume of his or her experience and accomplishments. Misstatements usually lead to rejection. Should we not expect a resume of sworn accuracy from politicians? We should also expect a brief written statement of the candidate's position on key issues, and how he or she intends to deal with them. If the candidate has been in a legislative role before, a complete voting record, grouped by category, should be provided including a clear description of what the purpose of the bill was and the rationale for the vote. It should also disclose campaign contributions from any parties benefitting from the vote. In the case of judges, comparative statistics of convictions, sentences, and repeat offenses for various crimes, or awards for civil cases, would enable me to make a more informed decision.

I simply don't vote for those whose records or positions are unclear to me. After hundreds of fifteen or thirty second ads attacking each other's character, I am left with the impression that neither candidate has anything to say about his or her own qualifications and so must have none. I refuse to vote for any candidate of any party who engages in this type of campaigning. Among their rights should be the reasonable expectation that things said about them are true. They who speak about others should have the responsibility for ascertaining the truth of what they are saying or to categorize their statements as rumors or speculation. That in no way undermines their right to free speech, the free expression of their opinions on any subject they choose. There is no place in civilized society for verbal abuse, threats, intimidation, or humiliation of others. Profanity is also in no way necessary for communicating our ideas. All of these stand in the way of effective communication, and only serve to divide us.

Conclusion

It should be apparent to anyone with an open mind that we have been conditioned to accept as fact concepts that cannot withstand close scrutiny when confronted with facts, figures, and historical evidence. In nearly every domain, some persons or entities have something to gain from promoting a particular viewpoint. Marketing and public relations firms, psychologists, political advisers and others have become expert at shaping our opinions. It becomes increasingly difficult to determine whether they are reflecting our opinions or we are reflecting theirs. In too many cases, their interests do not coincide with ours. Who are they? What do they have to gain? How do they affect us? These are all questions we must ask if we are to make choices that are in our own best interest.

Why are most nations on earth deeply indebted? The most common answer is that they spend too much, especially on social programs. How do we then explain why nations without social programs are often more deeply indebted than those that have good safety nets for their people? The answer must lie elsewhere. Most have inadequate revenues to meet their needs, so they run deficits, and that forces them to borrow. International investors love government debt because no one is willing to let governments default on their debts. They are the most secure investment, guaranteed by both debtors' and creditors' governments. The lenders typically impose conditions on the loans, including higher interest rates, lower taxes, privatization of public infrastructure, spending cuts, freeing of commodities markets, etc. These austerity measures invariably raise prices, lower revenues, increase unemployment, and throw the countries into recession. They fall into a perpetual debt trap. We are currently in just such a situation. If we default or continue to borrow beyond our means, interest rates will rise to attract additional capital, and the recession will deepen making the crisis even worse. The solutions being proposed as cures for our debt crisis feature spending cuts and tax cuts. Tax cuts reduce revenues directly, while spending cuts reduce revenues by increasing unemployment. Neither approach can work.

Why have tax cuts never resulted in economic recovery? Because revenues increase only when the tax base is expanded by full employment. Businesses do not expand operations, introduce new product lines, or hire new people in the absence of demand. This is evidenced by record corporate profits and cash balances in 2011, but very few of them are hiring. Demand is created by masses of people spending money. The Great Depression happened after the top income tax rate was lowered from 63% to 25%; the early 1970s recession followed a cut from 92% to 70%; the early 1980s recession followed a cut to 50%; and the 1990 recession followed a cut to 31%. A tax increase to 39.6% resulted in several years of budget surpluses. A return to a 35% tax rate preceded the 2001 and 2008 recessions. The explanation is simple. Cuts in progressive tax rates disproportionately benefit the already wealthy. Their tax reduction windfalls are invested in long term passive investments like government debt or mergers and acquisitions. They become "**lazy money**" that adds nothing to overall economic activity. Taxes should only be cut when the economy is growing and the debt is being reduced, and the cuts should be made in small increments.

Can deficit spending refuel an economy? Yes, but only if the spending is on domestic job creating activity by domestically owned businesses. The Great Depression was ended by massive deficit spending in support of our World War II effort which reduced unemployment to 1.2% by 1944. The Vietnam War helped reduce average unemployment to 3.5% in 1969. A massive effort to rebuild our infrastructure could have a similar effect today if we have the political will to raise taxes temporarily so the boost does not all come from increased debt. Infrastructure projects take time to plan and execute so we must be willing to sustain the effort for a few years.

Are there any short term actions that might help refuel the economy? Yes. We could raise the minimum wage to reflect a realistic living wage. Wage erosion is largely responsible for the decline in consumer spending. Establishing a sensible comprehensive immigration policy keyed to the unemployment rate would help prevent further erosion. Not since 1928 (just before the Great Depression) has there been such a huge disparity in earnings and wealth between the top 1% of income earners and everyone else. In healthy economies, money is kept flowing through all sectors. Money that flows to the already wealthy does not increase economic activity. By contrast, money that flows to lower economic strata gets spent immediately on goods and services.

Does increasing wages not result in higher inflation? Yes, but no growth is possible without inflation. Reread the chapter titled *"We Cannot Afford It"* for a more detailed explanation. A good analogy for inflation is eating. If you do not eat, you will starve. Eating builds muscle and bones so we can work. Eat too much and you will grow so fat that you cannot get enough food to sustain yourself. Excessive inflation most greatly affects people on rigidly fixed incomes. It reduces the value of everyone's savings, and causes loans to be repaid with cheaper money. That is why financial institutions resist inflation. If there is too little inflation, the economy stagnates and ultimately goes into recession.

Should not the private sector refuel the economy? The private sector will not expand their businesses in the absence of demand; consequently, refueling depressed economies must be done by governments. This raises the specter of big oppressive government. To my knowledge, there have been no examples of small government that have achieved long term success. All the greatest and longest lasting civilizations in history were compound structures involving a sizeable portion of their citizenry. The more people that have a vested interest in their government, the more they will support it. It is impossible to return to simpler times before there was much that required regulation. That was when doctors did not need medical degrees, fires were fought by bucket brigades, transportation was by horse or boat, there were no building codes, communications were handwritten, chemistry was in its infancy, and there was no electricity, radio, television, movies, nuclear power, computers, space travel, satellites, genetic engineering, etc., etc. All of these require regulatory input from a government strong enough to maintain control and permit orderly processes.

How can we afford to pay for it all? Someone has to pay for the necessary functions government performs. That requires sufficient revenues, and that means taxes. Since the purpose of business is to make as much profit as possible, large businesses are most resistant to taxes. Because of their disproportionate money advantage, over time they succeed in getting tax breaks and subsidies that reduce their tax obligation. Corporations have approximately three times the revenues of individuals, yet individuals pay more than fourteen times the amount of federal income tax than corporations in relation to their revenues. Our tax codes punish small businesses and individuals while allowing large international corporations to escape much of their obligation. Taxing on the basis of place of incorporation allows many corporations to escape taxes. It is time to level the playing field. In the chapter titled *"Fair Tax"*, I propose a new system of taxation that will do precisely that while eliminating budget deficits. It will significantly increase the disposable income of individuals; and, it will encourage the formation of small businesses which are the primary job creators in our economy.

Many of the chapters in this book deal with issues that, on the surface, are not directly related to economics. If you examine the data carefully, you will find that deregulation of the financial sector and huge tax cuts have drained working capital from the economy and contributed to current and past financial crises. Illegal immigration has had a very direct effect on unemployment, wage erosion and, consequently, poverty. Poverty has a direct effect on welfare cost, physical and mental health, family life, education, crime, abortion, and substance abuse. All of these are cost drivers to the economy. It cannot be fixed unless we deal with the issue of poverty, not by expanding the welfare state, but by creating employment opportunity.

Regardless of how well meaning and necessary reforms may be, negotiations between two diametrically opposed positions usually result in legislation that pleases no one. That is certainly true with the financial industry reform bill, health care reform bill, our tax codes, and the way Social Security is funded. The watering down of reforms is due to the need for campaign finances as often as a party's principles. It will take tremendous political will to bring about meaningful change. When most transportation and farming depended on horses, blinders were put on horses to prevent them from being distracted from what their masters wanted them to do. Overconcentration of news media ownership and extreme polarization of politicians allow us to see only what they want us to see. Taking off our blinders may be frightening at first, but it will allow us to see a world of alternate possibilities. I hope you will find some of the possibilities I propose to be well-reasoned and worthy of consideration, fully supportive of capitalism and democracy, and perhaps even achievable. I love this country!

"You write in order to change the world, knowing perfectly well that you probably can't, but also knowing that literature is indispensable to the world... The world changes according to the way people see it, and if you alter, even by a millimeter, the way ... people look at reality, then you can change it."

James Arthur Baldwin (1924-1987), American writer, poet, civil rights activist.